Praise for *Fall in Love with the Problem, Not the Solution*

"Waze founder Uri Levine has one of the rarest of all entrepreneurial traits: he has the skills and persistence to have launched multiple successful companies, paired with the self-awareness to know how he did it. In *Fall in Love with the Problem, Not the Solution*, he shares these hard-won truths with the rest of us. If you are curious about how Waze (or any of Uri's other companies) came to be, or are just looking for the actionable advice you can use to turn any idea into a reality, this deserves a place on your bookshelf. In fact, **it should be required reading for every aspiring entrepreneur.**"

—Marc Randolph, Cofounder, Netflix

"Uri's book is a window into the entrepreneurial mind that through passion, perseverance, and accountability can change the world. This book reminds us of the importance of always connecting with the end consumer, and provides the road map of tangible tips to build businesses. **Reading this book feels as if you're a mentee sitting with Uri to understand the next step in your start-up adventure—practical considerations combined with memorable mantras** that drive entrepreneurs to ask the right questions and optimize chances of success throughout their journey."

—Jenifer Fleiss, Cofounder, Rent a Runway

"Uri Levine provides unique insights on what builds enduring entrepreneurial success. The entrepreneurial path is a journey through a labyrinth of challenges that requires a passion for problem-solving that delivers timely solutions—**a must-read for every start-up that yearns to be a unicorn and beyond.**"

—Kiran Mazumdar-Shaw, Chairperson & Founder, Biocon

"Uri Levine was at the forefront of achieving a signature milestone in the history of Israel as a Start-up Nation. Waze was the first Israeli consumer app to blast through the entrepreneurial equivalent of the 4-minute mile barrier: a billion-dollar exit. Since then, Israel has produced dozens of 'unicorns,' but it was Waze that paved the way. And Uri just kept going, the quintessential serial entrepreneur. **When he gives you advice, it's time to sit back, listen, and learn.**"

—Saul Singer, coauthor, *Start-Up Nation: The Story of Israel's Economic Miracle*

"When Uri came on my podcast, it ended up one most popular of all time. **If you read this book, you'll quickly see why.** It's the most tactical, real, and entertaining guide to building a start-up you'll find. It walks you step-by-step through each step of the journey—from ideation to finding product-market fit to hiring, and all the way to how to exit your company."

—Lenny Rachitsky, Host, *Lenny's Podcast*

Fall in
Love
with **the**
Problem,
Not the
Solution

Fall in **Love** with **the** **Problem,** Not the Solution

UPDATED EDITION

A Handbook for Entrepreneurs

Uri Levine

Matt Holt Books
An Imprint of BenBella Books, Inc.
Dallas, TX

Matt Holt is an imprint of BenBella Books, Inc.
8080 N. Central Expressway
Suite 1700
Dallas, TX 75206
benbellabooks.com
Send feedback to feedback@benbellabooks.com

BenBella and *Matt Holt* are federally registered trademarks.

Printed in the United States of America
10 9 8 7 6 5 4 3 2 1

Library of Congress Control Number: 2022027904
ISBN 9781637741986 (hardcover)
ISBN 9781637746608 (paperback)
ISBN 9781637746615 (electronic)

Editing by Katie Dickman and Adi Barill
Copyediting by Scott Calamar
Proofreading by Madeline Grigg and Becky Maines
Indexing by WordCo Indexing Services, Inc.
Text design and composition by PerfecType, Nashville, TN
Cover design by Brigid Pearson
Printed by Lake Book Manufacturing

Special discounts for bulk sales are available. Please contact bulkorders@benbellabooks.com.

To the more than one billion users of Waze, Moovit, and the rest of my start-ups.
Without you, this story would never have been.

Contents

Foreword

Steve Wozniak, Cofounder of Apple

SPOILER ALERT: this book will change your life and become your "bible" if you are an entrepreneur.

I do a lot of public speaking, largely on topics of entrepreneurship and start-ups. At one conference, I heard Uri Levine speak. It wasn't that he was an exceptional speaker, which he is. I hear many exceptional speakers. But Uri had a casual style, like a friend, that made his material easy to follow and understand. I learned that Uri was the force behind the app Waze. We recognize apps that become a big part of our lives but few are like Waze, better than the other similar apps. If you care about quality and excellence, Waze is always spoken of in those terms.

People often look to me as an Apple cofounder for advice. I may have a lot of internal feelings, mostly related to personality, that I relate but in general, Apple is a bad example as a start-up. Apple was a rare case that doesn't apply to people starting companies. With Apple, there were extremely favorable elements of our success that you can't count on or control.

One product was our only successful one, earning money, for the first ten years of the company, and it wasn't even what people think. Our Apple II computer was the best, most usable computer in the PC early days, but who would buy a computer to do inventory and sales figures and employment in your home? Games were the key. Atari was starting the arcade industry right here in Los Gatos, California. In the hardware days, a game had thousands of wires with all the signals that the engineer understood and it could take a year for a new arcade game to be prototyped. I had a vision that these games would be much better when they were in color. The Apple II computer was the first time that arcade games had color and the first time that they were in software. A nine-year-old could use a simple language, BASIC, to make colors move on the TV screen and could complete a decent working arcade game in one day. That product led to great wealth for Apple, and to eventually change lives for all of us.

I don't have enough free time to read many books. But from the first pages of this book, *Fall in Love with the Problem, Not the Solution*, I had to read every word, taking handwritten notes on paper. I even noted many typos in an early draft. I could tell from the start that this book was very meaningful to me, but for a business book, it was natural and understandable. Uri uses metaphors of human life to get across his thinking in product and business terms. Entrepreneurs know that great passion for the products and company is necessary. Uri speaks of it as falling in love with the problem, not with money or yourself. He relates this love to dealing with personal relationships in ways we have all experienced. Falling in love with the problem means valuing the end user as the key to success, not even your own ideas and creations. I have always believed in this.

As to the need to create a product that strikes the first-time user deeply and emotionally, Uri refers us to the deep emotional feelings of our first kiss, something you never forget. I will use this as a guideline in my thinking from now on. It's worth the effort to connect with a user or investor this way. Recently in Berkeley, I was half a block from where I had my first kiss and this metaphor rang truer than ever. That's the emotion that a new product should bring out in first-timers, both investors and users.

Uri is not a dull lecturer, like so many are, but is an interesting professor who creates an atmosphere where you want to learn from examples that make sense. He does a great job of showing the importance of human personalities, as related to products and features. All through the book, Uri had principles (qualities) that guided him, alongside a lot of "formulas" that he used to figure out whether something was good enough or what the real value was, and the decisions you should make to profit from that value.

Uri states outright that he wants to take his successful experiences and help educate others to be successful, too. We all agree on the importance of entrepreneurship but the value of teachers and mentors cannot be overlooked. This is a strong principle to me as well and something I devote much of my life to.

All through the book, you find the reality of constant iterations to find the PMF: Product Market Fit. It doesn't come easy and is full of failures and retries. Uri relates this with his experiences with Waze and other start-ups, finding ways to solve problems in layperson terms. One thing I really like is that Uri falls in love with problems that ordinary people have in their lives. Once a product is good enough for "the rest of us," funding comes into play. Uri has numerous formulas to capitalize on a great product but not to turn people off with payment methods or amounts. All my life I wanted to create products that enhanced the life of normal Joe's, like with home appliances. In this book, I also found good approaches and even formulas for B2B dealing, Business to Business.

I feel very unusual in my thinking in a lot of ways but, I have come to realize, we all feel this way. Over my life, I have come up with principles for dealing with things, and even rough formulas that I use to guide me. These principles are in my head. I rarely speak of them with anyone other than my wife or closest friends. I fear that if I came to conclusions on my own, they aren't good enough for others to follow. True scholars must surely have better ideas. Throughout this book, I saw one confirmation after another that another, Uri himself, thought similarly as myself about many things. It actually startled me and is a strong reason that I love this book so much. To me, this is a bible of entrepreneurship that I will keep close at hand and refer to for entrepreneur ideas. Already I'm recommending this book to the countless entrepreneurs that approach me every day for advice. One quality that I have always admired is the ability to recognize when concepts from another (Uri) are better than what you have yourself.

I am in a couple of start-up businesses currently and already I started speaking principles in conversations with other founders of how we should proceed in our businesses according to this book. I used to like residing in the shadows but now I have the confidence to step up and take the lead in discussions with potential employees and investors. I use the same phrases and principles that I learned in this book. One person with confidence in a product can make a company go. In this book, I saw and agreed with the observation that investors decide in the first seconds if they want to back you. It starts with a simple story you tell the investor, that could even be made up or exaggerated, but that is a metaphor of the problem you are in love with. It is important to develop a good story (or more) that grabs others emotionally. The story should be like the first kiss to them. Uri makes clear that boring presentations with standard slides are not what sell to investors or clients.

With one start-up based on trackable location devices, Wheels of Zeus, I presented a story that was personally important to me. If my beloved dog got away due to a wireless gate failing, how could I know when it happened and where my dog was now? My emotions over this issue helped me in my product decisions. Why the name Wheels of Zeus? We started with ideas of tracking police cars via their own radios and started looking for company names that would translate to a web domain. We quickly found that even things like modernpolicefinder.com were taken. I got into the internet so early that I had a three-letter dot-com, woz.com, that I could license to this start-up. I silently thought, in our meeting, and blurted out Wheels Of Zeus (W-O-Z) and the other founders couldn't see why I suggested such a weird name. Only one thought it was a great name. Only afterward did I explain that we could use woz.com as our web address. It really helps to be light-hearted in your entrepreneurial endeavors.

Fall in Love with the Problem, Not the Solution is loaded with product and feature principles that lead to simplicity of use. I think about this every day with the technology products I use and relate to how important this is. If you are bothered by complexity and things not working when they should, you can relate to this. Steve Jobs used to quote Michelangelo that simplicity is the ultimate sophistication. It's too easy to get side-tracked as to value with infinite features possible. For years at Apple, if a feature couldn't be written in simple human understandable terms, our publication department could turn that feature down. It's how Steve Jobs guided the iPhone to not be confusing to himself. This book deals with the long search and many iterations to find the best balance of simplicity and features, which is always changing.

Quick decisions to back out of a new feature, or to fire the wrong employees—even founders—is conveyed with real examples. Delay can only hurt you, your company, and your users. In this, I have seen my own failures in a couple of start-ups, but this principle explains to me why it is important to replace many founders with true business leaders after a product is far along the PMF curve.

Read this book and take notes. Then you are ready in the best way to improve things for others with a product and company. You have my permission to Think Different and Change the World.

Introduction

At the end of May 2013, Google reached out to Waze, the company I had founded six years earlier, with a single-page term sheet. The price: $1.15 billion . . . in cash. Google promised that Waze would remain Waze, fulfilling its destiny to help commuters avoid traffic jams, and the company would be able to continue our operations out of Israel.

Google also said the transaction would be completed within a week.

We said yes.

It took ten days to complete the transaction, but that was still record time. While the transaction was a final one, the dialogue with the potential acquirer had been going on for the previous six months.

Somewhere starting in the winter between 2012 and 2013, Google reached out to us and said they "were interested in acquiring Waze." A little while later, they invited Waze's management into Google's "secret room," where they made offers and convinced companies to agree to be acquired. We didn't like the offer they made in December 2012, and we turned it down. In their second offer, six months later, the numbers were completely different.

Building a start-up is a roller-coaster journey with ups and downs. Fundraising is a roller coaster in the dark—you don't even know what's coming.

Closing a deal is an order of magnitude more, and negotiating multiple deals in parallel (especially those that are also a life-changing event for you) are the most extreme moments in the start-up journey. I promise to tell you more about the emotional roller coaster of a transaction in the "The Exit" (chapter 13 of the book), but there is one thing for sure: there is nothing like the first time.

I was part of another unicorn exit—the tech term for a company that is valued at $1 billion or more—for Moovit, which was sold for $1 billion to Intel in 2020, and there will be more, but the first time is so emotional, maybe because you realize it is a life-changing event, because of the extremeness of the roller coaster, and perhaps—in particular in the Waze case—because it was all over the news even prior to the deal, and so everyone felt involved.

The most interesting part of my life started just after the Google-Waze transaction. I left Waze immediately after the acquisition to build more start-ups, and this is what I have been doing since. All of my start-ups are about solving problems, doing good and doing well, and all follow the same method of building a start-up.

This is what this book is all about—my method of building start-ups and unicorns.

When the news of the Google acquisition went public on June 9, 2013, it stunned both the Silicon Valley and Israeli Start-up Nation investment communities. It was not just that the price of $1.15 billion was the largest amount ever paid by a tech firm to acquire an app maker up to that point. It was more a confirmation in the tech world that this five-and-a-quarter-year-old start-up from Israel was building something better than Apple, Google, Microsoft, and pretty much everyone else in the driving and navigation space.

Today (I'm writing this at the beginning of 2021), when you look at a $1 billion valuation, it is not a big deal. There are more than fifty Israeli unicorns out of approximately one thousand in the world. I just want to believe I was there at the beginning to set the mark.

People often ask me whether selling Waze for $1.15 billion in 2013 was the right decision, and if Waze would be worth way more than a billion dollars today. In my opinion, there are only right decisions or NO decisions. Because when you make a decision—when you choose a path—you don't know what it would be like if you had chosen a different path. Making decisions with conviction is one of the most important behaviors of a successful CEO and, in particular, in a start-up.

If you had asked me if Waze is worth more today than the amount Google paid for it back then, absolutely yes, but what we don't know is if Waze would have gotten there without the acquisition.

At the end of the day, it's all about our ability to make a bigger impact and help make the world a better place.

Waze was my first billion-dollar exit; seven years later was the second, Moovit—the Waze for public transportation—and I believe the next will be much less than seven years apart.

While luck counts for a lot in this space, let me define luck as "When opportunity meets readiness."

This book is about making you ready for that moment.

⁓

I am an entrepreneur and a mentor. Over the past twenty years, I have started and worked on and with dozens of start-ups and have seen both successes and failures. I love building companies that change people's lives for the better, and nearly always I start with the PROBLEM. If the problem is big and worth solving, then in my mind this is already an interesting company and a journey worth taking.

The other part of who I am is a mentor or a teacher. This is why I'm writing this book—to fulfill my destiny to teach entrepreneurs, high-tech professionals, and businesspeople how to build their start-ups with a higher success rate. To share my method for building unicorns and start-ups.

To an extent, if you were to take just one thing from this book, the one thing that will help you to make your start-up more successful, then:

- I did my share.
- I would ask you to pay it forward and teach, mentor, or guide another entrepreneur in need.

Fall in Love with the Problem, Not the Solution is organized around the key components of building a successful start-up, and I will share here my method (or my "cookbook").

Most of the chapters are organized around a combination of real stories, case studies from Waze and other start-ups and, in particular, the key take-aways, which you will find at the end of each chapter. In order to build a successful start-up, you will need to figure out product-market fit (PMF), which is nearly always the first part of the journey; determine your business model; and, of course, you must lock down a growth path. All these are phases in the lifespan of a start-up and are covered in chapters 3, 8, 9, and 10.

Some of the chapters are about the never-ending phases of the start-up—people, funding, investors, and users. In the operating phases of building a start-up, once you figure out growth, it is no longer the main focus anymore, but people, fundraising, managing your investors, and thinking about your users will always be there.

In chapter 1, called "Fall in Love with the Problem, Not the Solution," I discuss the trigger for building a start-up—a problem worth solving.

Chapter 2 explores the baseline of building a start-up—the journey of failures and failing fast. Chapter 3 provides a bit of a market perspective about successful start-ups—total disruption.

Chapter 4 establishes the underlying method of "operating in phases," the focus on the "main thing" of each one of the phases and, in particular, switching between phases.

Chapter 5a is about fundraising (for the first time), and chapter 5b is about managing your investors and the continuous journey of fundraising.

Chapter 6 is about DNA creation, people, and in particular firing and hiring (the order is not a typo). Chapter 7—just before figuring out PMF—is about understanding your users.

Chapter 8 discusses PMF and how to get there.

Chapter 9 is all about business models, business plans, and how to figure out the right ones.

Chapter 10 is about marketing and growth, which is yet another phase in building your start-up.

Chapter 11 dives deep into another aspect of growth—going global and becoming a market leader on the world stage.

In the years since this book was written, it seemed like 90 percent of my time working with my start-ups was spent on crisis management.

The four years that started with COVID-19 but continued with additional crises like the war between Russia and Ukraine, as well as the tech "bubble burst" in 2022, have brought us several significant global and regional crises.

While we've defined the start-up journey as a long roller-coaster journey of failures, it is also a journey from one crisis to the next.

This is why I added a new chapter in this updated edition. Chapter 12 is all about how to run your start-up during a major crisis. In this chapter, for the first time, I also provide a front-row view of crisis management with the personal testimonies of CEOs of three of my start-ups.

The final chapter, chapter 13, is about the endgame of a start-up—the exit: when to sell and how to make this decision, as well as whom you should consider in this decision, and so on.

At the end of the day, entrepreneurs are changing the world and making it a better place. Many of the most significant companies in the world today were start-ups not that long ago. It has only been a decade-plus for Tesla, Waze, WhatsApp, Facebook, Uber, Netflix, and many others. Google and Amazon are just twenty-plus years old. Apple and Microsoft are still younger than I am.

The next generation of entrepreneurs will make an even bigger impact, because they have more to rely on and there are more experienced entrepreneurs who can guide them.

Hopefully, this book will become instrumental in your success.

~

I speak at many events, such as technology, mobility, and entrepreneurship events, as well as academic workshops. One of the most rewarding experiences for me is that "Eureka!" moment when there is a spark and a change in the entrepreneur's mindset.

Some years back, in December 2016, I was invited to speak at an entrepreneurial event in Bratislava, the capital and main city of Slovakia, and the reasoning they used to convince me to come and speak at the event was that this was one of the first countries to adopt Waze successfully.

Indeed, when during presentations I show a video of how Waze maps are created, I always start with Bratislava. **QR code of the link to the video**:

I was the keynote speaker the first night. There was then a cocktail party on the second day and an all-hands entrepreneurs' lunch.

In my keynote, I told the following story.

I spoke with many entrepreneurs whose start-ups failed, and I asked them why. What happened?

While I believe the main reason is that they didn't figure out product-market fit, about half of entrepreneurs told me, "The team was not right."

So, I kept on asking. "What do you mean the team was not right?"

For that question, I heard two main answers. Most said, "We had this guy who was not good enough or that gal who was not good enough." So, "not good enough" was a major reason.

The other reason I heard often was, "We had communication issues" (which I actually would call a problem of "ego management"), where the team was unable to agree with the CEO's leadership.

Then I asked them the most interesting question of all: "*When* did you know that the team was not right?" All of them said, "Within the first month." One CEO told me, "Before we even started!"

But wait a minute: If all of them knew within the first month that the team was not right and they didn't do anything, then the problem is not that the team was not right. The problem was that the CEO did not make the hard decision.

Making easy decisions is easy, it is the hard decisions that are hard to make. This is why most people don't like to call the shots. If the CEO doesn't make the hard decisions, there is a major problem, and the top-performing people will leave (in chapter 6, "Firing and Hiring," I will explain why that is so).

My presentation continued a bit more, and then, at the cocktail party, a start-up CEO approached me and said, "Thank you, now I know exactly what I need to do—to fire my cofounder."

The event extended into the next day. The CEO reached out to me again and said, "It's done. I fired my cofounder. It was painful and I didn't sleep all night long, but once I announced that to the company, everyone approached me and said, 'Thank you, it was about time!' So, I know I did the right thing."

He even sent me an email later saying that the company was on the right path now.

That is when the first trigger for writing this book appeared and I initially thought I should share my knowledge and experiences with other founders, entrepreneurs, CEOs, managers, and perhaps all tech business-people to help them to become better.

~

For myself, it hasn't all been smooth sailing. Having experienced multiple roller-coaster journeys, the challenges and hardships on the way to success, I hope and believe that I can share more and different perspectives around the entrepreneurial journey in a way that will inspire entrepreneurs. More-over, I hope that the lessons I provide will increase your likelihood of being successful.

I consider myself an optimist. As an avid skier, people often ask me what my best ski vacation was. My answer is simple: "The next one." At the end of the day, it's all about our ability to make a bigger impact and to help make the world a better place.

Chapter 1

FALL IN LOVE WITH THE PROBLEM, NOT THE SOLUTION

I have not failed 700 times. I have not failed once. I have succeeded in proving that those 700 ways will not work. When I have eliminated the ways that will not work, I will find the way that will work.

—Thomas Edison

On the Jewish holiday of Rosh Hashana in 2006, I had taken time away with my extended family in Metula, a tiny town in the far north of Israel, about 120 miles from my home in Tel Aviv. As the short vacation came to an end, it was time for us to make the three-hour journey back home. We were a large group—driving ten separate cars—and the topic on everyone's mind was: "What's the best route home?"

There were only two routes from Metula to Tel Aviv—kind of like the 280 versus 101 deliberations when traveling between Silicon Valley and San Francisco.

In 2006, there was no way to know for sure which highway to take.

As my wife and I had four rather little kids at the time, we were the last ones to leave, and I was thinking, "If only we had someone driving ahead of us to inform us which roads were jammed and which were open."

But we did. We had all these family members ahead of us on the road. I started calling them up.

"How's traffic on your route?" I asked. "Any jams I need to know about?"

That turned out to be my "Eureka!" moment—the insight that led to the understanding that all I need is someone ahead of me on the road to tell me what's going on. That's what later on became the essence of Waze.

Many of my start-ups began similarly—being frustrated and then realizing that others share the same frustration and trying to find a way to ease it.

While none of my start-ups would have become successful without the leadership team, the trigger for me to start them was nearly always the same. I started Waze because I hate traffic jams. I started FairFly because I hate money left on the table. Pontera (formerly called FeeX) came into being because I felt I was paying too much in fees on my retirement savings, and Engie because I feel like an idiot at the mechanic. More about my motivations and what my companies do later on this chapter.

For me, it is always frustration that leads into understanding there is a problem. Then I try to figure out if it is a BIG PROBLEM—a problem worth solving. It is always the problem that triggers everything, and if the problem is significant, you can create a lot of value and become successful yourself by solving it.

This chapter tells the story of the beginning of many of my start-ups, always starting with a problem and then always remaining focused on that problem. At the end of the day, building a start-up is hard, long, and painful. You have to be in love in order to have enough passion to persevere through the hard parts of the journey. You are better off being in love with the problem you're trying to solve.

A START-UP IS LIKE FALLING IN LOVE

Building a start-up is very much like falling in love. In the beginning, there are many ideas you could pursue. Eventually, you pick one and say, "This is the idea I'm going to work on," much like you might go on many dates until you eventually find someone and say to yourself that this person is "the one."

At the beginning, you spend time only with that idea. This is when you think of the problem, the users, the solution, the business model—everything. Just like you only want to spend time with your new loved one as you begin falling in love.

When you finally feel confident enough, you start telling your friends about your idea, and they usually tell you, "That will never work," or "That is the stupidest idea I've ever heard."

I've heard that many times. I think that people don't say that to me so much anymore, but in the beginning, they used to say it a lot. Sometimes you take your date to meet your friends for the first time and they say, "That person is not for you."

This is usually when you disengage from your friends because you are in love with that idea, you are in love with what you're doing, and you don't want to listen to anyone else.

The good news is that you are in love, and you don't listen to them.

The bad news is that you are in love, and you don't listen to them.

But this is the reality, and it's relevant for many aspects of your life. If you don't love what you're doing, do yourself a favor and instead do something you do love, because otherwise, you'll sentence yourself to suffering. You should be happy!

It can be detrimental to ignore what others are telling you. Maybe your friends, potential business partners, or investors had something important to say and you didn't listen! But, at the same time, you must be in love to go on this journey. It will be a long, complex, and difficult roller-coaster ride. If you're not in love, it will be too hard for you.

Before we founded Waze, I had been working as a consultant for several start-ups. One of them was a local mobile navigation company, Telmap, that built navigation software for mobile phones and was offered as a service to mobile operators, which then offered it as a paid subscription service to their subscribers. It was essentially a B2B2C (business-to-business-to-consumer) company. Telmap licensed its maps from third parties such as the Israeli company Mapa and international mapping giant Navteq. Telmap didn't have traffic information, though.

I approached the CEO and shared my thoughts. The Telmap platform seemed an ideal one to carry out my vision.

"No one cares about traffic information," the CEO said, rebuffing what I thought was a brilliant idea. "They care about navigation. I don't think traffic information will be actionable."

By "actionable" he meant "we'll never be able to get people to use it enough to make it worth our while financially or to change their route accordingly."

Back then, the only way traffic information was used was with color-coding applied to the map—green meant there was no traffic, yellow meant there was traffic, and red meant the traffic was heavy. But that information was not particularly helpful. On busy roads and intersections, there is traffic every day between 8 AM and 9 AM and between 4 PM and 6 PM, and on the same road at midnight, there is no traffic!

I was persistent, though. Anyone who knows me is aware that once I get an idea in my mind, it's nearly impossible to dissuade me from pursuing it.

Telmap had 50,000 users at the time, all in Israel, and all using their mobile phones with GPS. I built a theoretical statistical model to show how those 50,000 random drivers would be enough to create actionable traffic information. It was a very simple model that turned out to be accurate later when we built Waze.

Here's how the math works: 50,000 users out of about 2.5 million vehicles in Israel (the number of cars and trucks on the roads at the time) was some 2 percent of the total. On a highway during busy hours, there are between 1,500 to 2,000 vehicles per lane, so 2 percent of that is a 30-to-40-vehicle sample per lane.

Now, if a highway is three lanes across, that would be about 90 to 120 vehicles per minute. If we could gather location and speed at all times, this would be a large enough sample to know what the traffic is like on that road.

I tried again to convince the CEO, but obviously I didn't make the claim strong enough to convince him.

While I stopped trying to convince him, I nevertheless carried the urge to work on this project for a while until, around a year later (it always takes longer than you would think), as a result of my background and my reputation as an advisor to start-ups, I was introduced by a mutual colleague to two entrepreneurs, Ehud Shabtai and Amir Shinar.

Ehud and Amir were working together at a software house that Amir was running. Ehud was the Chief Technology Officer (CTO), but in his "night job" he had built a product called FreeMap Israel.

The FreeMap Israel app was a combination of two parts—navigation and map creation. The app created the map as you drove and used it at the same time for navigation. It ran on personal digital assistants (PDAs), as there were no iPhones yet. As its name implies, FreeMap Israel was entirely free—both the app and the map.

Ehud had a problem that was similar to mine: He needed maps for his app to work, but it was too expensive to license them from a third party. This was a critical issue for both our visions because without maps it would be impossible to build a critical mass of users that would generate actionable traffic information. But a start-up couldn't afford the high prices the map-making companies were charging at the time.

Meeting Ehud and Amir was my second magical moment; it was when I knew I had found what I needed to complete my vision of an everyday "avoid traffic jams" app. I had an idea but no way to implement it. Ehud had the conceptual and technological answer for the cost of the map and a similar vision. In fact, Ehud was already multiple steps ahead of me. Mine was in theory; he had actually already built a lot of what was needed. The magic of Ehud's self-drawing maps that created a "free" map was a prerequisite for developing a free application that would encourage use by the number of users who were needed in order to generate accurate traffic data.

From the beginning of Waze, after we joined forces in 2007, it was clear that a GPS-powered mapping/driving/traffic app was exactly what we were going to build. We certainly realized that smartphones with operating systems (and therefore the ability to run apps) and built-in GPS chipsets were becoming more and more popular. What we didn't know back then was that Apple would revolutionize the business when it launched the App Store in 2008. That would in turn give Waze its biggest push.

There was even more magic in that the same app that gathers the data also uses it at the same time—it's the crowdsourcing of everything!

IDENTIFY A BIG PROBLEM—ONE THAT'S WORTH SOLVING

Start by thinking of a problem—a BIG problem—something that is worth solving, a problem that, if solved, will make the world a better place. Then ask yourself, who has this problem? Now, if the answer is just you, don't even bother. It is not worth it. If you are the only person on the planet with this issue, it would be better to consult a shrink. It would be much cheaper (and probably faster) than building a start-up.

If many people have this problem, however, *then go and speak to them to understand their **perception** of the problem. Only afterwards, build the solution.*

If you follow this path, and your solution eventually works, you will be creating value, which is the essence of your journey.

If you start with the solution, however, you might be building something that no one cares about, and that is frustrating when you've invested so much effort, time, and money. In fact, most start-ups will die because they were unable to figure out product-market fit, which in many cases happens when focusing on the solution rather than the problem.

There are many reasons to start with the problem, in addition to increasing the likelihood of creating value. Another key reason: your story will be much simpler and more engaging; people understand the frustration and can connect to that.

Start with the Problem

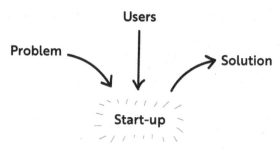

Find a **Solution** for Many **Users** with a **Problem**

Companies that fall in love with the problem ask themselves every day: Are we making progress toward eliminating this problem? They tell a story of "This is the problem we solve," or, even better, they narrow it down to "We help XYZ people to avoid ABC problems," whereas for companies that focus on the solution, their story will start with "our system . . ." or "we." If the focus is about you, it will be much harder to become relevant. If the story is about your users and a focus on the problem, it will be much easier to gain relevance.

WHY DO PEOPLE HAVE SUCH STRONG RESPONSES TO YOUR COMPANY IDEAS?

People are apprehensive about change. While you may have incubated the idea for a long while in your head and had time to embrace or adapt to the vision, for others it's brand new. Especially if you're a first-time entrepreneur, without name recognition, the change you're proposing can be so dramatic that it prompts a negative response. People need time to feel comfortable with an idea.

Starting a company is a leap of faith. If you're not willing to sacrifice— to give up on your current salary, position, and title—then you're not deeply enough in love. If you don't want to give up on a sport or a hobby, you don't have enough room in your attention to go on the journey of a start-up.

How do you know when you're ready to launch a start-up? When you're willing to sacrifice. That's the single most important metric. If you say, "I'll keep working in my current place of work but as soon as I raise capital, I'll quit and start my company," then it's not going to happen. You're not showing enough commitment. Which, by and large, will tell investors the same thing—that you're not committed. If you're not, then why should they commit?

WHAT IS THE PROBLEM YOU'RE TRYING TO SOLVE?

The key theme of this book is "fall in love with the problem, not the solution." A problem is easily defined. When you tell someone about it, that person should say, "Yeah, I have that issue as well!" In most cases, people will tell you their version of the problem and how frustrated they are when it happens to them. The more you hear other people tell you their version of the problem, the more you know that people perceive the problem as real, which means the perception of your value proposition will be real.

Now, if they describe their perception of the problem, and they also say there is value for them for the problem to go away, we are starting to look at a very painful problem. But before you rush into building a solution, you still need to ask yourself—and then validate with people who face that problem—either how painful it is (how much value there is in solving that problem) or how frequently they encounter it.

If you solve a problem people face daily—and, if possible, a few times a day, like during their commute to the office and back—you are on to something big. When Google was in dialogue with us about acquiring Waze in 2013, their CEO Larry Page said that Google is interested in a "toothbrush model"—something that you would use twice a day, which is exactly what Waze is.

Problems fit into a matrix with two axes: Total Addressable Market and Pain.

The Qualification Matrix

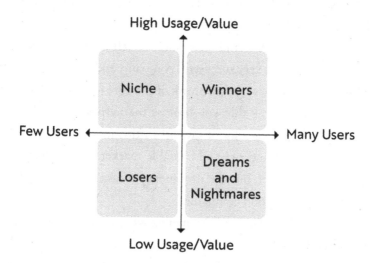

When thinking of a problem, look at this two-by-two matrix and ask yourself two questions:

1. How big is the addressable market? How many people have this problem? How many businesses suffer from this issue?
2. Then ask yourself the more important question: How *painful* is it? Pain can be measured by one or both of two factors: amplitude (really, really painful) or frequency (how often we suffer from it). Once you define your problem, go back to the matrix and see where it fits.

Let's look at each of the four quadrants in the matrix.

- "Winners" are easy to understand but hard to find. They're located in the upper right corner where there are many users and a high frequency of use (value)—think Facebook, Google, WhatsApp, and Waze. If you ask someone how they heard about Waze, it's most likely through word of mouth, from friends. All successful companies in the consumer space have seen their growth based on friends telling friends. If your product is used at a high frequency, the chance of this happening is dramatically greater because there are many opportunities to use the product and many more to tell others about it.

- "Niche" could be a very successful company, and one with potentially a huge impact for a very few (think of the cure for a rare medical syndrome). Or imagine that you build a marketplace of underutilized private jets. There is a lot of savings in this model, but it is relevant for a very small (and rich) addressable market. Niches have a small addressable market, but their frequency of use or value is very high. These are pretty good companies.
- "Losers" are in the area of the matrix where there are few users and low usage/value.
- "Dreams and nightmares" are the category of the addressable market of "everyone," but where there is low value or low frequency of use, e.g., a service to renew your driver's license. While going to the DMV (Department of Motor Vehicles) is always perceived as a waste of time, it only occurs once every five or ten years. People want to believe in their dreams, but in reality, these are nightmares because there is not enough value that can be accessed through the addressable market.

Problems can be measured by frequency of use, the magnitude of the frustration, the alternative cost, or time saved. Whatever the model, the solution may change several times along the way to product-market fit (which, quite simply, means that you've figured out how to create value for your users).

We'll explore product-market fit in detail in chapter 8.

The problem, not the solution, is nearly always the key motivation and reason for founding a start-up. Of course, there are successful companies that started without a problem, like the first social media start-ups or online gaming companies, but *my* approach is always to start there and not with the solution.

FIND YOUR PAIN POINT

How do you know if a problem is one you should pursue?

I always begin by looking for "the pain." For me, that's driven primarily by frustration. Yes, there may be other parts to that pain, but frustration is critical in order for anyone to act. If I run into something that I don't like or that makes me angry, I start to think about how to fix it.

My biggest recurring frustrations are wastes of time, like waiting in line (at supermarkets, in traffic jams, at airport security, waiting for the lift at a ski resort), and wasting money.

I hate it when I feel like I'm being ripped off.

The problem Waze set out to solve was how everyday drivers could avoid traffic jams—simple, straightforward, and relatable.

The story is similar in the other companies I've started or joined on the first day. Here are some of the pain points they address:

- **Moovit**—Deals with the frustration of waiting for the bus; it's the Waze of public transportation and it answers the same questions: How do I get from here to there in the fastest way possible (in this case, on public transportation)?
- **Engie**—Dealt with the frustration of going to the mechanic, where most of us feel somewhere between helpless and being idiots.
- **Pontera**—We started FeeX, which in 2022 changed its name to Pontera, based on the problem that people know very little about their retirement plans. Most people don't know how much they are paying in fees, nor what their expected retirement savings are. When I was young, my dad once told me that if you don't know how much you're paying, you are paying too much. It turns out that transparency, and acting on that knowledge, will help you to retire richer.

- **FairFly**—FairFly deals with the biggest secret in the travel industry: What happens to airfares *after* you book your flight. No one knows because no one compares prices afterward. Airfares change all the time—before you book your flight and also after you book it, so if the price drops, you can actually rebook the same flight at a cheaper price.
- **Refundit**—When you travel and go shopping in Europe, you're entitled to receive tax back on purchases made. That tax is not insignificant: it can average more than 20 percent of the purchase price. But when you're trying to get the tax back, it simply doesn't work. Maybe there are long lines at customs, or the store doesn't have the right forms, or when you ask where the tax refund office is, they will tell you it is in a different terminal. The result is truly frustrating. In 90 percent of cases, people fail to get their money back.
- **Fibo**—Filing taxes is complex and expensive in most places outside the US. As a result, a lot of money is left on the table. (Recall that I hate waste; money left on the table is certainly a waste.)

Let's look at a few of these companies in more detail.

PONTERA: RETIRE RICHER

The year 2008 was a bearish year and, not surprisingly, because of the economic crisis, when I got my annual statement for my retirement account at the end of the year, I found I'd lost around 20 percent of my long-term savings. Even worse, I discovered that I was charged 1.5 percent in management fees for *losing* that money.

I was frustrated, and not so much because I was paying fees but because I *didn't know* that I was paying those fees. I asked some of my friends; none of them knew either. If no one knows, that's the exact definition of a secret. A market with secrets, with unidirectional information, is calling for disruption through the creation of transparency. Then I started to dig deeper, and realized that no one understood how retirement savings work, or what the expected worth of their savings upon retirement is.

I came up with the idea for Pontera to help deal with the transparency of retirement plans and their fees. Obviously, the return is much more important than the fees, but when you look at the bigger picture, the net return is the nominal return minus the fees, compounded over the years between now and retirement. That makes up a very big piece of your retirement savings.

We started in Israel with the fees, and when we moved to the US, we made several rounds of changes in the product until we figured out the market and its needs. When we started in Israel, we quickly attracted users who could then see how much they were paying (and how they compared to people like themselves, which became a key "triggering event" for user acquisition and taking action).

We started in Israel focusing on fees and not the return because there was no way to compare returns back then, and we thought it would be easier to market and a call for action for our users. We thought we'd take the same concept to the US, but we discovered that the fees involved with "held-away accounts," such as 401(k) and 529 plans, were just the tip of the iceberg. It was then years of figuring out product-market fit again, and realizing that the nature of the problem in the US is very different. When you join a new employer in the US, your benefits often include a 401(k) plan. You can define your 401(k) contribution and choose where to invest it. In more than 80 percent of cases, people stick with the default investment, and that decision won't change over the years. This default is usually low risk/low return, and what's even worse, no one is managing or even overseeing your most important long-term savings. In fact, default 401(k) accounts result in much lower returns than managed accounts, and with the compound effect of it, the difference could mean retiring rich or not.

Pontera today is a platform for financial advisors to manage 401(k) and other accounts for their customers. Pontera is the bridge to better (richer) retirement.

FAIRFLY: SAVING MONEY AFTER YOU'VE BOOKED

When one of my sons was thirteen, I took him to Orlando on a bar mitzvah trip. After all, what thirteen-year-old boy turns down a visit to Disney World?

I booked an apartment in a vacation resort in Orlando for $120 a night, which seemed like an awesome deal. But a week before the trip I found out, to my surprise, that the resort was nearly empty, and the deal was now $120 *for the entire week*. I immediately canceled the first reservation and made a new one. I set myself a reminder to check again two days before departure, at this rate they might even pay me for going there, and yes, two days before the trip, it was now $120 for the week *including breakfast*.

This experience, I realized, also applied to an even more common example of prices changing after they're booked: airfares.

FairFly is another great example of turning frustration into a company. What happens to airfares *after* you've booked your flight? The reality is that you don't know because no one compares prices after the reservation is made. But airfares are still going up and down all the time. As long as the price drop is greater than the cancellation fee, it's worthwhile to rebook the same flight for cheaper airfare.

When I was at Waze and needed to schedule a work trip in New York, a couple of days after I made my reservation, another Waze employee asked to join me on the trip. I told him "sure," and I went back to Expedia to book his ticket.

To my surprise, I discovered that his ticket would be more than 30 percent cheaper than what I had paid for it!

I was traveling a lot at that point for Waze, and there were other Waze employees traveling a lot as well, so this was not an insignificant problem. The same goes for most large corporations. It turns out that the average price of airfare changes about ninety times from the moment you make your reservation until the day of the flight.

The bar mitzvah trip may have been the trigger for FairFly, but it was booking my trip to New York when I realized this problem—let's call it an opportunity—is truly systemic and not just a one-off occurrence or coincidence.

REFUNDIT: SIMPLIFYING TAX-FREE SHOPPING IN EUROPE

A few years ago, I was in Madrid with my wife. On our last day there, we wanted to buy something at a sporting goods store. I was already experienced in applying for tax refunds while shopping in Europe, and I knew it was a problem worth solving. I was looking for confirmation from an inexperienced user—my wife—and therefore asked her to go through the process with me watching.

While it seems like I was creating extra work for her, there is *nothing* more important to understanding a user's frustration than watching that frustration unfold. It is even more critical when you watch a new user trying something for the first time.

My wife asked the shop owner if he had the tax forms she needed. He did not have the right ones or at least claimed not to have them. As I looked around at the other people in line, my thought was that this seller doesn't want to waste time with my wife; he wants to sell more or serve more customers. At this phase, my wife was ready to give up, as most people would in such a situation, but I insisted we go to another branch of the store that had the correct forms.

It took us only about ten minutes to find what she needed. But she then waited over an hour for the forms. There was a line of about ten people with only one employee to handle the paperwork. An hour-long wait to save about fifteen euros was certainly not worth it, but the experience was very important to understand how painful the process is.

Eventually, she got what she needed.

When we arrived at the airport, we went through the second process of claiming the tax refund, which is to get customs to approve it. Surprisingly, it was rather smooth and quick, but then we had to visit one more office, that of Global Blue, the company that issues the refund, and there the line was simply too long, our time was too short, and we were unable to claim our tax refund before our flight.

That's the problem Refundit solves—the estimated 26 billion euros a year that are not picked up by the millions of tourists streaming to Europe (in pre-COVID-19 days).

I've heard so many stories of people telling me: "Ohhh, you should hear what happened to me . . .", "You wouldn't believe my story . . ." Trust me, I believe you.

By now, you've already realized that I don't like to leave money on the table, nor do I like to wait in line.

FIBO: TAX RETURN FILING IS COMPLEX AND EXPENSIVE

When I speak with people in different parts of the world, I often ask them: "How is it to file tax returns in your country?" Other than in the US, where it's not such a big deal—you can take your documents to the nearest H&R Block or file online using TurboTax—filing taxes is a real pain. I always hear the following: It is either complex, expensive, or both. It's certainly a big problem for a lot of people around the globe.

In the US, everyone has to file their taxes annually. It's mandatory. That's not the same in other countries where most people don't need to file a personal income tax return, relying on their monthly deductions. In Israel, for example, only 5 percent of the adult population files a tax return. In the UK, it's about 25 percent.

Can you guess what happens? If it is not mandatory, and it is complex and expensive, people simply don't file and, as a result, even when they're entitled to a refund, since they don't claim it, they don't get it.

In Israel, 80 percent of employees are entitled to get a refund, but they don't bother filing. The result is an astounding 10 billion ILS that never gets refunded. This pushes my buttons just like the problem Refundit solves. Not only do I not like money left on the table, but I also particularly don't like it if there are a lot of people who could enjoy that money!

In all these examples, I fall in love with the problem and it was an easy story to tell people. They immediately connected to the problem. But for all those cases it took me years to find the right team—Yoav, Eyal, and David at Pontera; Aviel and Ami at FairFly; Ziv at Refundit; and Roi and Dana at Fibo. Then the journey started and those teams were the ones that never gave up, and went through the roller-coaster and desert-crossing challenges.

WHEN THE PROBLEM DISAPPEARS

Problems don't usually disappear all on their own. But the *perception* of the problem could very well vanish. That's what happened with Mego, a start-up I founded to address frustrations at the post office.

Mego was born from my frustration of getting a note from the post office saying I have a package waiting for me.

In much of the US, this is not a problem because the postal worker will leave your package at your front door even if you're not home. If you live in a building, the package can usually be left with the doorman. In that respect, packages in the US are essentially addressed to a door, not a person.

In Israel and Europe, though, the package is linked not to an address but to a specific person. So, if you're not home when the postal worker visits, you get a red note informing you to come to the post office. Naturally, the post office in question is open for only a few and inconvenient hours usually, at the same time you have to be at work, and closes early. If this was not discouraging enough, there are also always long lines and never any parking.

The result: Nearly 100 percent of packages in Israel are not delivered on the first attempt. It's not much better in the UK, where only a third of the packages are delivered on the first attempt.

Mego gave the recipient of the postal service red note an alternative: For a small fee, you could scan the red note, scan your ID, and someone would go and get it for you. The cost: about five dollars per pickup.

We started the company in 2016 and began testing the service in Israel. People loved it. But in 2017, the post office made several changes that addressed some of the main problems. You could now pick up your package at local 7-Eleven stores or lockers in strategic locations around the country. At the post office itself, you could now make a reservation for a specific time via the postal service's app or via text message. This, too, addressed the frustrations its customers had. And the post office remained open until later in the evening (8 PM and sometimes even until midnight).

The Mego service still had value, but the perception of the problem went away thanks to the changes the post office made. If you were looking at this problem in 2016, you'd start the company, as I did. By 2017, you wouldn't. Sometimes it's all a matter of timing. We have since closed the company down.

Additionally, I have made investments in start-ups where I am not the founder, but like the idea and the CEO. My usual strategy in these cases is to join the board so I can contribute my time and expertise. These start-ups include SeeTree, Weski, Dynamo, Pumba, and Kahun.

MORE ABOUT SOME OF MY START-UPS

Besides the start-ups that I founded based on problems I fell in love with, I'm involved in half a dozen other start-ups, which I'd largely joined long before they had even started. In most cases, I helped the founding team or the CEO to get started, then invested, and then guided them throughout the journey and became a member of their board.

SeeTree is one of them. I have known the CEO for four decades, and when he was just starting to think about building a start-up after a long and successful career, I started helping him way before he started. I invested the first money in the company, and I am now on the board of directors (BoD).

SeeTree's magic is in the agriculture space and, as the name suggests, specifically in the tree grower market, where they help to increase yield dramatically. Growers who have millions of trees have very little information and certainly not actionable data on what's going on in their farm.

SeeTree's solution combines drones flying overhead with on-the-ground, individual-tree-level analysis to figure out if there is an issue with a tree and if so determine an actionable plan to restore production for that tree. At the end of the day, their efforts increase the tree farm's yield by 15–20 percent year over year.

WeSki is another start-up I'm involved in. I mentored the team at the Zell Entrepreneurship program, and have remained involved since then, through a major roller-coaster journey, which included a near shutdown, two years of service interruption due to COVID, and much more.

WeSki deals with my biggest hobby—skiing. Today, when trying to arrange a ski vacation, you have two options: buy an off-the-shelf package or do it yourself, often spending hours on the internet building your own custom package. WeSki is a Lego-like, build-it-yourself service, offering the flexibility of custom-made in a fraction of the time. If you're on the East Coast of the US, and thinking of going for a week-long ski vacation in the Rockies, I would suggest going to France, using WeSki to plan, and your trip will be much better and much cheaper.

The CEO of **Kahun** has been a friend of mine since high school. The CTO, however, has been a friend through middle school, high school, and military service, and worked with me at Waze. Both have considerable experience in the tech start-up world and have experienced a successful exit as founders of a start-up that was sold to Live-Person. They came to me with the idea about two years before they started, and I told them the problem they wanted to solve was real and big, and that whenever they were ready, I would be ready as well. It was another year and a half, or maybe even two years, until they officially started. I'm first money in (through my investment vehicle), on the board, and always available for them. The problem they are addressing is one of the biggest—data in the medical space. It turns out that most of the data in the medical space is in a form of text, such as books, articles, research, and so on. Kahun converts this text into data and creates an AI system for diagnostics, for prescreening of patients, and to help medical staff be better prepared.

FIND YOUR PASSION

Your passion for making a change must be greater than your fear of failure and the alternative cost. This is what I call the "entrepreneurship zone," because not every person with a great idea has the personality to build a start-up.

This won't be the same for everyone, but the common denominator is that you say, "I'm not going to continue what I'm currently doing. I'm willing to sacrifice, to take that leap of faith."

That's what I mean by "alternative cost." It's the price you pay to go on the start-up journey, either by turning down other options or leaving your current position.

Very strong feelings create emotional engagement that leads to passion. While in my case, frustration or waste could lead to it, in others' cases it could be love, hate, or revenge.

Nir Zuk, the founder of cybersecurity company Palo Alto Networks, was one of the first employees at Israeli cybersecurity giant Check Point Software, but he had a falling out with the management. He built his new company to compete with Check Point.

If my passion is avoiding frustration at all costs, his passion was revenge. It was even reported that he had a custom license plate made in California that meant "Check Point Killer": CHKP KLR.

Zuk may have the last laugh here: In 2021 Palo Alto Networks had a market capitalization (the value of the company) of $52 billion and in 2020 an annual revenue of over $4 billion, compared with Check Point with a market cap of "only" $15 billion and annual revenue of over $2 billion. In December 2021, Check Point was removed from the Nasdaq-100 Index. Palo Alto Networks replaced it.

The strongest form of passion is not for methods of making more money. Rather, it's about changing the world to make it a better place.

We thought that the value proposition of the Waze app was to find the fastest route and save time. But it's not. It's peace of mind. As I mentioned before, people mainly want to know their estimated time of arrival (ETA) when driving from Cupertino to San Francisco. They're less concerned about whether it will be faster on Interstate 280 or Highway 101. Eventually, in order to be successful, you will need to know what makes people tick. In most cases, this is about their emotional engagement with the problem, and the actual perceived value is likely going to be different than the perceived value in your story. For now, you need to find a problem that makes you tick, a problem you can fall in love with.

GOING BEYOND A "SAMPLE OF ONE"

Falling in love with the problem usually starts with a personal perspective. That makes sense: No one will try to solve a problem they don't care about. But it's important to switch your thinking to the experience of others, of the masses, so to speak.

As individuals, we are a very good sample . . . *of exactly one person.* We tend not to realize that there are other people who don't think like us. You do something in a certain way and believe it is the only way to do it, or you become attached to your perception of the problem and imagine therefore it's a problem for everyone. It's not. People are not all the same. There is not usually one right way.

If you hear the essence of the same problem described by multiple people from different angles, then you know it's a real problem.

Emotions are a powerful motivator for change.

When we set up Engie, it was because we kept hearing about the same problem: we feel helpless, or we feel like we are being ripped off, or we feel like idiots at the mechanic. Unless you are an expert in spark plugs and oil levels and the like, you're standing there clueless. And there's no clear price quote. Your repairs could cost $200 or $2,000. You don't find out the price until your car is already lifted on the rack.

You want a quote? "Let me open up the hood. Only then can I tell you." The reality is that in most cases what they simply do is connect the car computer to the diagnostic computer, and you don't even need to go to the mechanic for that.

You begrudgingly pay the bill, but you often feel like you're being ripped off. You're not, usually. Most mechanics are honest professionals, but the perception is there. Indeed, research we conducted for Engie shows that about three-quarters of people think they are being ripped off while, in fact, about three-quarters of the mechanics are professional and honest. The challenge is to sort out who's who in the larger pool of available mechanics. The uncertainty exacerbates the feeling of helplessness.

Here's a story I like to tell in my presentations. You go to the mechanic, and he says you have to replace the carburetor. So you agree. There's one problem: there is no carburetor in your car. Manufacturers haven't made cars with carburetors for a few decades now! That's how helpless we are!

The other problem with mechanics is there's no way to compare prices between different mechanics. When your car needs a new alternator and won't run, you can't exactly drive it around to the next nearest garage. If there's no way to compare prices, it means the market is broken.

We started Engie to deal with this broken market and the frustrations of getting your car repaired. We created a device that plugs into the data port of your car (all new cars built during the last twenty years have them).

The Engie dongle was designed to communicate with your smartphone and give you a real-time description in plain English of what your car's problem is. Is the air pressure in your tires low? Do your brake pads need replacing? It then displayed a list of available mechanics in your area with a price quote for fixing your vehicle.

The size of the market for car mechanics—how much car owners pay every year for repairs—is approaching $1 trillion. That certainly seemed like a market worth addressing!

We didn't think Engie would be used that frequently because cars, thankfully, are pretty robust, but we discovered that people were running the "check car" function on the app on a regular basis in order to have peace of mind.

The consumer side of Engie was awesome, with very high retention and high frequency of use. In fact, way more than we expected—about five to six times a month. When we initially tried to figure out the business model, we were aiming at a marketplace. Once the driver knew there was a problem with the car, we would ask for a quote for the repair from mechanics in the driver's neighborhood. The app provided the advantage of knowing exactly what needed to be repaired. It turned out that was not enough. It was a bit of a burden for consumers to renegotiate the quote from their local mechanic, but not enough to switch to a different mechanic. Further digging into it revealed a very complex market where consumers, mechanics, and dealerships have different perspectives on the market, and each one had their own agenda. We tried a different business model of remote diagnostics so your own mechanic would call you once there was an issue—proactively—but it was too late and too little.

At the end of a six-year journey, Engie was shut down. A big problem and a powerful story are very good starting points, but they're always not enough to become successful. We were able to figure out PMF for consumers, but we were unable to figure out PMF for a marketplace or for a retention tool.

We were close to the end of our funding and were in dialogue with some new investors from Asia. Then, COVID-19 hit, and the investors disappeared. We simply didn't have enough funding to continue or to find another investor.

It was as Michael Jordan once said: "I've never lost a game. I just ran out of time."

Obviously the Engie journey, like all other journeys, was a long, a roller-coaster journey of failures. There were ups and downs, including a change of CEOs (which today I think was a mistake), but the one dip that we were unable to recover from was the disappearance of the investor who told the company that he intended to invest and then disappeared. This, together with lack of support from the existing investors during the pandemic, brought Engie to its end.

EASY PATH—NOT FOR START-UPS

No matter what you do, building a start-up will be a very challenging journey, perhaps the most challenging journey you will ever take. There will be times you'll ask yourself, "Why in heaven did I decide to go on this journey?"

If you are not really passionate, if you're not really in love, you won't have enough internal energy to get through the hard parts. But if you're in love, you won't think about anything else.

What about building a start-up as a second job, or building it while you still have other major commitments? That's an easy answer. To go through the start-up journey successfully, you must put 200 percent of your time, effort, attention, and everything into the start-up and 0 percent into everything else. Nothing else works. You're about to embark on a roller-coaster, nightmare journey that will be so challenging that, if you don't start with enough passion, you won't get to the other side.

If you don't fall in love with the problem, you simply will not be able to get through the point when it feels like nothing is working and you're ready to give up.

STARTIPS

- Avoid the trap of falling in love with the solution. Instead, focus on the problem you're trying to solve.

- A solution-focused story starts with "My company does . . . " or "My system does . . ." A problem-focused story starts with "We solve the . . . problem." A user-focused story starts with "What we are doing for you is . . ."

- Find a BIG problem worth solving and ask yourself who has this problem. Then go speak with those people to understand their perception of the problem.

- Prepare for people to tell you your start-up "will never work" or is "a stupid idea." People don't like change and your new start-up is a change.

- How do you know that you're ready to launch a start-up? When you're willing to sacrifice—to give up your current salary, position, and title, and maybe your income, for the foreseeable future.

- As individuals, we are a very good sample of exactly one person. Only when you hear a problem described by multiple people from different angles do you know you are addressing a real problem.

- Work-life balance doesn't exist for founders, and in particular for the CEO in a start-up. If you fall in love with the problem, you will not want (or be able) to do anything else!

Chapter 2

A START-UP IS A JOURNEY OF FAILURES

If you've never failed, you've never tried anything new.

—Albert Einstein

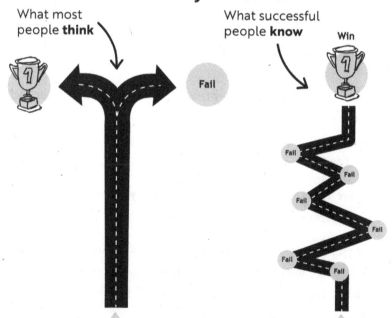

The Journey of Failures

What most people **think**

What successful people **know**

Win

Fail

Fail

Fail

Fail

Fail

Fail

Fail

Ben Horowitz is one of the most successful venture capitalists in the world, a partner in the Silicon Valley firm Andreessen Horowitz. Before he was a VC, Horowitz was CEO of software start-up Opsware.

Once he was asked, "Did you sleep well at night, being the CEO of a start-up?"

"Oh yes," he replied. "I slept like a baby. I woke up every two hours and cried."

Horowitz had experienced firsthand the roller-coaster journey that is common to all start-ups. There are so many ups and downs and, while all businesses in the world have ups and downs, the frequency of those in a start-up is much greater. They could be a few times a day, to the extent, I would say, if you don't like extreme sports, maybe a start-up is not for you.

That's because building a start-up is, at its essence, *a journey of failures*. You are trying to do something that no one did before, and even though you may be pretty sure you know exactly what you're doing, you don't.

In this chapter, I will establish the fundamental assumptions of building a start-up.

- It is a journey (with multiple sub-journeys).
- It is a roller-coaster journey.
- It is a journey of failures with continuous trial and error in each one of the phases.
- There is a very long period of no traction, which is the desert that you need to cross on your journey.

There are two immediate conclusions once you realize that building a start-up is a journey of failures.

1. If you're afraid to fail, in reality, you have already failed, because you're not going to try. Albert Einstein said that "If you've never failed, you've never tried anything new." In other words, if you will try new things, you will fail.
2. To increase your likelihood of being successful, you must fail *fast*!

If we agree that this is a journey of failures, then the best way to increase your likelihood of figuring out what works is simply to *try* more things, and the best way to try more things is to try them out *fast* and to fail fast so you have enough time (and run rate) to try the next thing.

For example, assume you believe that a specific feature is going to cut it, and you build this feature, release the new version, and then . . . it doesn't work, or it doesn't bring the results you were hoping. In that case, you should think immediately about the *next* feature that is worthwhile, and try and focus on that, rather than trying to optimize the current one.

That creates a very unique DNA for a company (a business culture or a set of values), where every underlying assumption is just a hypothesis and is worth trying—the sooner the better. If it works, that's it. If not, then it's on to the next hypothesis.

Even when you follow this path, and every new try or attempt is undertaken with a conviction that this time it is going to work, it is still going to be a very long journey.

The longest part of it is when nothing works. At the beginning, there will be a lot of excitement. You're creating something new. You have the first user or the first version, and maybe someone writes about you in the paper, and it seems like you are moving in the right direction. But then there is the realization that what you've built simply doesn't work. You try different things and it still doesn't work.

The Long Journey

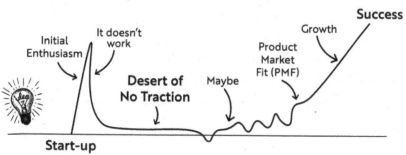

Imagine that you are crossing an endless desert. There is only sand around you. You walk all day and there is still only sand around you. You go to sleep and wake up and there's only sand. You do that day after day after day. You don't feel like you're making any progress, but you actually do make progress, taking one small step at a time, until eventually, you're out of the desert (if you haven't died beforehand).

The "desert of no traction" is the longest part of the journey. This is where you try everything, and nothing works. You build a product, and it doesn't work. You build the product, and it *does* work, but users aren't coming. You build the product, it's working, and users are coming . . . but they're not staying. Most of the start-ups that fail will fail during this desert journey.

When you're crossing a desert—whether it's the real thing or a metaphor for life in a start-up—there are two things you don't want to do:

1. You don't want to change directions, otherwise you might wind up walking around in circles. (Being potentially lost in the desert is not the time to "pivot.")
2. You don't want to run out of fuel. It turns out that fuel (or in the case of a start-up, your funding) is very expensive in the middle of the desert.

The first part of the journey of failures is always figuring out product-market fit (essentially creating value for your users). Once you figure out PMF, you buy yourself a ticket to the next part of the journey (which by itself is going to be yet another journey of failures), whether that's crafting a business model, going global, or learning how to scale.

The good news is that if you figure out product-market fit, you are on the path toward success. If you don't figure it out, you will die.

In each one of these parts of the journey, what matters most is how fast you recover and, in order to recover fast, you must start by failing fast. How quickly can you get back on your feet to try the next idea/concept/thesis? Entrepreneurs who adopt this method of failing fast will simply increase their chances of success.

When to pivot? Hopefully never, but if nothing works, you cannot figure out PMF, and users are telling you the problem is not real or that the value you're trying to create is irrelevant, then it is time to pivot. A pivot is not yet another experiment in your journey. It entails reconsidering the underlying assumption. At the end of the day, product-market fit means you are creating value for your users, and they are coming back. Figuring out PMF is about trying to get to this value so they will come back. Pivot is about changing either the users or the value proposition.

Let's take a deeper dive into Waze, which may look like a knockout success today, but until it got there, was a trial-and-error journey on multiple fronts—first for product-market fit, then for the growth process, and yet again for figuring out the business model.

In the case of Waze, though, there is a magic that is way beyond imagination.

A BLANK SHEET—THE MAGIC OF WAZE

Waze is today the world's most successful driving app, and in many countries, people won't even start their car before they start up Waze. What most people don't realize is that *all* the content used by Waze is **user generated** by other drivers. We crowdsource everything, not just traffic information or speed traps—those are obvious—but *also the map itself.* That's the magic of Waze.

Blank Page

When we started Waze, **the map was simply a blank page**. There was absolutely nothing on the map, not even a single road—just a blank page.

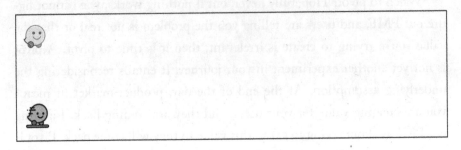

First Driver

Then, when the first user drove with the app, we collected the GPS data from the driver's device. If we take this data and plot it on the blank page, we can actually see the "trace" of the drive.

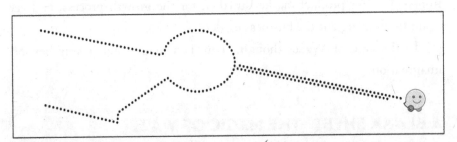

Many Drivers

Once there are a lot of drivers on the road, the GPS data from the drivers' devices creates something that starts to look like a map.

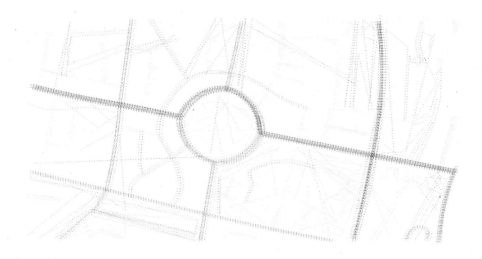

When you're looking at this picture (which, by the way, is from actual GPS traces in Tel Aviv from 2007), you can easily tell that there is something that looks like a traffic circle in the middle, and it is in fact a traffic circle.

You can look at the density of those GPS traces and tell the difference between a main road and an arterial street. If there is an intersection where no one is making a left turn, then no left turn is allowed.

If there are one hundred cars going in one direction, and no one driving in the other direction, that's a one-way street. Now, if there are one hundred cars driving in one direction and two cars driving in the other direction, that's a one-way street in Tel Aviv! When we launched Waze globally, we discovered that the 2 percent ratio of Tel Aviv is actually pretty good compared to some other places!

By crowdsourcing everything, we can provide real-time relevant information for people to use every day for their commutes.

Turning It into a Map

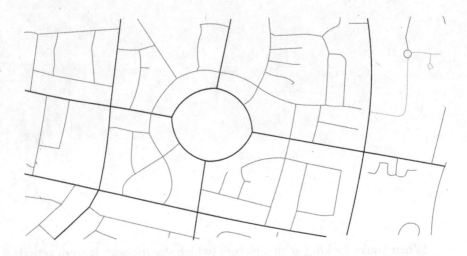

We've created the software that takes all these GPS traces from all users and creates the map out of it.

Map Editing

Then we enabled a map editing tool so that users can provide us with street names, points of interests, and house numbers.

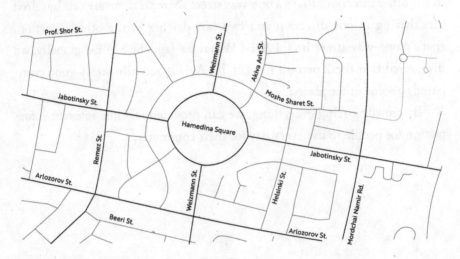

Driving Slowly

As we were tracking the GPS, if someone is driving slowly, we can figure out there is a traffic jam there.

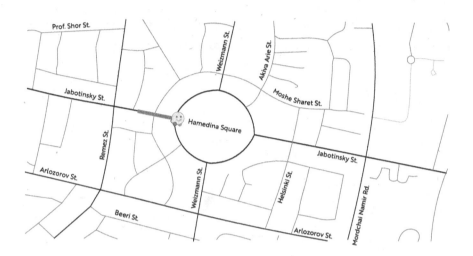

Traffic Jams

And once we have a lot of drivers, we can figure out where all the traffic jams are, and route people to avoid them and take the fastest route.

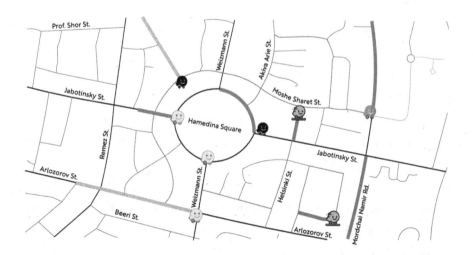

In this way, Waze is a social network of drivers, where all the content is created by the drivers.

Speed Traps and Driver Reports

On top of that, drivers were reporting speed traps, accidents, road hazards, and other real-time information that motorists do care about.

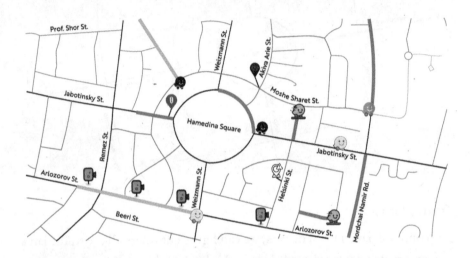

When I speak about this magical concept, people often ask me, "So, you mean that there was no map on the app for the first users?" To which I reply, "Exactly! There was nothing there." Then comes the more interesting question: "So, why would they use it in the first place? What was the value for them?"

The key question is not what was the value for the first user, but *who* were the first users? They were enthusiastic amateurs whose hobbies were GPS, GIS (geographic information system), maps, and navigation. These hobbyists cared more about the promise and the innovative approach of crowdsourcing, along with controlling their destiny, than the current state of the map. Think of the first users of Wikipedia, before there was any meaningful content.

"GOOD ENOUGH"

We worked on Waze for two years before it was good enough in Israel. In 2007 we were working on it as a project and not yet a company. In March 2008, once we received funding, we started the company, under the name Linqmap, which we changed in 2009 to Waze. We built the real-time app on a Nokia phone.

We went through multiple iterations until it was "good enough." One of the best ways to get to that point is actually to start with something that's *not* good enough and then iterate repeatedly until it is good enough. Your iterations are based on the feedback you get from your users.

Imagine the following: Two twin companies are starting on the same day and doing exactly the same thing. After three months of development, one of the two companies decides that their product is not ready yet, and therefore they continue development with the product now planned to hit the market in another three months.

The other company also decides that they are not ready but opts to get the product out to real users. Which one of those companies will be in a better position in three more months? It's simple. You do not make progress if you're not out there. If you don't have new information, you're not making real progress.

But what is "good enough"? If we define product-market fit as measured by one and only one metric—retention—then "good enough" is when your retention is sustainable and valid. (We'll discuss what to measure and target metrics in chapter 8.)

Going back to Waze, Israel is a very dense country. About nine million people live in a total area of about eight thousand square miles, similar to the state of Massachusetts. Plus, we already had those two years of gathering data and mapmaking during our development phase. In addition, we signed an agreement with a local fleet management company to provide us with real-time GPS data, which made the traffic information pretty accurate on the day of our official launch in January 2009.

All this made Waze "good enough" in Israel. We saw that the magic works. The map was created by the users, the word of mouth worked for growth, and the data accuracy was good enough. We were ready to launch the app globally.

We used the rest of 2009 to prepare (languages, servers, support) and launched the product globally toward the end of the year. The situation abroad was much different, however. We had assumed Waze would work much the same in other countries as it had in Israel. But that wasn't the case.

We turned the app on worldwide all at once, and it was a disaster. It was simply not good enough—really, it simply sucked—except in four countries: Ecuador, Slovakia, the Czech Republic, and Latvia. Everywhere else, people would download the app, try it, and give up.

When we first got up and running in North America, if you tried to go from your home to the office, with the limited map data we had and with few users running the app, Waze would give you an awful route. Instead of the obvious route (say Highway 101 from Palo Alto to San Francisco), it would offer to send you via the East Bay and Oakland, something that obviously doesn't make sense.

As Waze was crowdsourcing the information, if no one drove on your street, we were unable to take you to the end of that block because we didn't know if you were allowed to drive there! We used a base dataset from the US Geological Survey for our maps. But the dataset was outdated big-time. Moreover, it was not navigable, meaning there were no directions on the map with indications of what was a one-way street or where there were turn restrictions.

Since Waze only knows if a turn is allowed if other drivers have already made that turn, the map data was at this point highly incomplete. Drivers became frustrated, and understandably so. People using the app would see a road ahead of them and they could see the road on the map, but the app wouldn't take them on the obvious route, simply because the data wasn't there yet. The result was terrible. Actually, it was worse than terrible. To our shock and horror, we had more than 90 percent churn. That's when people try something only to give up on it.

In the consumer services business, as I've mentioned, retention is the *only* indicator of product-market fit. If users are coming back, you are creating value. You can't build a company if your retention sucks.

Waze tried multiple forms of triage. The company empowered community map editors in the US, as we had done in Israel. We even hired our own map-editing staffers who manually reviewed the routes people drove and corrected them every night to support the community map editors. We changed the algorithm powering Waze again and again.

There was a point in time when we wanted to upend the saying that you can "never get a second chance to make a first impression." So, once the community or our map team fixed a problem, we'd generate an app message to all users who had experienced that map issue. It would read something like: "We know you got a crappy route yesterday, but the system is learning all the time, and when you drove with the app, it learned that it could go that way, so it is worthwhile to give it another try."

We were hoping to regain the trust of our users, and we assumed that, as Waze was targeting commuters, if the map going to work and going home is now OK, we will have time until it will become good enough. We realized that "good enough" has an individual perspective: your good enough and mine may not be the same.

The goal was to reengage the user so that he or she would give us another chance. Think about it: You've tried Waze, it was a lousy route, so you drove your regular way. The next day, we already *knew* your regular way. The feeling was that the app was improving. Without users knowing that it is improving, they wouldn't give us the second chance we so desperately needed.

Every two to three weeks, we'd release a new version, trying to make it better. Every once in a while, we'd have a real breakthrough. In some of those new versions, we'd take a baby step forward. In some, it turned out to be a step backward. But whichever way we went, we would always speak with drivers.

This is one of the most important keys to your success, and I can't empha-size it enough: Listen to your users/customers and, particularly during the product-market fit phase, try to understand what *doesn't* work for them. This user feedback is the only thing that allows you to move faster, and it is the only thing that matters. Even though we could glean pretty good measurements out of our system, if you don't speak with users, you can easily figure out the "what," but not the "why." And in order to get to "good enough," you need to understand the "why."

This is exactly what we did. When we realized things weren't working, we immediately went out and spoke with drivers. They told us what didn't work, so the next version was all about fixing those issues. Each time we just knew, with 100 percent conviction, that this was it, that this version was going to make the leapfrog . . . and then *it didn't*. So, it was back to the next process of listening to the drivers and going into another iteration, again with the same conviction and determination . . . and then all over again.

Obviously, if we had known which one of the changes would compel the metaphorical frog to leap to the next level, we would have made those changes right at the beginning. But we didn't know. Every time we thought we knew, it turned out we didn't. Over time, the system improved, new drivers signed up, and the system became better and better. After a long journey of failures, through iteration after iteration, Waze finally took off.

The key takeaway: Building a start-up is a "journey of failures." You try one approach—be it a new product feature or testing your pricing model or a decision about scaling up in a new territory—it fails, and you move on to the next idea until you get it right. And then you don't change at all.

It took us nearly a full year of iterations, the entirety of 2010 until we reached the "good enough" level in the US and Europe with Waze. The magic happened one metropolitan area at a time—Los Angeles first; then San Francisco; Washington, DC; Atlanta; New York City; and then Chi-cago. In Europe, it was one country at a time: Italy first, then followed by the Netherlands, France, Sweden, and Spain.

HOW WE BUILT WAZE

When we started building Waze in 2007, the first version of the app ran on a PDA. You remember PDAs. No? Well, many years ago, there were dinosaurs, then PDAs, Nokia phones, and today we all have iPhones and Android devices.

Now, this "long time ago" is just a bit over a decade in the past. Imagine there is a time machine where I can take you with me back to 2007. That means that I would have to take away your iPhone, your Facebook, Messenger, WhatsApp, Uber, Netflix, and of course, Waze. It is unclear that you would survive!

It's quite incredible when you think about it: Everything that we are using daily is just one to two decades old.

If you used that time machine to go back to the prehistoric era, the days before Waze, and I told you what I was about to build, most likely you would have told me, "This will never work." That's if you were polite. Otherwise, you might say something more extreme like, "This is the stupidest idea I've ever heard!" Dramatic changes are really dramatic and therefore the first reaction is always the same. In fact, this is *exactly* what I heard when trying to raise capital for Waze.

Think about the top companies in the world today like Google, Amazon, Tesla, Facebook, Netflix, and many others. Most were start-ups just ten or twenty years ago. So much has changed in the last decade, and the next decade will be even more dramatic.

In the pre-Waze era, the navigation and mapping worlds were separated. On one side there were companies that made maps, like Navteq in the US and Tele Atlas, based in the Netherlands, which mostly focused on Europe. The process of creating a map back then involved using dedicated survey vehicles and an armada of paid professional cartographers who crafted the digital versions with proprietary mapmaking tools. Then, there were navigation devices like TomTom and Garmin that enabled turn-by-turn navigation (using the aforementioned maps). There were also map display companies like Yahoo, Google, and MapQuest that enabled people to view and search a map for directions but not to navigate in real time. And there were traffic information companies, like Traffic .com and Inrix, that collected data from fleets in order to color-code the map (red, yellow, and green, usually) to reflect if there was traffic or not.

Finally, there were some mobile apps—Telmap, Telenav, and Networks in Motion—that allowed mobile carrier operators to offer their subscribers navigation functionality for a fee. AT&T used Telenav, Verizon used Network in Motion, and Israel's Pelephone had partnered with Telmap.

Waze was the first company to combine all of those functions into a single product. We had a key advantage: The same app and server are used to collect data, process it, deploy it, and present it to the user. Since the feedback cycle is in real time, we were able to improve and move much faster than our competition.

Ehud Shabtai, who would become CTO of Waze (and whom we met in chapter 1), was working on his navigation and mapmaking app, FreeMap, when I hooked up with him and his partner Amir Shinar in 2007.

The story started when Ehud received a PDA for his birthday. Ehud's PDA included navigation software on it from a company called Destinator Technologies. It helped him get to places that he had no idea how to get to. Ehud is an innovator. So, it's not surprising that he quickly got hooked on his new toy. Destinator had an SDK (a software development kit) that allowed programmers to easily add functionality to the basic app. Ehud was a talented software engineer. He decided to add to it the ability to report where speed cameras were.

He sent a message to a popular online forum for PDA users called Pocket PC Freaks. "If you have a PDA with the Destinator app on it, please download my add-on, report any speed traps you see, then I'll send you an updated file showing where all the other speed traps users report are," Ehud wrote on the forum.

A few hundred people downloaded the app extension and got to work. It only took a few weeks before every speed cam in Israel had been logged into the database. It demonstrated that crowdsourcing could be truly actionable in creating navigation data, and it was the beginning of the crowdsourcing concept that Waze would eventually use.

The next phase of the evolution was that he realized that the map content is king and that those who own it control their destiny. He also realized around the same time that just as the community had crowdsourced the speed cam data, maybe they could also crowdsource the creation of the map itself. That was easier said than done. But Ehud was clever and comfortable with thinking outside of the box.

~

Ehud created FreeMap as a magical combination of a few functionalities. There was the driving app, the mapping app (actually, the same app), and a back-end server to compile map updates (every night, at first). He did this by writing much of the code himself, occasionally using off-the-shelves packages where they were available.

In a very abstractive and simplified way, FreeMap was a combination of a few main functionalities:

- driving and GPS-collecting application (running on a PDA)
- data sync and mapmaking (server side)
- map-editing tools (Web and app side)

Once the data was synced to the server, it would be compiled and shared with all the other drivers who had synced their driving data.

The crowdsourced maps were far from good enough, but they were actually pretty impressive for a proof of concept that crowdsourcing a map may work. This did have one major advantage over traditional maps: It was up to date in the most relevant areas for the users. A new intersection could appear on the map the next day. It was only later when we started Waze that we made the crowdsourced map work to a level of good enough.

~

When Amir, Ehud, and I met in May 2007 and they explained what they were doing, I immediately thought, "Wow, this is the missing link needed to build this real-time commuter tool I had in mind." I then explained my theory about real-time traffic. As it turned out, Ehud's model was two steps ahead of mine, as he had already made a few leapfrogs in proving the model works.

From a small base of just a few hundred users, we were able to prove the concept, the same concept that was later used by Waze—that you actually can create a map and traffic information entirely through crowdsourcing.

Waze wasn't perfect. As I described above, it wouldn't be even "good enough" for another three years. But the vision was working, and we could imagine how, with more users and more tools, we could in fact make it good enough.

The three of us got down to work. Ehud and Amir were at the time working at a software house called XLNet, where Amir was the CEO and Ehud was the CTO. We all realized that we should start by raising capital, as there was a lot of development needed and we required a super powerful team for it.

From that day in May 2007, we decided that Amir and Ehud would run the R&D and I would run the company, the fundraising, strategy, team recruitment, and so on. It required a leap of faith from all of us and the commitment to go through the journey. I left my job and they followed once we raised capital. That was critical for the establishment of Waze, which was essentially started that day.

A couple of weeks later, we decided to start the fundraising journey, with me leading as CEO. We raised capital only in March 2008, and formally started the Waze journey (even though it wasn't called that at the time).

During that initial time in the "garage," until we were funded, we made relatively slow progress. I was trying to raise capital (building the story and the business plan and running around to meet investors), while Ehud was still operating FreeMap and making some enhancements as needed.

We met frequently, sometimes at the offices of XLNet, but more likely in my mom's living room. My father had passed away a few months earlier, and she was rather lonely, on one hand, and the house was rather empty, on the other. So, we used her living room as our meeting room. It turned out to be a pretty good place for a start-up. Not only was it perfect for us, but it was also a major support for my mom in her grief. (At the same time, she was preparing us food and goodies throughout the day!)

In the summer of 2007, we started our fundraising journey. By the spring of 2008, we had raised $12 million. That was, of course, after another journey of failures. (More about it in chapter 5.) It doesn't sound like a lot today, but it was a very hefty funding round in 2008 in Israel.

WHY FAILURE IS IMPORTANT

Failure is not only OK but also *necessary*. It may be the most important thing to understand about building a start-up. By embracing failure, you increase the likelihood of being successful.

What matters most is how fast you recover—how quickly you can get back on your feet. If you're operating under fear of failure, you will break.

Basketball superstar Michael Jordan once quipped, "I've failed over and over and over again in my life. And that is why I succeed."

Canadian ice hockey player Wayne Gretzky made a similar point, joking, "I will miss one hundred percent of the shots I don't take."

The point is: You are trying to build something new that no one has built before, and even though you think you know exactly what you are doing, you do *not*. So you must try, again and again and again, until you find the one thing that does work.

The realization that this is a journey of failures is perhaps the most important thing that will help you to prepare for life in a start-up. If you believe you can simply build it and it will work, you are dead wrong! You will need dozens of revisions until your product becomes good enough. You run experiments until you get it right and only then can you move on to the next part of the journey.

If sometimes you tell yourself, "I should have done that differently," right then is the best time to do it differently. If you tell yourself, "Next time . . . ," guess what, next time is right now! TODAY IS THE FIRST DAY OF THE REST OF YOUR LIFE. It may be a cliché, but it's nevertheless true, for your own private life and even more so for your start-up journey.

I find myself mentoring many people—most of my CEOs, my kids, and occasionally others—and there is a very good reason for it: I like it. Perhaps my most important personality trait is that of an entrepreneur, but the second one, and pretty close to the first one, is that of a teacher. I enjoy teaching and therefore mentoring. That combination is pretty unique, but I feel equally rewarded whether I am building things myself or if I'm guiding someone else to build them.

This is, by the way, one of the key reasons for writing this book: I'm trying to help more entrepreneurs become successful, and I feel rewarded when I create value for others. While in general most of my guidance is around professional life, for a second, I want you to think about your personal life as well. For the sake of your personal life, do something that you love. This will keep you happy. If you don't do something that you love, now is the time to change it! You don't deserve to be miserable and, if you keep on doing things that you don't like, you will be.

If you tell yourself, "Next time, I will do it differently," then make "next time" *now*. It doesn't matter if this is about your relationships, the way you raise your kids, your job, your studies, or a hobby. If you know something needs to be changed, make that change *today*. We cannot change the past, but we can make changes today that will impact our future.

Teaching tolerance for failure is important not only in the start-up world. If you have children, encourage them to try different things. That will help them develop self-confidence. Fail and recover—this is one of the most important lessons to incorporate in your parenthood.

REFUNDIT: RESTART FROM SCRATCH

Here is a story about failing fast and restarting a whole company from scratch.

I founded Refundit, my company helping tourists who visit Europe to claim their tax refunds digitally, *twice*. Talk about a journey of failures!

I had been working with a team of entrepreneurs in the Zell Entrepreneurship Program at IDC Herzliya, a prestigious private university in central Israel.

The Zell program is a veritable factory for start-ups for me. Pontera (formerly FeeX), FairFly, Engie, and Fibo all came out of this program. It lasts for a full academic year alongside a student's standard curriculum requirements. Twenty or so of the very best students are selected to learn about building a start-up. They team up and launch a company during their studies.

At the end of the year, this is where the serious students are willing to commit; where we determine what they are giving up by going into the journey of building a start-up, and whether their passion for solving the problem is greater than the alternative cost.

For Refundit, the first attempt was during the Zell program, and it's when we realized that this journey was going to be longer than usual because of our dependence on European governments to approve a new method for processing completely digital tax refunds. This perception of a longer journey time created a much higher barrier (the alternative cost all of a sudden was quite significant), and so the team decided not to pursue the idea at the time. I put the problem aside for two years but decided to try it again after I got the attention of my friend Ziv Tirosh.

Ziv was running a bio-agricultural company that had recently been acquired by a Chinese firm. The company manufactured environmentally friendly pesticides; Ziv didn't know anything about tax refunds. In fact, he'd never tried to claim his VAT before.

"I didn't even know you could do that," he told me. "Go and speak with some travelers to Europe and get a sense of their experiences," I suggested. He did. He got back to me a week later. "I spoke with dozens of people," he reported. "You wouldn't believe the horror stories they've had." "Trust me, I believe them all!" I said. Ziv then flew to Belgium, bought a bike trainer in a small store, and tried to claim the tax refund. He was stymied just like I was. That was all it took for Ziv to get hooked. Shortly after, we started Refundit for the second time, and he became Refundit's CEO.

Why did I want to go down that road again with Refundit? Because this is a BIG problem to solve. Ninety percent of people do not get their tax-free refund and a total of nearly thirty billion euros in Europe alone is left on the table every year, not to mention the frustration and helplessness felt by many tourists. Under the leadership of Ziv, Refundit is certainly on the right path to making an impact and becoming successful.

Dov Moran is one of the great Israeli entrepreneurs. He built the USB drive, and afterward, started, funded, and engaged with many start-ups. One of those ended up unsuccessful. Big-time. In one of my meetings with him I asked, "How do you know when it is time to give up?" He thought for a second and then told me, "Never. Entrepreneurs will never give up." I think he's right, but I would add another point of view. If the problem disappears, then give up. If the team is not right and you're unable to do anything to change it, then give up and restart. The problem Refundit set out to solve was still there, it was a BIG problem, and Ziv's team is right.

FAILURE IS NOT A BADGE OF SHAME

Let me start with a story about a very successful CEO who didn't like to be covered by the press (he hated the spotlight). One day he agreed to sit down for an interview, and after a bit of small talk, the reporter asked: "How did you become such a successful CEO?"

The CEO replied: "Two words: right decisions."

That led immediately to the next question.

"OK, but how do you *know* how to make the right decisions?"

The CEO had an even shorter answer. "One word: experience."

That led to the final question. "So, how do you gain that experience?"

The CEO had a ready response for this, too. "Two words: wrong decisions."

Now, why is that so important? Because the fear of failure is usually what limits our ability to make decisions. That's why it's so important not to be afraid to fail.

Failure is no badge of shame in the tech world. The opposite, in fact, is true: A second-time entrepreneur has a much greater probability of success, regardless of what happened the first time, so the experience in that sense is worth the increase in the probability.

~~~

Experience is dramatic; it's key. So I don't care so much about your failure. I care about what you've learned!

Experience and failure play out for a company as a whole. Waze's algorithms work because they pack two years of failure into every line of code. What do I mean by that? One of the reasons Waze succeeded so much is our ability to detect traffic jams faster than anyone else. I often tell people that, because we collect the GPS trace data in real-time, we can tell the difference between a vehicle stuck in traffic and a vehicle pulled over at a 7-Eleven store. And therefore, we can detect traffic jams based on a single vehicle.

But in reality, this feature (detecting traffic jams based on single vehicle) was extremely complex to develop. We tried many ways, and it didn't work.

We tried to look at the trace difference (pulling into a gas station versus being stuck in traffic), and it didn't work. We wished it would determine where there were jams, but it didn't.

We tried averaging out a few vehicles, but that didn't work either, and in any case, we lost the "single-vehicle" determinant that way.

We tried asking drivers if they were stuck in traffic. That actually *was* helpful, but not helpful enough.

We tried to normalize the data, but it didn't work either.

We tried to use other data to support the decision, but that also didn't work.

Eventually, it was a combination of all the things that didn't work that allowed us to figure it out. Going through a journey of failures allows you to determine what to do by realizing what *doesn't* work and in particular *why it doesn't work.*

Start-ups that have lived the journey of failures and conducted many experiments over a longer period of time truly understand why they're doing things the way they are.

START-UPS THAT DON'T FIGURE OUT PRODUCT-MARKET FIT SIMPLY DIE

You've never heard of a start-up that didn't figure out product-market fit because they died unnoticeably. Some start-ups may *think* they figured out product-market fit, but they haven't. Remember, there's only one metric for determining you've locked down your PMF: RETENTION. Everything else, like customers willing to pay and partnerships with third parties, all those are great, but if your customers don't stick with you and don't keep on using your product, that means you don't create value for them, and that you will die.

Strong companies launch products and shut them down all the time. Google is famous for that: Google+, Hire by Google, Google Hangouts,

Picasa, Google TV, Google Reader, and Google Wave. They are constantly running experiments and making decisions based on the data.

Figuring out product-market fit is hard. It may be easier for established companies like Google. They have more time, resources, and access to the market that can keep their journey going for longer. Moreover, for the team trying new things within a large established company, the price of failure is minimal. "Hey, I still have a job at Google" (or whatever their existing company) is a common response.

But start-ups that don't figure out product-market fit, they simply die.

Once you figure out PMF, you're on the runway for takeoff (before that point, you're mainly taxiing on the ground).

There are four elements to increase your likelihood of getting to product-market fit:

- Fail fast so you have more time/runway for more experiments.
- Listen to your users.
- Focus on the problem.
- Make the hard decisions if needed.

LAUNCH BEFORE YOUR PRODUCT IS READY

I meet people all the time who are building a product. Often, they'll tell me their app or software will be ready in six months. I tell them, "You're totally wrong here. You should launch your product today, even if you're not ready, because you'll learn so much faster." You only learn when you have real users and real feedback.

You develop a very different approach when you get to use feedback at an early stage. It's much more effective than building the product to your satisfaction upfront and only then getting feedback. If the product is "done," you're much more reluctant to make changes.

It is also possible that, if you have heavily invested in the product, you might fall in love with your solution. You shouldn't! Falling in love with the solution means losing the practice of listening to your users, which is the only way to make progress in your journey toward product-market fit.

In fact, the best time to launch your product is when you'll be *embarrassed* by the quality of it. Yes, the product has to be so bad that you'll be mortified by the feedback. That's how you'll learn faster. You'll do shorter cycles, even at the beginning.

"But if I launch a poor product, I'll lose my users!" you might worry.

To which I respond: "Which users? You don't have any yet!" So, it's OK to disappoint those nonexistent users.

When you eventually figure out your product-market fit, after many experiments, the users will come. And if you don't figure it out, well, it doesn't really matter.

The role of your first users is to highlight the way for you. They will show you where to go with your product (and where not to go). If they are disappointed or screaming or churning, it's not a problem. Their role at this point is simply to point you in the right direction.

When your product eventually becomes good enough, they will forget they were ever displeased.

The other day, I was approached by an entrepreneur trying to build a neighborhood swap site for sharing lawn mowers, power drills, and the like.

"We'll be building the whole system using artificial intelligence," the entrepreneur gushed.

"Stop right there," I responded. "You'd be better off starting small and moving fast. For now, just create a WhatsApp group for exchanging items and listen to the feedback you get. You don't need to develop a full back-end server and do all the AI yourself at this point. Only once you've got your feedback should you start to build the product."

The founders actually listened to me and started a Facebook group and a WhatsApp group to exchange/swap items in their hometown. This turned out to be unsuccessful, as there was an underlying assumption that proved to be incorrect: The founders had assumed they needed critical mass—enough people in close proximity who were willing to share.

In reality, that wasn't what was most important. Rather, people were reluctant to share their frequently used items, and there was not enough demand for the infrequently used items, or they were too expensive to share. (There was a request for a Sea-Doo watercraft, which no one was willing to swap.)

The result was that, even without building an AI system to demonstrate anything, they were able to figure out what they needed . . . and much faster (in a matter of weeks and not years). The *only* way to make progress is by listening to your customers.

I once heard a story about how Dell started out like most computer companies. In one of the manufacturer's early meetings, CEO Michael Dell asked his team, "What are we going to do in this company?"

One of the guys wrote on the whiteboard, "We are going to do two things: 1) Build computers and 2) Sell computers."

Michael got up to the whiteboard and looked at it for a while, and then simply changed the order. "We are still going to do two things," he said. "We first sell computers and only then will we build them."

When you have a mindset of failing fast, every idea you have is a hypothesis that you need to validate.

In fact, when you think of a problem you would like to address, the first step is to validate if this problem is common and if you understand the perception of the problem *from other people* (your potential users or customers) rather than just your own "sample of one" perception.

So, rather than building it up front, from the get-go, simulate your software. Give it a manual back end so you can test the value proposition and the users' feedback before investing too much capital.

When we started Mego, the app that helps eliminate standing in line at the post office to get your package, we pulled off the biggest kludge of them all: we didn't develop a thing. Not a single line of code. No app, no back-end server, no infrastructure at all.

Instead of building an app to scan the note received from the post office and the customer's ID, we created a WhatsApp group and promoted it on Facebook. If you needed something picked up, you would contact us on WhatsApp. Everything was done manually, which allowed us to gauge market demand early and fast.

Essentially, the user would never even know that someone was reading the details and manually scheduling a pickup, rather than automated software. And let's be frank: users don't care.

When we started FeeX (which changed its name to Pontera in 2022), the plan was for you to upload a document, then OCR (optical character recognition) software would translate the image into text. In order to test the concept, though, we threw together a website in a hurry and we did all the OCR manually. A document would come in and someone in our office actually read it and wrote out what was in the image.

We did the same thing for Refundit—manually reading and typing in the data, long before we even considered developing the eventual OCR functionality.

This approach is exactly the same with each part of your journey, whether that's go to market, growth, business model, or business development. While most of the examples I've shared in this chapter are about product-market fit, this is still the case for any part of your journey.

When you build your go-to-market plan or your plan to bring users, I often see a one-line item, such as: "We are going to do PR," "We are going to use Google Ads," or "We are going to use Facebook to target our audience because we know these are thirty- to forty-year-old females who have a degree in X or Y."

In my mind, all those are very good ideas for conducting worthwhile experiments, but as soon as you figure out that they don't work, you need to have many more ideas lined up to try. The same is the case with business development; if you think that through business development you can bring a lot of customers (or users), then you would need to try many (and many more than you think) ideas until you find the one that does work.

With Moovit, we were looking for a business development partner to promote the app, and we thought that the best partner would be the bus operators themselves. We had already seen that word of mouth and paid user acquisition work, but we were looking for other growth engines.

We reached an agreement with the Metropoline bus operator in Israel to put stickers on the backs of every seat on all of their vehicles. At 9 AM the stickers went "live," I called our operations manager.

"What do we see so far? Any bump in users yet?"

"So far, nothing," he replied. "Let's give it a couple of weeks."

"No," I shot back. "If we see nothing today, then there's nothing there. If there is going to be a change, we'll see it instantly. We don't need to wait. If it's not working, no matter how hard we worked or how complex it was to do, it's time to put it to sleep."

This seems to be very different from the product-market fit experiment, but is it? It is still about failing fast; it is about understanding that the results are most likely to be obvious, even if you've invested a ton of effort into it. So, whether it's a new version of your app or a new campaign, the most important message is to always be ready to move on to the next experiment.

Running experiments means that you get a little taste of each part of your journey of failures. You get to test whether your underlying assumptions are correct. Gathering input before you commit to coding could cut a full year of development from your journey. Whether you've raised money or are still looking, that's not an insubstantial advantage.

ROADMAP: FAIL FAST!

Once you've accepted that failure is normal, inevitable, and actually something to be sought out, the best way to maximize this reality is to *fail fast*.

That way, you can jump back on the horse and try again. This is the only way you can increase the total number of iterations and therefore increase the likelihood of being successful.

Your road map is essentially a list of experiments you are going to do until you find the one thing that works.

Your go-to-market plan, user acquisition plan, and the vision for going global are all just experiments until you get each right.

If you have twenty different features you're considering, that means you will need to run twenty different experiments. And guess what: you will stop as soon as one thing does work.

Most entrepreneurs think that their product or app will need a lot of features. It's the other way around: The more features you add, the more complexity you create.

THE BIGGEST ENEMY OF "GOOD ENOUGH" IS "PERFECT"

How much time should you allocate to your journey of failures? Years! Not because you're doing anything wrong, but because two elements make a start-up a success: pure luck and getting your experiments right. If you get them right on the first try, you can move faster. And luck is always helpful.

Voltaire once wrote, "Perfect is the enemy of good."

I would modify that slightly for the start-up world: "The biggest enemy of 'good enough' is 'perfect.'" Good enough is usually enough to win a market.

Assume for a second that there is a good enough product in the market, which is measured by retention, so people are actually using it and are coming back. Now, you're building a better product, a perfect product. Your biggest challenge is to convince people to switch. Most people won't because what they currently have is good enough.

Agility must be the mindset of everyone in the company. It's not limited just to the R&D or product development team.

We always need to try new things and at the same time be ready to fail. It's true for individuals and it's true for organizations, too. The most important characteristic of an entrepreneur is quite simple: "Let's give this a try and see if it works."

FEAR OF FAILURE ON A SOCIETAL LEVEL

Fear of failure may be a cultural thing. In some countries, failure is not acceptable and, as a result, there are fewer entrepreneurs per capita than in other countries.

In Israel, for example, where failure is embraced, there is around one start-up per 1,400 people, while in Europe the number is one start-up per 20,000 people. Silicon Valley also has a low fear of failure, and as a result, more entrepreneurs per capita.

In a culture where the fear of failure is high, fewer people are willing to try. However, in a different place, where fear of failure is lower, more people are willing to try. The equation is rather simple: An individual will choose the entrepreneurship path if their passion is greater than the combination of fear of failure and the alternative cost.

I grew up in a home where, when I came to my father with an idea, even a crazy one, he would say, "Why don't you give it a try?" If it didn't work, there was no judgment, there was simply, "What have we learned?" Growing up in an environment like that decreased my fear of failure, but there was more to it than that.

Just imagine that you simply try more things, and if they don't work, you try different ones. That certainly helped build my self-confidence a lot and my ability to trust myself. In order to do it right, never forget: no judgment.

Obviously, this by itself doesn't create an entrepreneur. There needs to be more—the curiosity, intelligence, the not-taking-anything-for-granted attitude, and, very likely, a bit of a troublemaker personality. (Teachers hated me in high school; the number of times that I was kicked out of class is second only to the number of classes that I skipped.)

Remember that if you are afraid to fail, then in reality you already failed because you are not going to go on this journey. It doesn't matter if it's building a start-up or doing something you're afraid to do.

I speak at many conferences and events, some of which are geared toward entrepreneurs. In three to four different cases in Latin America, I was asked, "How can we become like Israel, the Start-up Nation, with so many start-ups per capita?"

The "what to do" is rather simple, but it starts with the realization that it is going to take one or two decades, and it requires perseverance in both decisions and action. After all, you're looking at a systemic cultural change of reducing the fear of failure. That will require a public, regulatory, and social campaign that encourages entrepreneurs.

Such a campaign should consist of the following:

- Create the regulation required for entrepreneurs. If an American invests in my start-up in Tel Aviv, there are no taxes for the investors in Israel. But if that investor puts his or her money into a Brazilian start-up, the investor will actually need to pay taxes in Brazil. It could be even worse; the investor may be liable in case of a failure.
- The media must encourage entrepreneurship. The message should be that entrepreneurs are true *heroes* because they are trying to change the world. It is not about who's successful. It's about who tries.
- Organize mentorship programs to guide entrepreneurs.
- Create a state/government/public fund to support the entrepreneurs, for example, to match one-to-one the dollar investment for new start-ups, so that if they can raise capital, the government will match that and as a result make the ecosystem more lucrative for investors.
- Encourage more people to become engineers. Encourage young people to study engineering. Meanwhile, allow engineering immigrants to start working at local tech companies.

Recall the equation: *Entrepreneurs will enter the entrepreneurship journey when their passion is greater than the sum of their fear of failure plus the alternative cost.*

Start-ups are an entirely different organism than established companies or government organizations when it comes to failure. In governments, no one will fire you if you don't make changes. On the contrary, if you do try something new and you fail, you might be fired.

Entrepreneurs, by contrast, undertake each new effort with the same enthusiasm, with the "knowledge" and belief that this time it is going to work. No matter how many times they've tried, entrepreneurs always hold the conviction that this time it will work.

That's what fuels the journey of failures—the passion, the enthusiasm, and the false "knowledge" that this time is it. That belief is the nature of start-ups.

How do you know which experiments to run and when? As we'll see in the next chapter, it always starts with figuring out product-market fit. From there, you add growth, scale, and business model.

Preparing to fail—and to fail fast—is the most important concept to internalize as you build your business. Let's say only 10 percent of your assumptions will work out. Eventually one will succeed and that's all you need. It's a change in mindset.

FAILURE IS AN EVENT, NOT A PERSON

Assume for a moment that there is something that you'd planned for, that didn't work out. If you ask, "Who's responsible?" then you're looking for a person to blame. That approach doesn't encourage the journey of failures or incentivize you to conduct more experiments.

Instead, you would build a very different DNA for your company if you asked, "What happened and what can we learn from it?"

Asking who is responsible builds into the company's DNA a fear of failure. It sends a signal to everyone around that if you try something new and it fails, you will be held accountable—and not in a positive way.

The reality is that it should be the other way around: Those who dare, win!

If you build into your company's DNA that the process is a journey of failures, then you'll always have one person who says, "Hey, I have a new idea. Let's try this."

This is the kind of behavior you're looking for. You want to encourage people to listen and ultimately to implement new ideas, even if—*especially* if—they fail. The most important thing is that someone decides to try something new.

CELEBRATE SUCCESS

Throughout a long journey of failures, it's important to celebrate. Every time we have even a small success, we celebrate it! You celebrate the first employee, the first user, the first version, the first office, the first everything. Then you can celebrate the tenth employee, the tenth user, the hundredth user, a thousand users, and so forth.

It's even more important to celebrate a major event that seems to be *negative*. For example, someone sues you for patent infringement. That actually means that someone cares that you are starting to make an impact. It's not just a "negative" patent suit. Rather, it means someone thinks you're doing something right or that someone thinks you need to be stopped.

Another celebration: If your system fails under load and your users are screaming, that means that you *have* users and what you're doing is important to them.

The best is when people come and say thank you for what you have done for them. You know that you have created value when they acknowledge how you've benefited them. Then you know that you've created something that is working.

SAFARI TIME

It's very important to understand how to build the right DNA of failing fast into your start-up. Perhaps the next (and last) story will help.

One time, two Israeli guys went on an African safari. Now, if you've ever been on a safari, you know visitors usually spend the nights in a lodge, where they're protected from the wildlife.

But these two guys were brimming with confidence. After spending three years in combat units in the army, the lodge seemed too tame to them. There was no adrenaline rush sleeping in a comfortable, protected bed.

So, instead, they decided to set up a tent and spend the night outside the lodge.

Sure enough, in the middle of the night, they woke up to the roar of a lion. It felt pretty close, and they realized that sleeping outdoors might have been a huge mistake.

The tent was just about a couple hundred meters from the lodge.

"Let's make a run for it," one of the two guys said.

"Yes, that's a great idea," the other Israeli replied, and he started to put on his sneakers.

"What are you, nuts?" the first guy said. "Do you think you can outrun that lion?"

The other guy replied, "No, no, no, I only have to outrun *you*."

Making mistakes fast means that you're faster than the market and faster than the competition, whoever (or whatever) that might be.

The "fail fast" approach is not about which thesis or experiment worked. It is about simply having more experiments and, as a result, increasing the likelihood of being successful (that is, finding the one that does work). Remember what Albert Einstein said (I love to repeat this quote because it's so important). *"If you've never failed, you've never tried anything new."*

The flip side: If you try new things, you will fail. And that's OK!

STARTIPS

- If you're afraid to fail, you've already failed because you're not going to try. You're too much in your comfort zone. That's true for individuals, organizations, and even countries.

- Make your mistakes fast. This is how you increase your likelihood of being successful. The faster you fail, the more experiments you can conduct within the same budget and time constraints. The journey of failures will last for years.

- Your road map, your marketing plan, your *everything* is just a series of experiments you keep on trying until you find the one thing that does work. If it doesn't work, then move on to the next experiment.

- Failure is an event, not a person. That's the only way for an organization to embrace failure and encourage fast recovery toward the next experiment.

- A second-time entrepreneur has a much greater probability of success than a first-time one. Engage with someone who has built a start-up before as your guide and mentor.

Chapter 3

EMBRACE DISRUPTION

> There's no chance that the iPhone is going to get any significant market share.
>
> —Steve Ballmer, Microsoft CEO, 2007

In 2007, Microsoft CEO Steve Ballmer got his hands on his first iPhone. In his typical blustery style, Ballmer blasted Apple's new product, especially when compared with what Microsoft had to offer. The iPhone had "no chance," Ballmer said. It's "a $500 subsidized item. They may make a lot of money. But if you actually look at the 1.3 billion phones that get sold, I'd prefer to have [Microsoft's] software in 60 percent or 70 percent or 80 percent of them than to have 2 percent or 3 percent, which is what Apple might get."

Ballmer's bravado is typical of what happens when something truly disruptive appears; it's initially dismissed as irrelevant, until the product eats away at the dismisser's market share.

To quote from another Microsoft executive, former CEO Bill Gates, "We are underestimating the far future and overestimating the near future."

The reason why is fairly simple. Between now and the far future, there will be revolutions, which we have a hard time envisioning. If we could envision them, we would create them ourselves.

The disruptor's journey is always the same. First, they laugh at you, then they ignore you, and then you win.

Well, you are not always going to win, but if you don't try, then for sure you're not going to win!

This chapter is about the perspective of disruption—how the market will change if you're successful and how big your impact will be. We examine how disruption looks to an innovator, existing industry (which doesn't see it coming), and what disruption is all about. The most important thing about disruption is that it is *not* about technology; it is about changing behavior and, as a result, changing the market equilibrium.

In what may be the most famous example of a misinformed dismissal, a fledgling start-up called Netflix in 2000 approached industry video giant Blockbuster, at the time worth $6 billion. There were Blockbuster stores on every other corner, more than there are Starbucks today. Netflix, meanwhile, just two years old, was on track to lose $57 million that year alone.

Netflix CEO Reed Hastings made an offer he was sure the Blockbuster head, John Antioco, couldn't refuse: purchase Netflix for $50 million. The Netflix team would then develop and run Blockbuster.com as the company's online video-rental arm. Antioco turned Hastings down. "Netflix is a very small niche business," he declared confidently. But at a Blockbuster internal management meeting, the team concluded the discussion by saying, "Whatever they can do, we can do better." The rest, as they say, is history.

Netflix went public in 2002. By 2010, Blockbuster had declared bankruptcy. And in the decade that followed, Netflix was not only synonymous with streaming video but has developed into a full-fledged movie studio, with a market cap in 2021 of $250 billion, some forty times higher than Blockbuster at its prime.

Netflix is a somewhat unusual story, given that they disrupted their own existing market. In its early years, Netflix would send DVDs by the

US Postal Service. They had essentially hacked the system—the post office could deliver packages in twenty-four hours, and the price was that of an ordinary stamp. By adopting a streaming model, the price is even more right!

Then there's the story of Kodak.

It was a twenty-four-year-old Kodak engineer named Steve Sasson who came up with the concept of the digital camera back in 1973. When he showed it to management, CEO Walter Fallon told his staff, "That's cute, but don't tell anyone about it." Did Fallon grasp that Sasson's filmless technology had the potential to disrupt Kodak's main business? It seems so, if only because Kodak's management went into reactionary mode, focusing mainly on the flaws of what Sasson had invented. It was too heavy, the resolution was low, and it took too long to process each picture. But you can't prevent a revolution by killing the messenger! Kodak had a patent for its digital camera technology, but it expired in 2007. Kodak sat on the patent for years. "We're in the paper and chemistry industry," the company repeated; a digital camera would simply be irrelevant to their core business. More-nimble competitors ate Kodak's lunch. Then smartphones disrupted even the competitors. Kodak filed for bankruptcy in 2012.

When Google was just getting started, the company had great difficulty raising capital. The company's cofounders, Sergey Brin and Larry Page, wanted to return to their studies at Stanford.

So, in 1998, they approached Yahoo (more precisely, they approached the Excite@Home division of Yahoo) and asked the latter to acquire their company, then known by the name of its core algorithm, PageRank. For just $2 million. Not $2 billion. Not $2 trillion. But $2 million.

Yahoo said no. Twice.

The second time was in 2002, and by that point, the price had jumped to $5 billion.

Disrupted POV

Blockbuster, Netflix	*"Netflix is a very small niche business."* **Blockbuster CEO, 2000**
Microsoft, iPhone	*"There's no chance that the iPhone is going to get any significant market share."* **MSFT CEO, 2007**
Kodak	*"That's cute—but don't tell anyone."* **Kodak CEO**
Yahoo!, Google	Said no for $2M

Yahoo's reason: They didn't want a search engine sending traffic off to third-party sites, as PageRank did. They wanted users to stay on Yahoo. By the time Yahoo realized the importance of third-party paid advertising revenue, it was too late.

Yahoo acquired another search engine, Inktomi, in its bid to topple Google, but the execution was sloppy, and Yahoo was eventually sold to Verizon's AOL internet business. The price: $4.48 billion.

Looking at the result today, you might be inclined to say it was a huge mistake. But you don't know what would have happened if they had said yes. We assume that everything would have stayed the same, but that's not necessarily the case.

I heard the same thing after Google acquired Waze in 2013 for $1.15 billion. People would often ask me if it was the right decision. Wouldn't the company be worth much more if we had kept it and sold years later? My answer is always very simple: There are right decisions and there are NO decisions. This is because when you make a decision and choose a path, no one knows what it would be like if you had chosen a different path.

Would Waze, with more than $300 million in revenue and about a billion users worldwide today, be worth more than it was in 2013, when it had just $1 million in revenue and about 55 million users? Well, of course it would, but what we don't know is if Waze would have become what it is today without that decision.

So, rather than think what would have happened to Yahoo if they had said yes to acquiring Google for $2 million (or years later for $5 billion), ask yourself instead, "Would Google have become what it is today under Yahoo's leadership and vision?"

That part we don't know, and therefore any statement about the decision being right or wrong is irrelevant. There are right decisions or NO decisions, simply because we can't predict what would have happened on the path we didn't take.

WHAT IS DISRUPTION?

People speak all the time about disruptive technology. They tend to think that it's a technology that dislodges market leaders by creating something that didn't exist before.

But disruption has little to do with technology. *It's about changing behavior and market equilibrium—that is, the way we do business.*

Disruption

Product	Price
	Market Equilibrium
Knowledge	Model

Think about Gmail. Before Google launched its email service, we used to pay to have a mailbox online. We'd pay a monthly subscription to our ISP (internet service provider) for accessing the internet and an additional subscription to have a mailbox for email. Google introduced Gmail, which at the beginning was not good enough, but after a few iterations became good enough AND FREE. No one can compete against good enough AND free.

My first email account was at Yahoo. Then, Google introduced Gmail and I signed up for the same email address but at Gmail.

Why am I telling you all this?

My Yahoo email address dates back to 1995 or so, and a couple of years back, someone asked me for my email address. I gave him the Yahoo email, and this guy just looked at me and said, "I know only two people that are still using Yahoo email, you . . . and my grandmother."

Google disrupted Yahoo on the email side, as well. Disruption can occur when offering a new product (which could be a derivative of a new technology), a new business model (on-demand electric scooters for rent like Wind, Bird, or Lime so you don't need to buy one of your own), or in Gmail's case, a new price.

Gmail is hardly alone. Uber disrupted the taxi business. Is there any great technology behind Uber? No, there isn't. It's simply introducing knowledge that wasn't available before. In Uber's case, that knowledge was about supply and demand: Who needs to go where, and what drivers are in your area right now to take you?

This transparency has been more important for drivers than their customers; the latter don't need to know exactly where their vehicle is, just that their ride will be there in five minutes. But for drivers, locating confirmed customers, rather than circling and waiting and wasting time, has been crucial.

Airbnb similarly confounded the hotel business. With thousands of Airbnb properties flooding the market, hotels have had to scramble to compete by lowering prices, offering more amenities, and emphasizing buffet breakfasts. Like Uber, there's no radical technology at Airbnb. It's the introduction of transparency to supply and demand, creating a simpler marketplace.

The iPhone's disruption was not the device itself, even though it was amazing. The real disruption was the ecosystem: the App Store, its community of developers, and the clearance at the store. That model started before the iPhone, with the iPod, where you could pay for and download a single song.

So far, we've mentioned three major examples of disruption: free (Gmail), marketplace (Uber, Airbnb), and ecosystem (Apple). There are a few more categories but, at the end of the day, each one of them created a market that is an order of magnitude bigger than what existed before.

ENTREPRENEURS AS TROUBLEMAKERS

Disrupters are always newcomers. They're the ones who have nothing to lose, so they'll take more risks. Incumbents and, in particular, market leaders don't disrupt because they have too much to lose.

But that's not the real reason. To disrupt something, we need to tell ourselves that what we're currently doing is wrong. For individuals, that's difficult. So just imagine how hard it is for organizations. It's usually impossible. No one likes to admit they're wrong. If someone proposes a disruptive idea, management will reflexively say, "This will never work." It is a "DNA limitation" of disruption and not the fact an organization has too much to lose that limits innovation.

Organizations that want to disrupt simply can't do so from within. They can only do it by investing in new organizations or start-ups that will disrupt their own markets.

Entrepreneurs are troublemakers in most cases. They don't take anything for granted. They're not "good corporate employees." As Kodak engineer Steve Sasson commented when he was put in charge of the project that resulted in the first digital camera, "It was just a project to keep me from getting into trouble doing something else."

Troublemakers usually don't fit into the DNA of large corporations, and in many cases, they simply leave. Maybe because they are trying to do something else or maybe just because someone wants to get rid of them.

I was fired from every place that I've worked. In the end, there was always the way that I wanted to do things (which obviously I thought was right) and there was the organization's way of doing things. So, in some cases it would end up as, "This is how things are done," and me saying it doesn't make sense and that we should do it the other way around. Usually that was the beginning of the end.

My longest tenure was at Comverse Technology—eleven years—and that ended with me being fired. A little while later, one of the executives at the company approached me.

"We have no idea how we let one of our most creative minds go." To which I replied, "You didn't let me go. You fired me!"

As long as the company was growing, I found my place there, and the organization was able to deal with troublemakers. But as soon as Comverse stopped growing, there was no more room for troublemakers like me.

My grandfather had *one* job throughout his entire life. Nowadays, we move around rapidly. The eleven years at Comverse were the longest so far in my career and most likely will be the longest ever for me. Most organizations will figure out how to get rid of the troublemakers, and in general, I would say most organizations should get rid of three types of people: victims, drama queens, and nonconformists (although keep in mind that most start-ups are born *because* of the nonconformists).

A BIGGER MARKET

The good news is that we can define disruption as a "change in market equilibrium." Now, by definition, the new market is so much bigger and better than the previous one, otherwise the equilibrium won't change. That's the beauty of the disruption: **the opportunity is much bigger than the threat.**

After Uber began disrupting the on-demand personal mobility business, the market grew tenfold. In this ten-times bigger market, there is room for Uber and Lyft and DiDi (China) and Grab (Southeast Asia), Cabify (Europe), and 99 Taxi (Latin America). There are three times more rides on medallion taxi (regular taxi service) today than there were before Uber. So, while all taxi stations in the world were trying to fight Uber's entrance into their markets, the reality is that the opportunity for regular taxis was bigger than the threat.

Online ticketing for tourism took a similar turn. It disrupted travel agents, who once could say simply, "Here's your ticket" and be done. There was no price comparison. Before the internet, how could there be? Now there is.

Transparency, perhaps more than anything else, creates disruption. Information is available for everyone. Initially, there might be fear that your business's profitability will go down, but transparency often creates a bigger market than before, one with much higher demand.

MARKETS WHERE INFORMATION IS MISSING

Some markets are simply calling out for disruption. These tend to be markets where information is missing, markets that are asymmetrical, and laden with regulations that don't work.

Think of places where you don't know how much you're paying, or you don't know what you are paying for.

Medical services in the US are about five times more expensive than they are in Germany. It is not that they are better in the US. They are simply more expensive. Obviously, this is an industry calling for disruption.

The CEO of TomTom, Harold Goddijn, once told me, "If your market is going to be disrupted, it will be disrupted." The key question is whether you will be disrupted with it, or whether you'll enjoy the newly expanded market.

Goddijn's comment came during the very early days of Waze when I was trying to engage the mapping and navigation company's CEO into a barter deal. My offer to him in 2010 was very simple. He was asking for our maps in Latin America.

"Great," I said. "We can give you Latin America maps if you give us the maps for the US or Europe, where our maps are not yet good enough." The CEO gave it some thought but eventually said, "No, our maps in the US and Europe are much more valuable than your Latin America maps." To which I said, "Well, you're right—Europe and the US are much more important to us, but what about for you? If we do not exchange, you will be losing the entire LATAM."

The second dialogue Waze had with TomTom was in 2012. We already had major traction in the US and Europe by this point, and TomTom had lost their biggest customer, Google, in the US. TomTom asked for traffic information.

"OK, give us your maps and we will give you our traffic," I said. I even extended the offer. "We can also give you map updates and therefore keep you relevant in the map space, if you would give us the GPS traces in real time so we can improve our traffic," I proposed. TomTom again gave it thought and again said no. "If we give you our maps and you're a free app, we are disrupting our own market," the CEO said. "Your consumer market doesn't exist anymore," I replied, "now that there is Waze and Google Maps, which are free. You are not free, so your consumer app will die anyhow." "Yes," the CEO said, reluctantly, agreeing with my assessment, "but WE are not killing it."

They were not alone. Once we realized how Waze works, it became clear that more users create better data, and better data retains more users—a virtuous cycle. And the key question was how to accelerate the flywheel by bringing more and better data.

While Waze creates its own maps, it takes time. If we could rely on existing maps and just bring them to up to date and keep them there, we could move *faster*. That was one of the key business development dialogues we had with many small or local mapmakers around the globe. Our partnership with Location World in Latin America was one of them.

Those conversations were always the same. I would tell them what Waze was doing and how the map was created by crowdsourcing the information, and then I'd come with a proposal.

"Why don't you give us your map, and we will provide you with map updates constantly, and we will share the revenues on selling maps and traffic."

Usually, this approach was made in places where our maps were not good enough yet. After all, if we were already good enough, we wouldn't need their maps anymore.

The initial feedback was nearly always the same. They would say no, they have an asset, and we don't, and our system is not proven yet.

"You're right," I would say. "Our map was not good enough in Ecuador and Latvia and Chile and Colombia and Israel and Italy and Malaysia and a long list of other countries, but now it is good enough. It will become good enough here as well, and then this offer will no longer be relevant." There was more to argue.

"You will not be able to compete over time with the big guys (Nokia and TomTom) and certainly not with Google, which can pour many more resources into this project than you can. We are your future in terms of keeping the map up to date."

When this argument didn't work either, I tried one last one.

"Look," I said. "There are two options here. One, my thesis works, and Waze will become successful here. If so, your only way to survive is through cooperation. Or two, my thesis doesn't work, and Waze is unsuccessful here and then it doesn't matter either way. Do you really want to be in a situation where you become irrelevant in the market, and you could have done something about it?"

It ended up that we had many data partners, including in India, Brazil, the rest of Latin America, and Europe. In addition, tons of fleet management companies signed on; the barter with them was "Give us GPS data and get traffic information data in return." Occasionally, this barter didn't work but they were ready to sell us the raw data, which we converted into traffic information that was so valuable for us. This raw data was literally nickels and dimes (an active GPS of a vehicle cost somewhere between a nickel and a dime per vehicle per month).

WAZE'S DISRUPTION

The existing map and navigation companies initially dismissed Waze.

"Your product is simply not good enough," they told us.

Why?

"You don't have the same validation mechanism that we have," a business development person at TomTom told me. I heard the same thing from Nokia.

What they meant was that, because Waze's maps are created by crowdsourcing, there was no way of knowing if someone had inserted the wrong data into the map.

I had a response.

"If it's a problematic area with a lot of people, they will figure out the problem and fix it," I said. "Conversely, if the area is rural and mostly unused, no one cares about the error."

"That's exactly why your product will never be good enough!" came the response.

DISRUPTING THE DISRUPTOR

Even Waze may get disrupted someday. Waze is an app for drivers. If self-driving cars become the norm and there are no more drivers, then we won't need Waze anymore!

How does TomTom feel about Waze today? I had the opportunity to meet TomTom's CEO a few years ago. He called me a "son of a bitch." But happily.

"Why aren't you angrier?" I asked him.

"If disruption is going to happen, it's going to happen, and I'm glad it was you," he replied. "Now the market is bigger. And, de facto, you have helped us to focus not on trying to compete with a phone app and not even with other navigation devices."

Indeed, when looking at the market today, everyone in the navigation space is making more money than before. Waze's phone app, for example, while working beautifully, is insufficient; many people want Waze to run on their large in-car screens. That creates a bigger market for everyone. There are more cars with in-car navigation systems than ever before.

For existing companies whose markets may be disrupted and who want to embrace change and be prepared for disruption (or in other words to increase their likelihood of building something that will be sustainable in the future), the insight that "if disruption is going to happen, it *will* happen" puts them in a much stronger position going forward.

There are two questions to consider in order for this future to come about.

- What will make my company irrelevant five years down the road? If you can answer that, then someone else can, too, and right now they are building a start-up that will in fact make you irrelevant. If you can figure it out, you need to start working on the new, disruptive direction *today*.
- What are the assets you have that, if spun differently, can become even bigger than what you have today? If any of your assets may be spun differently for a bigger business, you should start today, but you should spin that off, or do it outside of your core organization. You can only try these methods:
  — You can spin off a company.
  — You invest in an outside start-up that can actually answer these questions.

Let me give you a few examples.

Let's say you own a coffee shop, a local one, in an area where there are other coffee shops, and you think your espresso is better. You make money from selling coffee, yet the other coffee places around you provide their customers with gift cards or 10+1 loyalty cards.

What if you completely change your business model and sell a subscription—a "drink all the coffee in the world that you want" package? That's disruption through a business model. The everyday coffee drinkers will come to you (although they may or may not buy the other things that you have to offer).

You've also realized that there are a lot of people coming to your coffee shop to work, and they stay there for many hours, ordering just one drink and taking up a chair and a table for half a day or even more.

Your thoughts are clear: "I need this place for other customers. I need these people to buy more, so I will limit their stay to one hour."

I would suggest a completely different way to look at it.

You have customers coming for specific purposes. Instead of making that purpose your new business model, you want them to go away. But what if you added much better desks with better chairs and potentially a private "phone booth" for making calls, and a printer—essentially everything one would need for an "on-demand office"?

You could try different business models. For example, a daily or a monthly flat fee. Provide your customers a power outlet and fast internet and you've found a different way to use your assets to make money.

WHY CAN'T EXISTING COMPANIES CHANGE?

Why don't existing companies disrupt their own markets? While we want to believe that they have too much to lose, let's break it down. We want to imagine that they are thinking of their own business, but it's not the business—it's the organization.

There are three challenges for the organization:

- **DNA**—Larger corporations have less risk-taking in their DNA. No one ever gets fired for making the obvious choice.

- **Lack of entrepreneurs**—Remember, entrepreneurs tend to be troublemakers; they don't last long in large organizations, so you either got rid of them already or they simply left.
- **Ego**—Say, for a second, that you have a $1 billion business across three geographical divisions and two product lines, and your top leadership team consists of those five leaders (running those five P&Ls). What exactly are you going to tell them? That you're going to create another division in the company to build your future and that this future is more important than the company's main line of business? Or that you are building another P&L that is going to lose money in the next five years? It's a leadership dilemma: If you decide this new division is more important, you'll have a problem with the existing part of the organization. If it is not important, though, the new division will bleed cash until killed sometime in the future (and way too late).

I recall a dialogue with the CEO of a company telling me that he thinks his market will be disrupted and his current offering will be irrelevant five years down the road.

"This is great," I said. "You can start the change now."

I was surprised when he said, "I can't. I can't get my management to do something around it." I offered to help. I was even ready to go and meet the management, but he said, "You're crazy! You are going to tell them they will die if they don't change. They will freak out. They are all very respected leaders and you will tell them they have no future without changing direction. No way can I allow that." And then he asked if I had any other suggestions. "Yes," I said. "Go to your chairman and resign."

TELMAP MISSES THE OPPORTUNITY TO MAKE AN OFFER . . . FOUR TIMES

When we were raising money for Waze for the first time (our seed round), I reached out to the Telmap team. Not because of Telmap but because of its main investor. We were thinking, since we know he likes the space, he might be a relevant investor for us as well.

That investor was the majority shareholder of Telmap, and also the majority shareholder at Mapa, the local mapmaker in Israel. So, we went back to the Telmap team together with his investor and the CEO of Mapa. This time, we were thinking that he would be interested in investing, but it turned out he was mainly trying to figure out if we were competitive with them.

We heard later that Telmap was considering offering us $1 million for the concept and the three of us. (This was in 2007, so it was before the company was even established.) The funny part is that, back then, we might have said yes if the offer would have allowed us to build our dream.

This was the second time I had pitched Telmap. The first time was a year earlier when I offered the CEO the opportunity to build crowdsourced traffic information into their maps, and he said that traffic information is not actionable and therefore no one cares about traffic and turned us down.

Our third meeting was somewhere in 2009 after we had launched Waze in Israel and had a few tens of thousands of users. Telmap at the time had more than 150,000 subscribers through local mobile operators. We reached out to them with an offer. "Why don't you share with us the GPS data from your users, and we will provide you with traffic information," I proposed, taking a page from our discussions with TomTom. Waze was still very young, though, and Telmap couldn't see the upcoming revolution. Telmap said no, again.

One reason that Telmap didn't consider us a competitor was that, although our maps in Israel were in large part good enough and up to date, in many other cases, they were not good enough, and there was a glitch right where Telmap's offices were. You see, close to Telmap's offices (in Herzliya, Israel), there was a T junction and Telmap was the first building to the left of that T. Since we hadn't yet added all of the house numbers for that street, we made a rough calculation that their office was fifty meters to the right of the T. So, when people used Waze to get to Telmap, Waze would tell them

"Turn right" rather than "Turn left." "It's not good enough. It needs to be perfect," the CEO told us, justifying Telmap's decision.

In 2010, we had what would turn out to be our final conversation.

We were starting to look toward the international market and Telmap had some customers in Mexico. We thought about expanding there using Telmap's installed base, so we approached Telmap about a possible cooperation. This time they were interested, but with one condition: stop competing with us in Israel.

That is, we wouldn't be allowed to play in our own backyard.

At this time, we had more users in Israel than Telmap, and we were growing rapidly (we were definitely "good enough") while Telmap was bleeding users.

We, of course, couldn't agree to this condition and we turned them down.

When you create something completely new, at first people will laugh at you. Then they'll ignore you until finally you win (or they lose, depending on the perspective).

That's the common response to nearly all of the tech disruptors in the world.

The first rejoinder is always, "This will never work." It doesn't matter if it's BMW saying that about Tesla, Microsoft criticizing the early iPhone, or Blockbuster believing that whatever Netflix could do, they could build better. The incumbents simply don't think what you're doing will happen . . . until it's too late.

TRAFFIC JAMS—STILL CALLING FOR DISRUPTION

One last note about disruption and Waze. We started the Waze journey to address traffic problems and to help drivers avoid traffic jams. That was in 2007. However, we are still stuck in traffic today, even more than we were in 2007. So, to an extent, I failed with my mission (or maybe it's better to say that I'm not done with it).

Lately, I received an accusation that Waze actually creates *more* traffic jams, because it empowers drivers to drive, even those who are afraid. If this is the case, I'm even happier about the creation of Waze. Empowering people is certainly much more rewarding than saving time!

Does that mean existing corporations are doomed? Of course not. They are evolving. Think of Microsoft, for example. Their moneymaker was DOS, then Windows, then Office, and today it is very different. Can they ride a disruption wave? It's much harder, but possible if they spin off or invest in disruptors.

STARTIPS

- Disruption is not about technology but about changing market equilibrium and the way we behave or do business.

- Free is the biggest disruption of all.

- Disrupters are almost always newcomers. Incumbents don't disrupt because they have too much to lose.

- Disruption is good; the opportunity is much bigger than the threat.

- Disrupters hear the same feedback over and over: "This will never work."

Chapter 4

OPERATE IN PHASES

The main thing is to keep the main thing the main thing.
—Stephen Covey

I f you don't figure out product-market fit (PMF), you will die. But wait a minute; if you don't raise capital, you don't even get to live, and if you don't have a business model, no one will invest. What's the use in reaching PMF if you are unable to bring users? This chapter tries to set in order the different phases of a start-up and, in particular, how and when to move from one phase to another. For each one of the phases the keyword is FOCUS: You must deal with this phase only by not dealing with anything else.

THE "ALL OVER PHASE"

When you start your "falling in love" cycles, you think about your new venture from multiple perspectives: the problem, the solution, the market, the business model, funding, and the go-to-market (GTM) plan. You have everything organized in your mind so you can already draw that plan.

Then you start meeting people.

At first these are friends and perhaps colleagues or businesspeople. This is what I call the "all over phase"—the early beginning where you are trying to capture everything in your mind (the company, the team, the product), and, as a result, your focus is spread all over the place.

While we already established the underlying assumption that many (if not most) of the people you meet at this point are going to say your idea is not going to work, they may have their own reasoning. It will sound like:

- "I don't have this problem," which is good, as it is a sample of one person. But in many cases, your listeners will abstract and then generalize about the problem, so that it winds up sounding like "No one has this problem," or "I don't know even a single person that faces that problem."
- "The solution does not address the problem—it needs to be X, Y, or Z" or "It is not that simple."
- On the business model issue, you will hear a lot of pushback along the lines of "I wouldn't pay for it," or with abstraction and generalization: "No one is going to pay for it."
- "I've already met start-ups that are doing exactly that."
- "Google can do that in no time," or "My friend is the chief engineer at XYZ and they are already working on it."

Your next step, then, is to find more support for your claim, to address each of the objections, and to validate the problem, the solution, the market, the business model, and the competition. At this point, you think you're ready with your story and you go to meet investors.

I've originated many start-ups and can say that this is usually the mindset. You validate a little, get the main answers, and move to the next part of the validation. Right now, it is all in theory, and we know that the difference between "in theory" and "in reality" is much bigger in reality than it is in theory.

So, in your mind, you already have great answers to many of the challenges of product-market fit, go-to-market plan, business model, scale, growth, going global, etc., but you haven't validated any of them.

Then, you meet investors, and they really rock your boat. They tell you things like, "We don't think this business model will work, so we are going to pass on the opportunity."

They may be right or wrong. It doesn't matter. What you actually heard is something completely different than what they meant.

For example, you heard, "Once you figure out the business model, we will say yes," but they didn't say that. They simply said no.

Or they will say, "You don't have users yet, we will wait," and you hear, "Show us one thousand users and we will say yes."

The challenge is to not misread them. They are saying no, and you're hearing, "If you will show us users, or paying users, or a working version in this and that market, we will say yes." The problem is that you're no longer sure about your plan. If they say they don't believe in the business model, do you need to prove it now? Or should you stick with the plan that product-market fit is first?

Or if they say there is no market in Israel, should you start in California? Does it mean you should change your plan?

This is where you get confused. So, what is it that you need to work on?

The product?

Acquiring users?

Validating the business model?

Showing that the competition is not that scary?

Do you do a deep dive into one of those areas? Work on all of them in parallel? If you can only work on one, which one?

Here's an even worse scenario: You already raised a pre-seed or seed round (first early investment), and you are working on product-market fit. You are not there yet, but you think you're very close.

You meet investors to raise your seed round, and they give you all sorts of input about the business model, competition, growth, and globalization, and you think that you need to satisfy their concerns.

YOU DON'T!

Your job is to deliver results: a product or a service that is generating value. Not to make the investors happy.

But wait a minute. If you deliver, won't they be happy?

You should tell them, "This is my plan, product-market fit, business model, growth, and in five years we will go global." You have to convince them by showing that you know what you are doing, and they will be happy if you deliver on your projections.

The "all over phase" ends when you have conviction about your plan, including the timing and sequence of your phases and, in particular, which phase should come first. Then, no one can distract you anymore. You have gathered enough feedback for your underlying assumptions that you feel convinced that this is how it is going to work. It doesn't matter if you're right or not, you just need the conviction at this phase.

Recall that this is a journey of failures, and you will validate your underlying assumptions later. You are trying to get to this comfort level in many aspects—validating the problem, the perception of the solution, a business model, your go-to-market plan, competition, budget, etc.—so that you can answer the first and second levels of questions.

So, if someone asks you about competition, you can name three to four potential competitors and why you're different (not better but different). Or if someone asks you about the business model, you say you have an Excel table with a five-year forecast, and at the end of the day, you will earn one dollar per user per month. You don't need to execute anything. You just create presentations, Excel sheets, and other supporting documents.

Occasionally, you will validate things with your users.

For example, if you believe you can attract users for a parking solution via Facebook in Timbuktu, then try it. Place an ad there as if there is a product and see if people care. (Saving you time to search where Timbuktu is—it is in Mali, in sub-Saharan Africa, and there are Waze users there.)

FOCUS IS THE KEY

The real plan is easy: Stick to the phases and operate by them.

In the early days of Waze in 2009, we were looking to get confirmation for our business model. At the time, we were under the impression that we would be selling data, maps, and, in particular, traffic information, as it can help mobility dramatically.

I met many municipal chief engineers and asked them, "What if we could tell you how long it takes to make a left turn in each and every traffic light in the city, every day of the week, and every hour of the day, in real time and you can readjust the traffic control system and improve dramatically the traffic in the city?"

In other cases, I met with logistics companies and said, "Our traffic information can help you improve your timing and fuel efficiency, allowing you to make fifteen percent more deliveries per truck."

One company in Israel liked this idea.

"What if we install Waze on a dedicated tablet that will be used by our truckers?" they asked.

Now, this was 2009, so what I was calling a tablet was, more precisely, a PDA running the Windows Mobile OS.

We liked the idea, too, so the deal was nearly ready. Best yet: We didn't need to do anything for them. We just enabled the no-tilt feature, so the display remains horizontal even if the device is vertical, for the PDA, and they were ready to pay us per truck per year. It wasn't a lot of money, but it was still pretty nice: ten dollars per truck per year.

For a company with five thousand trucks, that's $50,000 a year.

So far, it sounds awesome. The company started its test drive (literally). Two days later, they came back and said it didn't work.

"What doesn't work?" I asked.

"Waze takes our truckers through 'no-trucks' roads," was one response we heard.

Or "The route didn't have sufficient clearance at an overpass. We need your map to include this data."

We went back to the drawing board and realized that our model couldn't provide this data. We are a commuter app, and the crowdsourcing information that the trucks cared about was not at all what the commuters cared about.

In our dialogue with the company, we responded that we could not do what they'd requested, because we don't have the data. That was a challenging interaction: Our business model was to sell map and traffic data, and here was a real customer ready to pay a lot of money for exactly that.

The logistics firm was persistent. They suggested a ten-times-higher annual subscription price, and we still said no.

Then they came up with an intriguing offer.

"If you can create a sales-agent travel algorithm [a part of the program that deals with routes that have multiple stops, in case a salesperson needs to visit twenty different places in a day], we will make that double."

It was a million dollars a year and, since Israel is rather small, we realized that we could actually do that—we could map by ourselves all the overpass and underpass clearances and get the no-truck restrictions from other sources. The sales-agent algorithm looked like something that we could do on a small scale (with a maximum of twenty stops per day).

We called for a management meeting and asked ourselves, "Should we?"

One voice said, "It is not a big issue to develop, and it is one million dollars per year."

But another voice said, "Our mission is to help commuters avoid traffic jams, and therefore we should remain focused on solving the problem for the commuters. Right now, we are in the phase of becoming global and not making money."

There were a few days of arguments, saying things like, "Wait a minute, this is only one trucking company, there are four million truckers in the US and, if they all pay one hundred to two hundred dollars a year, this is a big business."

The argument back: "If we change either the value proposition or the target audience, then this is a new company or a pivot, which basically means we no longer believe in the problem we are trying to solve."

We ended up saying no—no to truckers, no to bike riders, no to pedestrians, no to public transportation, no to anything that wasn't commuters. The one-million-dollar-a-year deal that we could have in 2009 was higher than the revenues of Waze in 2009, 2010, and 2011, and was about the same order of magnitude of revenues we made in 2012 and 2013.

Over the years I have told this story to people, and I am always asked, "Why not both?" And the answer is very simple: **focus**.

A start-up, in order to be successful, needs to do one and only one thing right, and to increase the likelihood of doing so, it needs to say no to everything else. Focus is not only about what we are doing; it is about what we are *not* doing! These are the hard decisions to say no to.

The main thing is to keep the main thing the main thing.

What's the most important stage in a company? Is it product development? Raising money? Acquiring users? Business development?

The answer is that each one of these is the most important until it is completed, and then it's *not*.

Focus is about doing one thing at a time.

When you're fundraising, nothing else is as crucial as that. The day after the money is in the bank, fundraising is irrelevant (until the next round).

When you're building your product for the first time, the most critical person on the team is the product lead. When the product is done and you've achieved product-market fit, you might not even need the same product organization anymore as the company shifts toward marketing or business creation. While, for a second, I would say that product development is a never-ending story, which is true, the main phase of achieving product-market fit and therefore creating value for the users or customers is done once the product is developed.

It's the same outside of the tech space. Once you figure out how to ride a bicycle, training wheels are no longer required. They are simply not important anymore.

OPERATING IN PHASES

This idea of directed focus is called "operating in phases." The first thing to decide is what to focus on, which means deciding on the MIT (the most important thing). If you don't figure this out, you can't move to the next phase. The strategy and leadership are about deciding on the MIT; the execution is about delivering it.

Let's look at fundraising as an example. It's usually the most challenging phase for a start-up. If you fail in this phase, you will most likely die (well, your company will). It's very different than any other phase in a company's life. It takes so much attention and energy that it's very hard to do other things during this period of time. There's a super high adrenaline rush, and then it ends. We occasionally want to think about it as zero or one, but it turns out there is a lot in between as well, for example raising less money than desired.

Raising money for your start-up is like refueling your car before you set out on a journey. If you don't have enough (or any) fuel, the journey ends.

But the purpose of the journey is not refueling. The goal is to get somewhere. Filling up the tank is simply a necessary evil. And once you've got the fuel you need, you don't need to worry about it again for a while.

Now, during the fundraising phase of the start-up journey, you'll be running from one investor to another—hearing no, no, and no—until, before you know it, you've invested six to nine months into this process. Eventually you close a deal and, on the day after, everything you went through for those nine months, including all the highly charged emotional engagement, is no longer important. Now you have to go on and build the product.

Another way of looking at operating in phases: It's like driving with a stick shift. If you don't depress the clutch when you're shifting gears, the gearbox will scream in protest. When you shift gears in a start-up, you have to readjust everything. First comes setting the new top priority—the new most important thing. The second is what to do about people and their roles.

START WITH PRODUCT-MARKET FIT

Your start-up strategy always begins with product-market fit, and let me spell it out for you: If you figure out product-market fit, you get to live. If you don't, you will die. After product-market fit, the order of the phases can vary. Each phase takes approximately two to three years. Some phases after reaching PMF can be done in parallel.

Can you figure out scale before figuring out product-market fit? Well, just imagine that you can bring millions of users, but your product does not create value for them. In that case, they will simply churn.

Can you figure out a business model before product-market fit? Not really. Even if you convince someone to pay for your product, if you subsequently don't deliver consistent value, they will churn, cancel their payment, etc.

~~~

For each phase, a different part of the organization and therefore a different member of your team will be the most important. For example:

- If you're trying to figure out monetization, then your chief revenue officer will be most important.
- If you're working on scaling up, the chief marketing officer will be paramount.

Once you've completed a phase, the position that was so key may not even be required in the company or may be at a different level of importance. And that person might transition into a new role.

Phase transfers are dramatic because what is changing is the MIT. An unavoidable derivative of that is that some people will become more critical to the company and others will be less critical, even if just a day earlier they were all deeply involved in what had been the start-up's MIT.

When I first presented it, people's first reaction would be "What do you mean seven to ten years to figure out the phases? I thought it would be much shorter, and my business plan suggests I will make a $100 million in year five." Well, think of all tech giants that were started in the previous four decades. Google, Amazon, Netflix, Tesla, Facebook, and fifty or so others. Then, consider the combined value of all those successful tech companies. How much of it was created in their first decade? The answer is 4 percent. That's it. Most of the value, 96 percent of it, was generated after they figured out PMF, business model, and growth.

PRODUCT-MARKET FIT PHASE (PMF)

This is so critical that it bears repeating: The most important phase in the evolution of the company is PMF. If you create value for your users, then you are on the right path. If you don't, you will die.

PMF is measured by one key metric: retention. Occasionally you will have other key indicators, like monthly active users (MAU) or other usage metrics.

During this phase you should focus all of your efforts on achieving value creation for your users; nothing else matters. Nearly nothing should be done on other fronts, like business development or marketing. The result is a very lean organization and a small budget. The entire road map of the product during this phase focuses on improving retention (and most likely conversion on the way to retention). This phase is so dramatic I've devoted a whole chapter to it (chapter 8).

MULTIPLE MITS AT ONCE

It's possible to have multiple MITs during the same phase. PMF is the key, of course, but it might not be enough; you may need to figure out retention and conversion in parallel. Or you may need to raise more money *before* you've reached product-market fit. Or you've achieved product-market fit in your home country but other territories present unique challenges that require tweaking, or an entire redesign. (Think an app in China vs. the US.)

Trying to work on multiple phases at the same time, on the other hand, is almost always a recipe for disaster, in particular in the early phases of a company, although, occasionally, it is a necessary evil. What happens is that you spend too much money on different tasks while you still don't have PMF. If you're not operating in phases sequentially, you could easily spend what money you do have too early. Moreover, you'll feel pressure to beef up the organization—marketing, sales, support.

So, you're not just increasing spending, you're increasing the *commitment* to spend, and it can be very hard to slow down.

If before you had ten people in the company, now you have twenty, and the monthly burn rate has doubled. You've also shortened the amount of time your cash will last by 50 percent. If this happens before you figure out product-market fit and you have to go back to basics, you'll discover you've already spent the run rate you have.

If you are not operating in phases, then you're spending money for nothing and not making progress. Remember, if you don't have product-market fit, most likely you won't be able to raise any more capital. If, in the seed round, all that was necessary was that the investors like the CEO and the story, as the company becomes more mature, you also need your investors to believe that the CEO can *deliver* on the story.

It's no longer about the story. It's about making progress.

An important caveat: If you weren't able to figure out product-market fit, it's possible to raise another seed round (not a series A or B round). Then go out and speak to prospective customers, telling them what you'll do and what you'll charge. You can usually get a feeling for when something is going in the right direction. But going ahead and *building* something at this phase is wrong.

BE CAREFUL NOT TO HIRE TOO EARLY

If you're in the product-market fit phase, there's no reason to hire a chief marketing officer or a chief revenue officer yet. It would be a waste of time and talent to hire someone good when they have nothing to do yet. They'll just leave. Or, even worse, they will deliver on their objectives!

For example, the VP of business development will engage with companies that deliver results that you don't need right now, and that will slow you down in reaching product-market fit.

Let's say that this VP of business development will bring a distribution partner that will bring millions of users. What will happen next? Most likely, those users will churn because the product is not there yet, and the distribution partner is going to be pissed.

This is even more dramatic when you have your founding team in place. Ask yourself: Do we really need that function right now? In many cases there will be investors pressuring you to move fast and hire a lot of people. You should hire only those you need, and know exactly what you expect them to deliver in the next ninety days.

The most dangerous moment for a start-up is when you *think* you've figured out product-market fit even though you really haven't. But you don't realize that, so you say, "OK, it's time for sales," and you start building out the sales organization in your start-up. You hire a VP of sales, a chief revenue officer, and a bunch of sales staff.

You're now at a burn rate three times that of before, and you're going to run out of cash rapidly. Then, because your customers are displeased that the product is not good enough, you go back to R&D. But what do you do now with the sales organization you spent six months building that's costing two-thirds of your capital and who don't want to sell your product because the customers are not happy with it?

This creates a vicious circle: You're spending too much, there's nothing for the salespeople to sell, and you run out of cash too soon. By the time you realize this, it's usually too late to take action to reduce your burn.

You need to do iteration after iteration of your product before you ever hire a single salesperson. Until then, the CEO will do some sales to engage the market to get feedback, but for a sales organization or, even more importantly, the sales machine (the sales team and the sales mechanism), it is too early. PMF must be achieved first.

The first five or so business deals (particularly for B2B products) a start-up makes will generally be completed by the CEO. *Only* after those initial sales are in place should you consider building a sales organization to replicate the process.

Your MIT will constantly vary depending on what phase you're in. If you need to hire two really good engineers to build your product, then hiring them becomes the MIT.

SIMPLICITY IS KEY

Getting to product-market fit generates value. But as I noted above, you don't need to actually build something to get to that point. I recently heard a claim that 78 percent of Americans will not complete a transaction if they need to download an app for it. For a moment, assume that the data is biased. Even so, every step along the way adds complexity, and complexity creates more barriers for users, and you simply are going to lose more of those users.

Speak with customers (and prospective customers); they will tell you if what your company is aiming to accomplish is a problem that's important for them, one they will pay to solve. That will give you the clearest indication of whether a problem is worth solving.

Traffic jams, for example, are a major problem. If I tell you up front that I can solve that for you, without even showing you a product, you'll say yes.

What's more challenging is making sure that *access* to the value is simple enough. The fact that your product does X, Y, or Z doesn't mean that your users can figure out how to do all that. The product may be too complex.

Achieving simplicity will take iterations. You might have thought it would be a good idea to require registration before using the product. After all, you want to capture that user data for marketing and advertising purposes. But if you lose 50 percent of your users because they don't know what they're registering for, are not yet comfortable sharing their personal information (or *any* information), or simply because the process is long, you've not built a simple-to-use product.

If this is a B2B product and you've just cut a deal with a customer for $100,000, then it's probably OK to have on-site training to explain how to use the product. But for everyone else, especially in the consumer space, simplicity reigns. Otherwise, no one will use it.

Think about ten years ago getting a new phone. You opened the box and there was a thick manual and beneath it was the phone.

Think about unboxing an iPhone. There's no manual in the box at all. That's simplicity!

(More about simplicity in understanding users in a chapter 7.)

I admit that switching phases can be frustrating because you've just reached your objectives, you have a product that creates value, and everyone is happy. And then you have to roll up your sleeves and start all over again from scratch. Even though everyone is pretty pleased by what you've achieved so far, it may be irrelevant for the next phase of the journey.

Understanding how to manage these transitions can mean the difference between success and failure.

DON'T GET BUMPED

In 2009, a mobile device product called Bump became one of the fastest-growing apps of all time. By 2011, Bump had reached number eight on Apple's list of the all-time most popular free iPhone apps. Big-name investors like Sequoia Capital and Andreessen Horowitz jumped on board. Bump was listed among *Time* magazine's "50 Best Android Applications" for 2013. That same year, it logged a total of 125 million app downloads.

And yet, by the beginning of 2014, the app was discontinued; it vanished from iPhones and Androids entirely. What happened? Quite simply: Bump had not achieved product-market fit. Bump was a deceptively addictive app: It allowed you to exchange contact information (as well as photos) by physically "bumping" two phones together. It was sexy, easy to use, and fun. A later version allowed you to share photos with your computer by bumping the phone to your keyboard. But there was no reason to keep using it. Bump's value was very limited; it was the definition of a one-trick pony, doing only one thing (doing it well, admittedly, but that's not enough).

What Bump had going for it was distribution. It went extremely viral. But that was not enough to compensate for the product's shortcoming.

It wasn't all bad, though; Bump was acquired by Google in 2014, and the team moved over to the search engine giant to work on new projects there.

Why was Bump so attractive for tier-one VCs? Well, we already realized that building a start-up is a journey of failures, and that each one of the phases is going to be a journey of failures by itself. Now, think of this journey as climbing a mountain. Ascending to the peak is hard and you try many different ways until you get to the top. And only then do you realize that this is not *the* mountain, it is just a mountain on the way to the summit. But you can only see it once you climb toward the first peak. So, you refocus your efforts and climb this one, only to realize that this is still not it—there is another mountain beyond this ridge that is much steeper and even harder to climb.

While figuring out product-market fit is essential, the hardest phase of all is figuring out growth—how to bring users. This is why Bump was so attractive. They figured out how to bring users (to an extent, they climbed the summit using a different path). The underlying assumption was that they would be able to figure out their value, but once they figured out viral distribution, it was perceived to be the jackpot and they got stuck.

BUILDING A UNICORN—THE STARS ALIGN

To become a market leader and a unicorn you need to align all the stars.

Product is
needed and used

Market is large

LTV is high
(business model works)

User growth and
globalization are figured out

The X factor
(coolness)

What seems to be rather simple is in reality much more complex because, when you start, all these stars are a complete mess.

Product is
needed and used

Market is large

LTV is high
(business model works)

User growth and
globalization are figured out

The X factor
(coolness)

The challenge to aligning all those stars is that each one of them is complex and requires a lot of effort over a long time and, in many cases, is by itself a journey of failures.

The alignment must be done one by one. Each star represents a phase along the journey of failures. You finish getting one star stabilized and then you go on to the next. Meanwhile, you have to watch the previous stars to make sure they don't get misaligned.

You simply CANNOT move on to the next star until product-market fit is complete.

Which phases come first and which come next? When I was young, my father once told me that there is only one justification for a revolution—if it turns out to be successful.

Most consumer services will try to figure out their growth after PMF. If they are successful, they will be able to raise capital based on growth, and likely they will become unicorns relatively fast. If not, they will go on and try to figure out their business model so they can feed the growth with money.

Business-to-business companies need to figure out their business model *before* growth. To a certain extent and in some cases, that business model may be part of product-market fit.

If, for B2C businesses, the main metric is **retention**, for B2B it's whether a customer is coming back to buy for a second time. That indicates increased engagement such as buying after a trial or renewal of the agreement for another period of time. This second engagement is a sign that you've figured out product-market fit. **Renewals** are the B2B equivalent of retention.

When it comes to globalization, it depends on where you start. If you're in a big country with a big market, like the US, Russia, Brazil, Japan, China, Germany, Indonesia, or India, you don't need to think about your strategy for expanding beyond your home country, at least not right away. The market is large enough and, at any given time in the next five years, for the question of "Where should I go?" the answer will be still "here."

If your company is based in Israel, Sweden, Estonia, the Netherlands, or other small countries, though, globalization is more important to tackle earlier. You don't have a whole lot of choice when you're located in a small market. You need to think of becoming global on the first day. As it turns out, in many cases, start-ups from small countries became global faster.

Aligning the stars is a slow and laborious process. You can't grab all of them at once; you must figure each out one by one and only then move on to the next one.

Moreover, when you are in the process of aligning them, remember that the stars are moving all the time. Once you switch gears and focus the company on a new part of the journey, there will likely be some degradation of the service level or satisfaction of the users as a result of refocusing efforts.

The good news is that it is going to be minor, so even if you are going to lose users, it is not going to be a lot.

It can happen when you're in the process of going global, as well. If you go to a new market that is dramatically bigger than the original market, you could wind up losing traction in the original market because you're not focused on that market anymore.

FREQUENCY OF USE

For consumer products, once you've gotten to product-market fit, the usual next phase is growth. Frequency of use is the key to success. If your product has a frequency of use of a few times a month or more, then you should aim for 30 percent user retention after three months.

That is, out of all the customers who used the product for the first time in January, by April, 30 percent of those should still be there and using the service. That's a good place to be. If you are close to that, then there's room for improvement and you might very well get there.

If you're at just 3 percent, though, you're not there and you still have a very long journey ahead of you. While you can certainly slice and dice the numbers any way you like, you cannot bluff the users; if you don't deliver value, they won't come back.

Frequency of use is so powerful for many reasons. One, if people are using your product often, it is obvious you're creating value for them, and therefore you're likely to have higher retention and a greater chance of figuring out product-market fit. Two, your growth is likely to be solved as well, because with word of mouth, every time someone uses the service, it is an opportunity for them to tell someone else about it.

You're in the car together with someone, they see you using Waze, and they ask, "What's that?" You tell them and they get hooked, too. The fact that you use Waze every time you're driving gives you many opportunities to share.

With Moovit, it was exactly the same. People were waiting at a transit station and someone who was using Moovit would say, "The bus will be coming in three minutes," and other people would ask, "How do you know?"

If your frequency of use is high, once you figure out product-market fit, your next phase is always growth.

If your frequency of use is low, however, then you'll need to jump to the business model phase instead of growth. Why? You always need to acquire users. But you have no word of mouth. It will take you a long time to figure out growth, and you probably won't have sufficient funding to get to that point. (If you have both word of mouth and frequency of use, it will take a shorter time to figure out growth.)

If you have three years of runway in your funding, you may still be able to grow, even if the frequency of use is low. But if there's no word of mouth possible, then you may need to pay to acquire users. More likely, you'll have twelve to eighteen months of runway and therefore time to figure out the business model so you can raise more capital and then go to the growth phase.

Think about how you first heard about Waze, Google, WhatsApp, Facebook, Uber, or any other app that you're using on a regular basis. In more than 90 percent of cases it's because "someone told me." That's the power of word of mouth. In reality, word of mouth happens only for services or apps that are used very frequently.

CREATING VALUE IN B2B

Let me define "business model" as the following: *What do you get paid for by the customer, and how much?* In general, these two have to tie back into the value that you create. As a rule of thumb, you should be able to get anywhere between 10 percent to 25 percent of the value you create.

So, let's say that you help companies save money. If you save them $1 million a year, you should expect the deal to be on an order of magnitude of anywhere between $100,000 and $250,000. The model itself (what customers are paying for) should be simple enough to explain and hopefully will increase over time (in terms of users, usage, etc.).

Once you figure out this part, it has to tie back into your business model.

- If this is the model, is the market large enough?
- Can you be profitable?
- Does it make economic sense (also called unit economics)?

In the buyer's mind will be the following formula: *Is the ratio between value and price reasonable?* If so, buyers should be OK with giving your product a try.

How do you quantify that? Ask yourself: What do you promise you'll do for your customers? Make money for them? Save money? Shorten their time to market? Those all have value.

FairFly, as B2B software, does exactly that. It helps travel managers measure and monitor their travel expenditures, and therefore can save them up to 10 percent of their travel budget. If you think of a large corporation, this might be hundreds of millions of dollars in annual travel budget dollars and therefore tens of millions of dollars in savings (value created by FairFly).

The value proposition is very simple, as is the business model: If we save you $X, give us part of it.

If you're building a back-end software system that will increase a customer's sales by $1 million, then you might be entitled to 10 to 20 percent of that as the fee for your service.

You might think that pricing on a variable scale could be beneficial to capture new customers. For example, you might be tempted, especially at the beginning of your journey, to offer a customer a price that increases depending on how much money you save for that customer.

CEOs will tell you, "I like that. We share risk. If you don't create value, you don't get anything." But your potential customer's CFO will be much more circumspect. "You're saying I won't know how much I'll be paying you next month? No, I want a flat fee. I want to know that every month I pay you X and that's it. If we save more or do more business, then we can renegotiate the deal."

Every deal will be slightly different when you're in the B2B world, although, after a while, you'll start seeing the same types of deals pop up. Some will be flat fee, some risk/reward, and others will have a minimum or a cap. The model will become more straightforward over time, although it will always have variants. You'll still make deals where you lose money, but hopefully there will be fewer and fewer of them.

B2B deals are negotiated one deal at a time unlike off-the-shelf B2C products.

PHASES AND UNICORNS

How long does it take to become a super success—a unicorn with a valuation of $1 billion or more?

A list with Israeli unicorns, gathered by the Israeli business publication *Calcalist* in December 2020, showed that the average time for building a unicorn is thirteen years. Nearly no one gets there in less than ten. Even for the most successful companies, it takes a long time to figure out all the phases.

- Microsoft took five years to figure out its product-market fit. The company launched in the mid-1970s but only came into its own in 1980.
- It was ten years for Netflix to figure out product-market fit.

- Waze started development in 2007 (or 2006 if you go back to Free-Map, which started earlier). When did we figure out product-market fit? Not until the end of 2010. That was relatively quick—only three and a half years.

If you're not aiming to become a unicorn, can you do it in less time? Unfortunately not. It will always take time. We hadn't figured out the business model for Waze when Google acquired us. So, even though our journey as an independent company ended after just six years (or five and a quarter if you count from our official inception until the acquisition date), if we'd stayed on our own, it would have taken us many more years to figure out the business model.

On the day of the acquisition, Waze's revenues were about $1 million on an annual basis. In 2020, that had jumped to more than $400 million. (To put things into perspective, Google would call that $0.4 billion.)

Why does it take two to three years per phase? Because of the journey of failures. You bring your hypothesis, test it out, if it works, that's brilliant and maybe you can even shorten the phases. But usually, it takes multiple attempts to get there.

Is there a way to speed things up? Yes. Measure fast! Then you'll know. If you analyze your metrics before you conduct any experiments along the journey of failures, then you'll know. Figure out what you need to measure so you have the tools in hand before you start to build your product.

Remember how my dad used to say that the only justification for starting a revolution is if it turns out successful? That's true. People only respect you if the revolution works out. But we don't know up front what's going to happen. To gain the strength to persevere, you need to *believe* that what you're doing is a noble cause. The nicest part is that you dramatically increase the likelihood of the next revolution to succeed if you try this one.

SPAMOFF: A CASE STUDY IN BEING TOO SUCCESSFUL

A few years ago, my son Ido started a company in Israel called Spamoff. Naturally, I mentored him and invested in the company. The goal was to stop the spam we all receive via SMS text messages. We went into the journey charged up. Here's an injustice we can fix!

We built a platform to leverage recently passed legislation in Israel that made sending spam messages illegal and that allowed the recipient of such a message to sue the sender for NIS 1,000 (about $300) *per message*, without needing to prove damages.

As in many cases where authorities try to provide a service to the public, it was too complex. Our platform simplified the process and allowed Israelis who received SMS spam messages to nearly automatically file a lawsuit. All they had to do was to upload the screenshot of the message; the system then submitted a form to the small claims court. Some of this was done manually at first while we were still developing the platform and proving the concept.

We launched the service in 2015 through a Facebook page where we offered followers the opportunity to use it. The response was overwhelming, with many people asking to file a lawsuit through Spamoff. Shortly after that, Geektime, an Israeli tech website, came across our service and published an article that brought us thousands of users at once, which was at the time way more than what the company could digest, or in other words, way too early for us. We knew immediately that the need was there.

Our start-up received immediate pushback. The spammers naturally didn't like the model. If before they could send millions of messages a day and there were maybe ten lawsuits as a result of it, we filed two hundred lawsuits *in the first month*, and it was more like a flood, growing to one thousand a month. That rocked the boat of the spammers' business models.

We then got a new type of pushback we didn't anticipate: The courthouses and judges were suffering from overloads. Those one thousand claims a month were about 15–20 percent of what the court dealt with, so all of a sudden, the justice system had to invest 15–20 percent of its cases in dealing with spammers.

With 15–20 percent of the claims to small claims court now being generated by a machine—our machine—the judges were feeling overwhelmed and found all sorts of reasons to dismiss the claims we filed, including claiming that the fact that the process was automated somehow made it faulty. (By the way, a large portion of the lawsuits were settled out of court, so the overflow was not as bad as they thought at the time.)

We tried to fight, but we didn't have enough funding. It would have been a long process, and in fact, one of the claims went all the way to Israel's Supreme Court, where we finally won. But it was too late for us. We had no choice but to shut Spamoff down.

Spamoff is a good example of a company that operated in phases but where operating in phases is not enough. With Spamoff, regulation and the justice system were the main obstacles on its way to success.

If you ask me today, knowing what I now know: Should we still have started Spamoff? Yes, because it was a fight worth waging.

What would we have done differently? We would probably have engaged the legal system *beforehand* and tried to build the service together with them.

Spamoff, in one aspect, was a huge success, and today there is just 10 percent of the SMS spam that was originally in the country. My only regret is that I lost money, as I was the only investor.

SHIFTING PHASES IN LATIN AMERICA

When Waze began to expand outside of Israel, it was a nightmare at first. One of the few regions where we gained some traction was in Latin America, and that was largely because we had a great partner in Ecuador who also took us to Colombia, Venezuela, and Chile. We were promoting the BlackBerry, which was the most common smartphone in Latin America at the time.

This partner was a company called Location World, which specializes in telematics for connected cars. Location World also had mapping capabilities, which instantly made our maps in the region more accurate. If it were not for them, we might have died; they gave us the leapfrog to move into the future.

The deal with Location World was that we would make the maps, and they would resell them. They actively handled business development for us.

But when we changed our business model and started selling advertisements to make money, Location World became completely irrelevant. Selling ads was not something they knew much about. They were willing to give it a go, but while they were amazing in the early days of building data and users, we were looking for an experienced partner in this space.

They were not happy.

"We feel like a donkey that carried a carriage up the hill and now that you're going downhill, you're telling us we don't need you anymore since the carriage can go downhill all on its own," they complained.

"We are so grateful for everything you've done," I assured them. "But think about it completely different. Our carriage can go down the hill *faster* than the donkey. If you don't move aside, that carriage will run you over!"

I proposed an alternative arrangement.

"Come and sit on the carriage with us. You have equity in the company. You'll be successful that way." And indeed, over their years of engagement with Waze, they made a lot of money. And we're still friends.

You might think that the US is the most important market, but relative to size at the time, Latin America was for Waze (and also for Moovit) much more successful.

The point of this story is that the different phases have to come at the right time. Location World was critical to Waze's success in 2010. They became a very good partner in 2011 and a less relevant one in 2012. As the company progressed, their relevancy decreased to the level where they became unnecessary. It could have been the same with an employee, a group, a manager, or a founder, and it is likely to happen when shifting gears, too.

THE START-UP AS AN ORCHESTRA

The biggest challenge for a CEO is to make sure the organization is changing along with the phases. In that way, a CEO is like an orchestra conductor. Each player in the start-up orchestra—sales, marketing, product development—is important on its own, doing their job at the right time.

You start with the piano, add some violins (so now the piano is no longer 100 percent of the soundscape), and later maybe add drums and trumpets. During the intermission, the pianist may go home because there is no need for a piano in the rest of the event. A mature organization has all the pieces in place. It needs to play in harmony. Each player realizes that what they're doing is only a part of the whole.

The inability to move from one phase to the next, to flow with these dramatic changes, to staff the orchestra at the right times to create the right rhythm, is one of the key reasons start-ups fail.

WHEN IS THE TIME TO SWITCH GEARS?

Get ready to switch gears when any of the following happen:

- when the metrics are right
- when your retention objective is achieved at product-market fit
- when the sales cycle is shortened by figuring out the business model
- when you reduce your user acquisition cost to either zero or way below the lifetime-value of a user for growth

What are the right numbers? We will discuss that in the product-market fit, growth, and business model chapters. Your challenge is to act according to the numbers and not according to a gut feeling, and to lead the company to shift gears when the numbers are right. I've seen too many companies moving to the next phase too early . . . and also too late.

STARTIPS

- What's the most important stage in a company? They all are—one at a time.

- Successful start-ups and entrepreneurs operate in phases, usually one at a time. Product-market fit always comes first.

- Each phase takes two to three years. After the product-market fit phase generally comes scaling up and monetization (business plan).

- Trying to work on multiple phases at once is almost always a recipe for disaster. You'll wind up spending money for nothing and not making progress.

- Start by deciding on the MIT—the most important thing. Phase transfers are particularly dramatic because what's changing is the MIT.

- Not every staff person, including the founders, will make it to the next phase.

- Be careful not to hire too early. Otherwise, your talented staff will have nothing to do, and so they'll leave.

- Getting your first customer to buy for a second time is an excellent indication of product-market fit.

- You can charge 10 to 25 percent of the value you provide to your customers.

Chapter 5a

RIDE THE FUNDRAISING ROLLER COASTER

If building a start-up is like a roller-coaster ride, then fundraising is like a roller coaster in the dark—you don't even know what's coming!

The "all partners" meeting with Vertex Ventures was scheduled for a Thursday morning in late November 2007. It was one of many meetings Waze would have with investors, and it was the third we'd had with Vertex, a clear indication of interest on their side.

We were seeking our first round of financing for Waze, which wasn't even formulated as a company at that point and had no paid staff. I was already full-time on the fundraising mission. In short, we needed this money to hire people and shift gears to start our journey.

The meeting in November with Vertex would be the first time all their partners would be present. Previously, we had met with Ehud Levy, our main contact, and a few other Vertex team members.

Ehud was very enthusiastic about what we were building, but he needed to sell it to his colleagues, in particular to Yoram Oron, the fund manager and the sole decision maker there.

We had already received dozens of "noes" from other VCs. Their reasons had by this time blurred, so I wasn't even sure anymore who said what.

Many of those reasons—if they had reasons at all—were entirely irrelevant or demonstrated a disconnection from the story we were telling.

Some others actually made sense.

"You think that people driving in their cars can create a better map than Navteq or Tele Atlas?" was one such response, referring to two of the leading GPS mapmakers at the time.

"If you don't know where my house is, it will never be good enough," was another.

"How do you know if someone hasn't created incorrect information? Don't you need to have someone to validate everything?"

"Users will never share their locations. There are privacy issues."

"Why does the world need another navigation application?"

And to me personally: "Why do you think you're the right guy to lead this?"

One of the key factors with VC decision-making is "user perspective." It is very unlikely for the partners in a VC firm to invest in something they don't think they would use themselves. The whole concept of crowdsourcing was too much to digest for many of the investors we met.

While the understanding of ideas like "WE are smarter than ME," and "the wisdom of the crowd" was accepted well, the thought of someone actively contributing via an app where the map and the app itself were not good enough just didn't resonate with them.

We needed to create a wow effect, one that Yoram would think was working "like magic." Even if he didn't believe he would actively contribute anything himself to the map, we needed him to believe that someone else would.

I came up with an idea.

"Let's make sure that all the partners' houses are on the map," I said to my partners, "so if they ask us to navigate to their homes, it will work." I hoped they would indeed ask, but if they didn't, then I would gently push them, so to speak, in that direction. My plan was to ask Ehud Levy during the meeting where his house was and then show it on the map. Hopefully, after that, someone else would want to try as well.

I called Ehud Levy and asked him for a list of addresses of the Vertex partners. When he asked me why, I told him that I wanted to make sure that when we ran our demo, it was in the actual neighborhood of one of the partners so it would feel real.

"The most common first address for people to test is either their home or office," I explained. I promised to erase the data.

Ehud sent me the list later that day, and we simulated drive and map creation close by to the area where each of the partners lived. We created multiple map-editing sessions that generated information for the neighborhood near the partners' homes.

In that way, not only was the house number of each of the partners on the map, but there were multiple other houses on the same street, and the next street, and so forth. As a result, we knew we were ready for someone to ask, "Is my house on the map?"

We arrived early so we could set the stage. I always set my stage: I want to sit where the screen is, so people are still looking at me when I present and, especially, so I can look at them even when they are looking at the slide deck.

We started by showing the map/navigation on the large screen.

"So, you're telling me that my house may be on the map?" Yoram Oron, the managing partner asked. It was exactly what I was hoping for.

"Well, I don't know where you live, but tell me your address and let's find out," I replied.

It was not even a white lie, because I personally didn't know where Yoram lived. But I did know that his house was on our map.

We typed in Yoram's address. And there, truly magically, was his house, appearing on the screen.

The partners stared at the map, but I was watching Yoram. I studied his face. The moment his house appeared on the map, his eyes changed. The sides of his mouth twitched up. The only way I can describe it is pure dollar signs.

It was at that moment that I knew the deal was ours.

A week later, we received a term sheet from Vertex for $2 million.

That wasn't the end, though—far from it. The deal would not close for another three months and, by that time, two other investors had signed on and the investment jumped to $12 million.

If a start-up is a roller coaster and fundraising is a roller coaster in the dark, then closing a deal is like a roller coaster in the dark going backward! Did I enjoy the roller coaster? I like speed and I like extreme sports. But what I learned would prove to be invaluable for the dozen companies I founded after Waze.

If you're looking for funding for the first time, this is certainly the chapter for you. Fundraising is very different from anything else that you've ever seen before. Imagine that you would need one hundred dates to find "the one." In fundraising, this is exactly the case. You will need to be extraordinary; this chapter will tell you how to become such an extraordinary fundable entrepreneur.

Think about the following: At the end of the day, an investor is going to invest in a new start-up and a first-time entrepreneur only if they like the CEO and they like the story. Make your story shine!

TELLING A GOOD STORY

After Waze was acquired in 2013, I was in a meeting with a partner from one of Israel's leading venture capital firms. I asked him how long it takes to decide if he likes the entrepreneur or not.

"Do you want the real answer or the right answer?" he asked. "The real one," I replied. "I've heard the 'right one' answered enough times."

We were sitting in a small conference room. He looked at me. Then he looked at the door. Then he looked at me again and then back to the door.

"That fast," he said. "Before they even sit down."

This is how quickly you make a first impression. After that, it is a matter of a few minutes to either solidify or change that impression.

Now, if this is the case, then in the story you're about to tell, you have to start with the strongest point at the beginning. Otherwise, by the time you get to it, they may have already made up their mind!

I asked investors on several occasions regarding early-stage companies: "Why did you decide to invest in this start-up or *that* start-up?" I heard a consistent answer. It was either "I knew the CEO from a previous start-up," or "I liked the story and I liked the CEO."

From this, we can draw two main conclusions:

1. *I liked the story*: You have to **LEARN how to tell a good story.** A good story is about emotional engagement and not about facts. You are trying to engage the investor to want what you're making, as we did with the "magic" at Vertex.
2. *I liked the CEO*: You need to be at your best, and appearance *does* matter. So, **the CEO goes to the first meeting ALONE.** That way, no one else is on the stage with the CEO to take away the spotlight.

A colleague once told me a valuable story about storytelling.

"A friend of mine went running on the beach last night and, after five miles, he thought that going into the refreshing Mediterranean Sea would be an awesome idea. It was already late, so there was no one on the beach. He thought that, if there is no one there, he can go naked to swim and cool down. So, he took off all his clothes—even his watch—and went into the water. After a few minutes, suddenly, he ran into a shark. So, he pulled out his knife and stabbed the shark . . ."

This is where I stopped him.

"Wait a minute," I interjected. "Where exactly did he pull his knife from?"

"Do you want a story, or do you want facts?" he responded.

The story illustrates an important point: If you tell facts, you make your audience think. If you tell stories, you make them imagine and feel. If you want them to invest, they need to imagine, and become emotionally engaged.

How do you tell a good story? You're trying to create emotional engagement and make them imagine they are part of it. Therefore, the story needs to be authentic. Making up a "use case"—a common part of business plans and marketing documents that describes in detail who a product's users will be and exactly how they will use it—doesn't fly.

Telling someone else's use case can still create the authenticity you need, but the most important thing is to make the listener (in this case, the investor) believe he or she is part of the story (that is, you want them to think: "It can happen to me"). They need to "feel" the story, even if it's not exactly true.

ZEEK: IT STARTED WITH A MICROWAVE

When we were creating Zeek, a start-up that helped customers make the most of in-store credit, we wanted to present several use cases.

Now, while use cases can be very helpful tools, they can also be very dry. They're not stories.

I was the chairman of Zeek, and Daniel Zelkind was cofounder and CEO. Daniel asked me how to convert his new company's use cases into stories. I made up one for Daniel. It went like this: In our kitchen at home, we have a space for a microwave oven with a custom-made cabinet. There is a wood frame around the oven, and only the door and control keys are visible.

One day the microwave broke and my wife (now ex-wife) told me it was urgent to find a new one. Because I understood the immediacy on one hand but also that the microwave needed to be smaller than the frame size or else it wouldn't fit, I carefully measured the size before I went to the store to buy a new unit. I was very lucky and managed to get the very last microwave of the size I needed. I took it home, unpacked the appliance, removed the frame from the cabinet, slid out the original oven, and placed the new one in its place. I then put back the frame, lowered the old microwave into the new box, and schlepped the box and the microwave out to the trash room. Finally, I checked to make sure the new microwave was working.

That's when I realized that the microwave oven door was one-eighth of an inch wider than the frame.

When telling this story, I use my hands to demonstrate the width of the frame, how I carried the heavy box to the trash, and the size of the stray cat that I scared from the garbage room. At this point, you're hopefully starting to imagine you are part of the story and it feels authentic; you share the frustration.

That's not the end of the story, though. When I went to return the microwave to the store, the salesperson was not particularly helpful. "We don't carry any microwaves in the size you need," he told me. He said he would be happy to give me store credit. "What do you want me to do with store credit?" I responded. "I need a microwave that fits this space. You don't have one. So, I have nothing else to buy at your store." I ended up buying a second microwave at a different store. Now I have two microwaves: one in my house and the other one that is "store credit."

Put all together—the feeling of helplessness, the realization that I'd wasted time and money, the expected reaction of my wife—and you have a full-blown story that explains why we need to have a marketplace for store credit.

That was the genesis of Zeek.

The story worked because of its great details. Indeed, when reading the story here in print, it might feel a bit like there are too many details, but it's the details that create the authenticity you need. (When you're telling the story, you may skip some of those details if you feel the message was conveyed.)

Moreover, the sense of frustration inherent in the story made it sound authentic and emotionally engaging. It's easy to imagine yourself in the exact same situation. In fact, Daniel even asked me what my wife said after the microwave fiasco, so there was a moment in time when the story sounded so real, even he forgot it was all made up.

Daniel began using that story in all his pitches. I think at some point he may have come to believe it happened to *him*, so much so that the story boomeranged around on me.

I had made an introduction for Daniel to pitch the venture capital firm Sequoia. He met with one of the partners, Gili Raanan, whom I knew since our days together in the IDF's 8200 intelligence unit and, later on, in several other places including the board of directors of Moovit.

I had already told Gili the microwave story. Then, it turns out, Daniel did, too.

"It's so funny," Gili said to me as we were debriefing the pitch. "Your CEO had the exact same microwave story as you. He even used the same hand movements!"

It doesn't matter where the story comes from. If the CEO can throw his or her "all" into the story, to make it authentic, to create true emotional engagement so that investors can imagine themselves in the story—maybe they're frustrated, maybe they're angry, maybe they want revenge—that makes all the difference.

Remember what I said before: Investors are users as well. If you're an investor and you don't think you're going to use the product an entrepreneur is pitching, you won't invest.

So, when you, the entrepreneur, are crafting your story, see if you can find out beforehand more about the investor you're meeting with. If your product is software for kids, ask if the investor has kids at the right age. Maybe they have nieces and nephews. The investor must imagine *someone* he or she knows using the product.

REFUNDIT'S STORY

The Refundit story is even more powerful than Zeek in the sense that Refundit addresses a different kind of frustration: trying to receive a VAT refund (usually called TAX FREE) when traveling to Europe.

As we noted in chapter 1, residents from non-EU countries visiting the European Union are entitled to get back any VAT paid on items purchased while there. But in 90 percent of cases, people fail to get their money back. Perhaps there are long lines at customs, or the store doesn't have the right forms, or maybe the desk at the airport was closed. There is always something that doesn't work in the process.

Refundit simplifies this so that all you have to do is use an app to scan your receipts, passport, and boarding pass to get your money back.

When I tell this story to investors, it always triggers something about their own frustration with the process. They often share with me anecdotes about what happened to them personally. It's exactly what happened to Ziv, Refundit's CEO, when he spoke with users and tried to buy a bike in Barcelona.

This is the most important part of telling a story: listen to the feedback, then once the investor is engaged, highlight and empower that connection.

An investor once told me, for example, "I never stop at the tax refund, but my spouse always does." You can use that feedback to respond with something like, "Wow, that's even worse! At least for your spouse there is a reason and, hopefully, some refund will come out of it, but you have to wait around, doing nothing. It's simply a waste of time. Refundit can save you the time and frustration of waiting for your spouse."

DEMOS AND SLIDE DECKS

What if you're nervous or don't feel you're a great speaker? Can you show the investor a video demo of how your product works instead when you come to do your pitch? No! It will only annoy the investor and you will have missed a ninety-second chance to tell your story live. What kind of first impression does that make?

But these videos are critically important when the story is being sent by email. Most of the investors you'll meet are not sole decision makers. They have an organization to support them. When done right, a video can be the best way for them to share information among themselves.

Let's talk about those ninety-second YouTube demos for a moment. They're becoming increasingly common these days. I've noticed that many are using "elevator music" as filler instead of telling the story in words. This is a terrible waste of time and opportunity. Someone gave you ninety seconds of their attention and you played them elevator music? When people send me videos like that, I often ask them who made their videos. When they tell me, I respond that they should fire that person!

A live demo is a completely different scenario. You're there physically and you have a listener that you can see, sense, and talk to; it is a key opportunity to tell your story. Here's an important tip: Make a complete separation between what people see on the screen and what you tell them in your own words. They see the product while you tell them the story. In the end, they will have heard the story and will sense that they have seen the story working. Don't fall into the trap of explaining what they are seeing or what you're doing as you move the mouse. That's a missed opportunity. Instead, tell a story that creates emotional engagement.

Creating a professional video (not a demo video) is worthwhile, however. If you do create one, be sure to add subtitles or a transcription in addition to the story being told, so that people can watch the video even in a quiet environment. It will also make it easier for you to change the language of the subtitles if needed.

When you craft your slide deck, the two most important slides that are overlooked are the first and the last (that is, the title slide and the end slide). That's probably not what you expected! In most presentations I've seen, the title slide says nothing other than the name of the company, that this is an investor presentation, and the date. Yet, this slide is going to be up and running longer than nearly any other slide in your presentation, and you've used it to say absolutely nothing.

Instead, use your title slide to deliver one simple, powerful message. Explain the problem, present the opportunity, or set a statement so that when you later tell your story, it will be considered a fact. For example, "We address a $400 billion broken market," "No one can do that better than us," or "Ninety percent of people hate visiting the dentist."

I said "nearly" about the first slide, because the last slide, the one that usually just says, "thank you," is likely to be staying on-screen even longer—so use it to recapture your key message. These two slides will be viewed for the longest period. Tell your audience something you want them to remember.

Last but not least, in your story, if you are solving a problem, start with the *who* and the *why* and get to the *what* at the end. It's the same process that we saw in chapter 1 about identifying a big problem worth solving. *Who* are you solving the problem for? That's your audience. *Why* are you building it? That's the problem. The *what* is the solution.

When you give your initial investor pitch, remember again that the CEO is the *only* one who should be in that meeting (unless the investor specifically asked for the team). It is not an ego thing. If a VC decides to invest, it is because they like the CEO and they like the story.

What happens if you bring more people to the meeting? There are two options. They actively participate and therefore take part of the time/attention/shine that should be on the CEO. Or else they say nothing, and then one could ask: What exactly is their role in the room?

THE DANCE OF ONE HUNDRED NOES

Every start-up struggles to raise capital at the beginning. Only 15 percent of start-ups (those that have already formed a company and perhaps have raised some pre-seed money from angels) ever get to a seed round.

Waze received dozens of noes before Vertex made its offer. You could call this the "Dance of the One Hundred Noes."

Why one hundred? Think of it this way: A VC partner will meet between one hundred and two hundred companies in a year. Yet, the VC partner will invest in only one to two a year. That's 99 percent no for 1 percent yes. So, having to pitch ninety-nine times doesn't mean you're doing a bad job. It's just how it works.

This is very different than when you're figuring out your product fit. If you speak to twenty people and they all tell you that the problem you're defining is not a problem for them, well, then your perception of the problem might be wrong and there's no reason to move forward. But if you speak with twenty investors and they all say no, it means nothing; keep on pushing up that hill. Now, don't get me wrong, it is very discouraging. People who you expect to know something about start-ups tell you no and no and no and no. You cannot allow yourself to get discouraged. Figure out how to improve, and move on to the next one.

In fact, you're making progress in two aspects: your story improves, and your resilience and perseverance increase.

Let me reiterate this point because it's crucial. Imagine you're trying to score a hoop from three-quarter court in basketball. You stand at the foul line and try to score by reaching the basket on the other side. If you think you can make it with the one shot, you shouldn't be building start-ups, you should be playing for the NBA. But if you try one hundred times, you will eventually get a chance to make it.

There's a reason venture capital firms are so selective. Seventy-five percent of all VC-backed start-ups fail, according to a Harvard Business School study. In Israel, 40 percent of VC-backed companies generate zero capital returns. In the US, just 6 percent of companies create 90 percent of the capital returns.

But occasionally, a VC will find success, maybe even a unicorn. Venture capital firms are looking for a specific kind of company—one that will be worth a billion dollars someday or that's playing in a multibillion-dollar market. They call this investment "the fund maker." It makes up for all the losses. The ratio of unicorns to start-ups was in 2014 1:1,500, and, while much better, still just 1:800 in 2021—that is, just one out of every thousand (give or take) start-ups will become a unicorn.

A VC partner doesn't want a company that will just double a $5 million investment. They want ten, twenty, a hundred times the return. If the VC doesn't think you have the possibility of being a fund maker, the VC won't invest.

This is another reason why it's so important to put the strongest point at the beginning of your story. If the VC's job is to say no because this is what they do in 99 percent of cases, then their patience deteriorates over time and they are generally in a rush to jump to conclusions. Start with the strongest point so the VC's conclusion is the right one!

Who should you approach at a venture capital firm? You can go for the low-hanging fruit—the first-line analysts whose job it is to speak with entrepreneurs. My advice: don't. Only the partners in a VC firm can say yes. It's useless to speak to anyone else. The most an analyst can say is no.

WATCH OUT FOR INVESTOR BULLSHIT

While you dance the Dance of the One Hundred Noes, watch out for investor bullshit. Here are some examples:

"In all the deals we do, this is how it's done." Really? If one of my kids came home and said, "But Dad, all the parents of the kids in my class allow them to do this or that," "All," "Never," "Always," "Nobody"—you shouldn't take them literally. Same with investors.

"We never invested in something like that" or "We never invested at that price" should be read as "Well, we did, but we don't want to tell you." If you're a first-time entrepreneur, it's really hard to call an experienced investor's bluff. "All" and "never" terms are almost always investor bullshit.

"People will never download it."

"We think the trajectory of the market will slow down."

"We believe that your product is for such-and-such type of investor, not us."

I call bullshit. It's all investor speak for "I don't like your idea" or "I don't like you, but I don't want to tell you."

One of the most common bullshit objections every entrepreneur will hear at one point is "Google can do that." It's rarely true. Because Google is focused on building its own business. They don't care about yours. And if they decide they do want to eat your lunch, they're going to have to go through the same or a similar journey you took to get to where you are now, which if you've got the right product-market fit, is not trivial.

When Nir Erez, cofounder and CEO of Moovit, was first trying to raise money for the company in 2012, one of the objections he heard again and again from investors was that Waze would most likely go after the public transportation space. After all, Waze had already perfected crowdsourcing traffic jams for commuters.

"They can do it in no time," the investors would say.

Which was pretty funny, because I was already on Moovit's board of directors. That allowed me to tell investors straight out: "No, Waze cannot do it in no time! Our users and theirs are completely different audiences. Waze users drive cars. Moovit users don't."

As with Google, it is a matter of focus, and focus is not about what we do, it is about what we *don't* do. Our focus at Waze was on commuter drivers, which means we don't do public transportation, pedestrians, or horse riding. We don't even do skiers or bike riders (even though I am both of those).

It's the audience that drives a company. Put another way, it's not so much **what** we're doing but **why** and **whom** we're doing it for. Waze and Moovit were never competitors, even though some investors would say we were.

If you get into such an argument of back-and-forth counterclaims, many of the entrepreneurs I've met will try to prove the investors wrong. If the entrepreneur receives a detailed email explaining why the firm is not investing, the entrepreneur tends to reply in length about why the investor's arguments are inaccurate or irrelevant.

Don't even bother. Just say "thank you for considering us" and continue down your list of one hundred VCs. Remember that they said no because they didn't like the story, or they didn't like you.

Some VCs will send you a thoughtful email explaining why they are not going to invest. Simply reply with a "thank you" and a note that "we will update you with relevant news." A VC that doesn't return your emails? Move on. If they want to invest, they will call you.

KEY INVESTOR INDICATORS

How do you know if an investor is interested in moving forward? Here are what I call the KIIs—the "Key Investor Indicators."

- If they're speaking about the deal, they're interested.
- If they're asking who else is looking at the deal, they're interested.
- If they're asking who the previous investors were or if they want to see your capitalization table (which shows ownership percentages and equity dilution), they're interested.
- If they begin to offer advice on how to change your presentation, it means they want to present it to someone else in their fund, so they're interested.

At one point, I took Waze to the same investor, Atomico, four times. Each time Atomico had a different objection. It started with "it's too early," which is actually a good answer. It means they don't believe your story yet, but if you can show them that it works with real-world data, then they'll be OK.

Atomico didn't invest but we liked them, so we went back for the B round. This time, Atomico said, "What you've done so far is amazing, but we think the valuation is too high."

Valuation is an estimate of what a company is worth. If a VC invests a certain amount at a low company valuation, the VC gets a larger percentage of the company than if the investment is made at a higher valuation. Higher valuations also mean that previous investors—and the company shareholders—are "diluted" less, that is, the percentage of the company they own remains higher. We met with Atomico again for the C round and Atomico repeated the same mantra.

"Your progress is amazing," they told me. "We didn't believe you would get that far. We wish we would have invested in the previous round, but this time your valuation is still too high."

"OK," I replied, "but next time around you're going to say the same thing."

Atomico never got in before Waze was acquired by Google. However, they were a great help in our business development progress in Brazil.

JUST A FEW MONTHS LEFT

The truth is, Atomico wasn't alone, at least when it came to our second round. Waze had a very tough time raising money. We had been very successful in Israel, but our progress was slow in the US and Europe, where the only countries in which we'd built any traction were Latvia, Slovakia, and the Czech Republic. We'd done well in Ecuador in Latin America, as well, because of an amazing partner we had in an automotive technology company called Location World.

The VCs in Israel all said no. We met many of them, showing how we'd progressed, and they were using the app in Israel. But our global figures were insufficient and there was no clear business model.

Nor were any of our existing VCs interested in investing additional money—this is how little support we had.

"If you can sell the company today for $20 to $40 million, you should," one of our early investors told us.

It was a challenging time for Waze. It was 2010 and we were pretty close to the end of the cash we'd raised from the series A. We had maybe a few months left. The entire management team decided to take a salary cut to avoid having to do an across-the-board reduction, so the other employees were not affected.

GOOGLE MAKES AN UNEXPECTED MOVE

It was around that time that Noam and I had dinner with one of the partners at Khosla Ventures, a large Silicon Valley VC whom we'd met several times. We were preparing for an all-partners' meeting the next morning where we would be presenting, and looking for funding for our B round.

Usually, when this happens, it is a clear indication that the partner really wants to invest, so he is briefing you before the all-partners' meeting. He also wanted to show us how valuable his firm could be (another clear indication that they are interested).

The partner then added that he knew our only potential competitor was Google, but that we shouldn't be worried, because he had spoken with his contacts there, and they told him they are at least two years away from having their own maps and free turn-by-turn navigation.

The next morning, I opened my computer to check the latest tech news and received a very unpleasant surprise: Google had announced turn-by-turn navigation in the US, replacing TomTom as the map source.

Noam Bardin, Waze's CEO, and I met for breakfast.

"Should we even bother to go to the all-partners' meeting?" he asked earnestly.

We went, but Noam was right: Google's announcement stopped that large investor's interest in Waze dead in its tracks.

Ultimately, by the time we were done with the B round, there were several dozen VCs who said no. B rounds, in many cases, are based more on traction and execution rather than story alone. Our team was amazing, the model (where it worked) was incredible, and our story was very powerful. But with no traction in the countries that mattered, it was hard.

Except for one company: Microsoft. The tech giant had a worry that dovetailed with ours. They were afraid that someday they might want to build their own mapping product and, now that Google was expanding its map functionality, what if Google would refuse to license maps to Microsoft?

Microsoft's fear became our savior. The company led a $30 million round in Waze, which also included Qualcomm Ventures, at a $70 million valuation. It was even higher than what we were hoping to get!

So, what started as a disaster—Google announcing turn-by-turn navigation in the US—spurred other companies to look for a mapping alternative . . . and we were the alternative.

It also allowed us to focus. Instead of trying to compete with Google on search within the map, we concentrated on commuting, which was not Google Maps' strength.

Microsoft's investment, which was not publicized at the time as it was below their reporting threshold, came just in time. We were just a month away from shutting down the company and firing everyone. That was our B round, and it was enough funding for us.

FOMO AS A FUNDRAISING STRATEGY

For Qualcomm, I used the power of FOMO—the "fear of missing out"—to convince them to join. Initially, they claimed our valuation was too high. I spent many hours with them, as they were hesitating. In one particular meeting, they told me how they'd skipped an investment opportunity in Twitter when the valuation was just $55 million. (At the time of writing in 2021, Twitter is worth $34.4 billion.)

A week later, they asked me to join an all-partners' conference call and to present over video. My last slide said just one thing: If you could roll back time, would you invest in Twitter at that $55 million valuation?

FOMO does work in a lot of cases!

Microsoft would eventually launch a navigation product on its Bing search engine, but with Navteq's maps (by that time it was Nokia), not ours!

The Dance of the One Hundred Noes can be exhausting. It can be debilitating to hear no after no after no. You may want to give up. Many before you have.

You might say at the beginning: "I'm strong, I can hear fifty noes and I won't stop." But after twenty noes, you feel yourself breaking.

Don't. If you've got a good story and you're a likable entrepreneur, you only need one yes out of a hundred.

THE TERM SHEET

A term sheet is a letter of intent from an investor that summarizes the terms of their potential investment in your company. It might look like the holy grail, but it is just a milestone along the path to the funding round. Most likely it will become an investment, but there's still a long way to go

Negotiating with an investor is an unfair fight from the get-go, especially if you're a first-time entrepreneur because you come with zero experience and you're facing off with someone who's made dozens of deals.

It's more than just that. If you already got them to like you and to like the story to the point where they want to invest and are ready to give you a term sheet, then you might be worried that appearing inexperienced at this phase could cool them off. You aren't sure if the right approach is to play hard to get or simply to give in since the thing that scares you the most is losing the deal.

Imagine buying your first house. You receive the mortgage agreement from the realtor and realize you have no clue what half the details in the contract are about.

Don't be afraid to ask for help. It's more than that, actually: You will need help and someone that you can trust to guide you through the entire process of fundraising (at least for the first time).

Do you have an attorney already on your team who can take the time to explain it all? The lawyer can explain to you each part of the term sheet and what the range of common practice is.

Or maybe you know a CEO from another company who could take a look, someone who's been there before? (A fellow CEO is the best choice to be your guide.) Otherwise, how will you know what parts of the terms are negotiable? (The answer: pretty much all of them.) The sweetest position to be in is when you have a term sheet but you're still able to "shop" your company to other VCs and ultimately receive multiple term sheets. This is more common than you'd think.

An investor might want the deal, but if there's a better deal out there to be had from a bigger firm, the original investor might be happy to participate rather than lead. It's an issue of ego management. Investors are happy to join with a more reputable VC, which will increase the likelihood of the deal being successful, increase the funding available for the company in the future, and, in particular, increase the VC's prestige, as the firm will have co-invested with a better or more prominent organization.

There are three phases to the term sheet process. The first phase is "term sheet discussion," in which the VC will tell you they want to give you a term sheet and will highlight the specific terms. This can be overwhelming if you're not ready. The VC might be discussing things that you're not familiar with. And you might feel uncomfortable admitting that. If I were to debrief you afterward and you told me, "The VC wants to give us a term sheet of $X million at $Y million valuation," and then I asked you what the other terms were, you might squint your eyes and be really confused.

If, however, I was to debrief the partner at the VC, he or she might say, "Oh yes, the CEO agreed to all the terms, including the liquidation preferences and veto rights that we asked for."

In the second phase, the VC will actually issue the term sheet. Now you are in "term sheet negotiation." Before you sign, it is nonbinding. This is perhaps your biggest opportunity to improve the company's position, as you can keep shopping for your start-up. You will negotiate with any additional VCs from a position of strength because you know you can't lose—you already have a term sheet in hand! In this situation, treat every pitch like practice and aim higher.

The third phase comes once the term sheet is signed. There is usually a no-shop clause, although having others join the round might be possible. Even though a signed term sheet is still officially a nonbinding agreement, it will infrequently be withdrawn. Maybe one out of fifty in normal times and one out of ten during stressful periods. One notable exception is if you're in the middle of a COVID-19-type period, and then anything can happen. During the pandemic, I have seen more term sheets withdrawn than in my entire career.

Even once you have a signed term sheet, it's still possible to shop around or to bring in a new investor with a better deal (whether that's better terms or a better fund). You can always renegotiate the terms with the first investors.

Another option: Wait three to four weeks for the no-shop period to expire and then get a new term sheet. I would add that the no-shop term is fairly weak. I've never heard of an investor suing a company for violating this term or not accepting the investment.

To get the deal you want, you will need to say NO to the deal that you don't want.

With some of the younger start-ups I've mentored, I have sent them to speak to an investor that I know won't invest (maybe because the fund is already after the investment period, maybe because they don't like me), just so they can practice their story (and get used to hearing some more noes).

The more you find yourself invested psychologically and timewise in a negotiation, the less you're willing to walk away from the deal. But it works both ways: the investor is also less willing to let the deal go. So, stop thinking only about your side and consider their side as well. If you're invested, so are they. If you've invested legal efforts, so have they.

Once you receive a term sheet, don't hesitate to sit down with someone who can explain to you each and every part of it. The challenge, however, is in the meeting before the term sheet. Most investors will meet with you to discuss what's in the term sheet. The following table outlines important paragraphs in a term sheet and how to read them, as well as what is common practice, what's nasty, and what are the favorable terms.

TERM SHEET

Key Terms	What You Should Pay Attention to on Term Sheets
Investment Amount	How much is invested? If the lead investor is only part of the round, you want to make sure you can close the round (formally) with this part only. So, for example, if you are raising $5 million and the lead investor is investing $3 million, you would really like this term sheet to say the round is at least $3 million and up to $5 million. Otherwise, your round is not completed until you find the other investors.
Securities Offered	Most of the investment would be of preferred shares, as opposed to common shares (yours). The preferences of the preferred shares are usually in case of a liquidation event and special rights, as will be described later in the table.
Company Valuation	This is the main deal, together with the amount that constitutes the transaction ("How much for how much?"). Valuation defines how much what was built so far is worth. There is no methodological way to define it, so most likely it will be negotiated based on your alternatives. It is defined as pre-money valuation, which is the value of what was created so far, and together with the investment amount, that forms the post-money valuation—the value of the company once the round is finalized. There will be an immediate derivative of this valuation, which is PPS (Price Per Share) and number of shares in the company (prior to the round).

Company Valuation (continued)	Mathematically, this is: pre-money valuation = PPS × number of shares prior to the round. And then the company issues new shares to the investors at the same PPS in a total amount of the investment amount.
	One note: It is important to realize that while ISO/ESOP is critical to attract and retain employees, it is mostly used by the investor as a way to lower valuation. ISO/ESOP allocation requires issuing more shares, a new share per option, essentially increasing the number of shares and therefore lowering the PPS. So, a $10 million pre-money valuation with 10 percent ISO/ESOP is actually less than $9 million. It is common practice that ISO/ESOP allocation comes from current shareholders and not new ones. To have better negotiation leverage you will need another competitive offer.
Pre-emptive Rights; Right of First Refusal; Co-Sale	Pre-emptive rights—The investor will have the right to participate in the next round to maintain its holding; so, for example, an investor with 10 percent of the company that participates in the next round can maintain its 10 percent position. While it may seem fine that all they want is to increase their position, it may discourage the next investor. Or, even worse, the next investor may ask for similar terms!
	Right of first refusal—The investor has the right to invest under the same terms as a new investor. For example, if a new investor in the next round offers you X money at Y valuation, the current investors may say: if these are the terms—I'm leading.
	Co-sale—If there is a sell transaction by any shareholders, the investor has the right to join that transaction with similar terms. It is very important to make sure that founders' shares (secondary) are excluded from co-sale rights. So if the founders are selling, the investor doesn't have the co-sale right.

Liquidation Preference	The investor has priority over common shares (or lesser shares) in case of liquidation. In its essence—last money in, first money out. There are four levels of liquidation preferences.
	1. No liquidation preferences—All shares are the same.
	2. Nonparticipating—The investor may choose the investment amount (plus interest) or the worth of the shares.
	3. 1x participating—The investors first will get their investment amount (with or without interest) and then get the worth of the shares.
	4. Yx participating—The investors will get Y times their investment amount and then the worth of their shares.
	This might be nasty. Common practice is nonparticipating 1x, and most likely with interest rate. So, in case of an exit, the investors may choose either their investment amount plus interest or the worth of their shares.
	Please see further elaboration at the end of the table.
Board of Directors	There is a common practice that the investors become part of the company's board, which makes sense. Recently, I've seen more and more investors join as observers on the board of directors so that they receive all the information and participate in discussions, but have no voting power and no responsibilities.
	Your objective is to keep the number of board members to a minimum. The more people on the board, the more you will feel you need to provide answers and satisfy everyone, and board meetings will become more of a hassle for you.

Anti-Dilution Rights	What happens if there is a down round in the future? (There is a 30 percent likelihood of this happening.) Broad base is common; full ratchet is nasty.
	Let me explain full ratchet. Assume your last round was $5 million at $10 million pre-money, so essentially the investor is one-third of the company and the founders are two-thirds (forget ISO for a second). Now, time is challenging. You haven't figured your PMF yet, and you're running out of cash, the market is bearish, and the best term sheet you can get is to raise another $5 million at a $5 million pre-money valuation. The new investor will have 50 percent, and everyone else will be diluted to half of their holding, right? If there is a full ratchet anti-dilution clause, then the existing investor (from the previous round) is protected and therefore maintains its one-third, and the only one who suffers is you. There is an even more challenging part. The new investor will look at the cap table and realize that after the round (which is essentially another seed round), the founders will have about 15 percent, which is way too little, and this may result in walking away from the deal.
Voting Rights; Protective Provisions	This is tricky—it lists veto rights for the investor. Some make sense. For example, you cannot violate an investor's rights even though the common shares are majority shares, so you cannot terminate the liquidation preferences of the investor, or you as the majority of the board and the majority of the shareholders want to decide on your annual bonus.
	Other voting rights may interfere with the smooth operation of the company—for these, you should disagree. Regardless, you want to prevent veto rights being placed in the hand of a single entity.

No-Sale	Ohhh, this is painful, as it touches your own pocket and tells you when you can sell secondary shares and for how much. But it also makes sense that you don't sell your shares immediately after the investor invests and then they lose their bet.
	Common practice would be to permit selling up to a certain amount per year and up to a total of a certain amount (30 percent is reasonable).
Founders' Vesting	This seems to be more painful, but actually, it is something that you really want. It basically says that, if you leave soon, you can take only a portion of your shares—it's a lockup/retention model for the founders. This is dramatic; further elaboration follows the table.
Expenses	Wait a minute, are you telling me that part of the investment amount will be used to pay the legal expenses of the investor? Yes, this is what I'm saying exactly. It looks absurd but it is common practice. And when it says "up to $X," simply change that to "exactly $X," otherwise they will waste your time to justify X.

OK, so what about the vesting?

Just imagine that an investor puts money into a company of three founders and one of the founders leaves the day after. That person is still a major shareholder, but in reality, that founder just screwed the other founders and the investor badly. The investor trusted the team to deliver.

Now, not only is it unclear if the team can deliver, but there is also no team, or at least not all of the team. Therefore, most investors will demand a vesting model in which, if a founder leaves within a certain period of time, some of his or her shares can be repurchased by the company.

This makes sense. You're doing the same with your employees, giving them ESOP (employee stock option program) or ISO (incentive stock options), vesting over three to four years and, if they leave, the unvested options return to the pool. So, in the term sheet, we realized the investor is going to demand it, but in fact, it is more critical for you than you think it is. You usually think of just one perspective, your own. But for a second, I want you to think that another founder is leaving, or you find out that one of the other founders is not good enough and therefore needs to be released. You want that vesting period now, so that you will have enough shares to hire a new leader to replace the founder that left.

Forget how much you trust your team right now. Just remember: About half of the founding teams will not last three years. And your most important mission now is the success of the company and not the founder that left.

I have a few start-ups that extended the vesting period. They realized that the journey is going to be long, and they wanted a mutual commitment, so they extended the period from three to four years, and then further to another period of three years.

What if there is no such clause in the term sheet? Add it! After all, the next-round investor will add it, and then it will only start in the next round, whatever that period of time is. If you add it today, the next investor is less likely to change it.

This is the truth for most clauses in the term sheet: if there are no liquidation preferences, the next round leader will create one, so you are better off having something fair today that is likely to last.

Liquidation preferences—how does it work? Let's demonstrate it rather simply. Say the seed round was $5 million, the A round was $20 million, and the B round was $50 million, and all had liquidation preferences of 1x participating, and each one of them is holding 20 percent of the company and common shares are 40 percent of the company. Now, there is an offer to acquire the company at $100 million. At first, you think that the common shares will get $40 million, which means $X million for you, a life-changing event. But looking down into the liquidation preferences, you realize that $75 million will go back to investors and only then you will divide the rest, so it is 40 percent out of $25 million, about $10 million for the common shares, not $40 million.

Liquidation preferences are helpful in a bullish market to satisfy very high (unreasonably high) valuation. Say there is a company trying to raise $500 million at a $10 billion valuation and that the $10 billion is somewhat disconnected from any economic reasoning, but hey, it is a bullish market and someone will take the deal. An investor may offer $500 million at $10 billion valuation, but with 2x or even 3x liquidation preferences (participating or nonparticipating). (2x or 3x means that the investors will get at least double or triple of the investment amount.) Now say this company, later on, goes public at a $5 billion valuation (or is acquired at this amount). While the valuation is way lower than the previous round, the last investor is still making a lot of money (2x or 3x).

A CATHOLIC MARRIAGE

Sun Microsystems' cofounder Vinod Khosla once said that "70 percent to 80 percent of venture capitalists add negative values." So be discerning!

Why are investors so bad? It's probably a matter of setting expectations. You would expect that their main task would be to help their start-ups, but, actually, it is very different.

VC partner roles are:

- to select start-ups in which to invest, that is, managing the deal flow,
- to raise capital for this or the next fund, and
- only then to help existing companies, and only those who show traction.

If you're struggling and expect them to help, be aware that it is not their top priority. It also depends on whether an investor was previously a start-up person. In the distant past, many venture capitalists were money managers, not company managers. Nowadays, many partners at VC firms are former entrepreneurs. You want that type of investor; they've experienced the journey of failures and they understand it. They won't get scared or spooked easily. Entrepreneurs have been there and done all of that already.

Once you get in bed with an investor, it's like a Catholic marriage—there's no way to get rid of the investor. They have all kinds of rights that, in most cases, will put them in a stronger position than you. It's OK to think about the dark side and ask yourself: If things go badly, do I really want this investor to become a part of my company?

Investor and Netscape founder Marc Andreessen noted that the "particular investors who are going to be on the board for your company are just as important as who you get married to."

While you're negotiating, the investor will do their due diligence on you. They'll check into your references and make sure the story you're telling holds up. You should do the same. Do due diligence on the investor, too, because at the end of the start-up journey, there are only two types of relationships between investors and founders: You either love or you hate each other.

Ask a seasoned entrepreneur what he or she thinks about the company's investors after his or her journey and Catholic marriage with those investors have ended. The entrepreneur will either say, "I'd take this investor again anytime," or "I'll never take this investor." (The investors are saying the same thing about you, by the way.) The reason for all the love or hate is usually not about the results, but the personal relationships.

Here's a tip on how to conduct your due diligence: Speak with half a dozen former CEOs/entrepreneurs in whose companies the VC has invested previously. They should be investors who are no longer involved so that the entrepreneur can speak freely. The main question that you need an answer to is how the VC behaved when the company was in trouble. You, too, will undoubtedly experience challenging times, and you want an investor that will back you up during the hardships of the journey.

A lot of entrepreneurs ask me what I think about a particular investor. My answer is the same as I'd give for any other recommendation I'm asked to make: I can only say what I know, based on what I've seen. I can think of someone as very smart, who makes a good impression, but only after being together through a crisis would I be able to let you know what I really think.

One of the most important behaviors of a successful CEO is perseverance, someone who doesn't get scared and will never give up. As an entrepreneur, I would love an investor that behaves the same way.

MOVING SLOW AND FAST

How fast will a VC move on a deal? The answer is: usually, not very. It depends on their agenda, not yours. In many cases, it's to their advantage to move slowly. As time goes by, they may want to reevaluate whether they still want to do the deal. They may want to see if other investors might be interested first.

Think about it: The dialogue about valuation already happened before the term sheet. It might take another month to sign it and another two to three months for closing. During this period, the VC has learned more (much more) and might decide to walk away from the deal. Meanwhile, while you're making progress, it's not at their expense. And even if you're making significant progress, the terms won't change in your favor, unless you say no to the deal.

That all changes if investors believe they're about to lose the deal. Then they will move very fast. That's what happened to Waze a few days after we received the term sheet from Vertex, as well as during the subsequent term sheet negotiation. I met Shraga Katz, a general partner from Magma (another leading Israeli VC), through an introduction from Shmulik Wasserman, CEO of LiveU, which had developed a technology to upload broadcast-quality video on the move. I was helping Shmulik at the beginning of LiveU's journey, and Shmulik had previously worked for Shraga.

Shraga was pretty interested. We met on a Saturday evening and the next morning, Magma called. I spoke with Yahal Zilka, Magma's cofounder and comanaging partner.

"How are you progressing with the fundraising?" Yahal asked.

I told him we were in the midst of multiple discussions and that they were going well. He then indicated that Magma would be interested in Waze, too.

"But is it still relevant?" he wanted to know.

"If you can move fast enough, then yes," I replied.

He kept on digging. "What's fast enough?"

"Well, I plan to sign a term sheet by the end of the week," I said. "If you can match that speed, let's meet."

We met on Monday, Tuesday, and again on Wednesday.

On Thursday, they offered us a term sheet and we began to negotiate.

In order words, within four days, Magma had sent us a term sheet of their own, only this time it was not for $2 million but for $6 million, and at much better terms.

I contacted Ehud Levy at Vertex and told him about the second term sheet.

"There's still room for you," I said. "But it's at a higher valuation."

I expected Ehud to be upset, to feel that we'd gone behind his back. Instead, he responded simply, "Send it to me and I'll take a look."

To my shock, he signed and returned the document in ten minutes.

There are two critical learnings here:

1. VCs can and will move fast when they are about to close the deal.
2. They will forget everything about valuation and the amount of money they're planning to invest if they feel they are about to lose the deal.

That wasn't the end of the "moving slow, moving fast" story for Waze. We signed the term sheets with Vertex and Magma in December 2007, with the expectation we would close at the end of the year. In fact, it wasn't until March 2008 that the deal was finally done.

What happened in between? First, we never stopped negotiating. We completed negotiation with yet another VC before we turned them down. Then during the due-diligence phase, Magma came up with a new demand. "Instead of $6 million, we think you will need much more," Yahal said. "Let's raise the bar to a $12 million funding round. We will invest $4 million, Vertex will invest $4 million, and a new investor will chip in for the remaining $4 million."

We were happy that Magma believed in us so much, but this new plan actually put the entire funding round at risk. What if we didn't find another investor? Magma made a few introductions, and we ended up meeting BlueRun Ventures at the GSM World Congress in Barcelona in February 2008. They decided to join.

But as we started to finalize the documents, they got cold feet and pulled out.

"We saw someone else doing crowdsourced maps in the US," was the excuse. (Remember what I said about fundraising being like a roller coaster in the dark?)

It turned out to be a simple hack where someone had added a layer of available real estate to rent or buy over an existing map, but in some ways, it was more a challenging setback because we realized that, if this scared them off, then they don't really understand what we are doing.

The clock was ticking, and I began to fear we wouldn't have a deal in the end.

Ultimately, we talked it through, and BlueRun Ventures got back on board for the full $4 million. The deal finally closed in March 2008 for the entire $12 million. We were at last ready to start the company.

WHEN IS THE RIGHT TIME TO RAISE CAPITAL?

The simple answer: when you can, and if you have good traction and can raise more, do it! The more the merrier. The challenging times (either because of traction or the market) will only make it harder.

At the end of the day, think about fundraising as refueling your car for the journey ahead. Without fuel, there can be no journey, but it is only a small part of it. Immediately afterward, you need to think if you have sufficient fuel (i.e., funding) for the journey or if you will need more.

If you need more, that's a major task to manage. Ask yourself: What will make us fundable for the next round? What will build your objectives in such a way that you achieve your goals with enough cash in hand so that you have time to raise new money *and* breathing room for slowdowns (in achieving fundable milestones or in the market).

Remember what I said in chapter 3—when you're fundraising, nothing else is as crucial. The day after the money is in the bank, you need to shift gears entirely toward execution of the plan.

That turns out to be one of the biggest challenges in start-up strategy in general.

Imagine the following: As CEO, for the last six to nine months you were completely focused on fundraising. It took a huge amount of effort and attention, and you were 150 percent invested in it.

Then it's over.

The next day you certainly want to—and should—celebrate, but the day after, you have to dive back into execution, building the product, crafting your go-to-market strategy, and firing and hiring.

Over the years I have learned how very critical it is to maintain the execution plan of the start-up while at the same time the CEO is distracted by the fundraising process. Execution *must* remain on track, in particular, to feed the fundraising cycles. Investors may like your story, but they are still expecting to see progress. If you can show them progress within two, three, or four months, then they will be game to continue. If not, they will pass and move on to the next investment.

How do you do ensure progress is made? Keep your management team out of the fundraising process. They don't need to hear all the rejections. That's discouraging. Only the CEO should suffer the hundred noes. Let the management focus on execution.

How much money should you raise? Think about your next fundable milestone. How long will it take you to get there? Add six months for fundraising afterward and another six more months of spare—that's the amount of money that you need to raise. If there are opportunities along the journey to raise more, then raise more!

Are there fairy-tale stories in fundraising? Actually, yes, sometimes the process is much easier, particularly during the "honeymoon period" after you've just raised cash. There are also stories where closing a new round was a matter of weeks or took just one meeting. One time, I called up a previous investor and told him I had an idea and he said yes on the spot.

But don't count on these. Yes, if you're a successful entrepreneur with a track record of exits, it will be easier for you. But otherwise (and normally), it is always hard.

STARTIPS

- The most important key to an investment is that the VC likes the CEO and his or her story. Therefore, the CEO goes alone to these meetings and practices the story to perfection. Storytelling is about emotional engagement; you want the investor to imagine he or she is part of the story.

- Investors form impressions fast—in a matter of seconds—before the entrepreneur even sits down. Start with the strongest point you have before the investor forms his or her opinion.

- Tell an authentic, believable story, not a dry series of "use cases."

- Make sure you have a **big** market story—if you're not a "fund maker," if you can't be a unicorn, then you're not relevant for a VC.

- Investors are users, too. If they don't think they will use your product, or they cannot relate to someone who will, you'll have slim chances of getting an investment.

- VCs are slow, until they think they're going to lose the deal.

- Raising money is a "Dance of One Hundred Noes." Be prepared to be turned down again and again. The ratio of yeses to noes can be very discouraging.

- Watch out for key investor indicators. These will tell you if an investor is interested in moving forward.

- Don't try to negotiate a term sheet on your own. It's an unfair fight. Don't be afraid to ask for help. Find mentors who can guide you.

- If the deal isn't what you want, walk away. Investment is like a Catholic marriage—there's no way to get rid of your partner.

- Go straight for a partner at a VC. It's useless to speak with a first-line analyst whose whole job is to say "no."

Chapter 5b

MANAGE YOUR INVESTORS

If building a start-up is a roller-coaster journey, then fundraising is a roller coaster in the dark. You don't even know what's coming. Closing a deal would be in the dark, upside down, and in reverse . . .

R aising money for your company is not a once-and-done event. It's ongoing and repetitive. Once you've accomplished the seed round, there are then the A, B, C, and more rounds. When raising capital, you get "engaged," so to speak, and managing investors, the board of directors, conflicts of interest, liquidation events, secondary shares, etc., are going to be ongoing issues. To plan for future fundraising events, I have developed an algorithm that helps you build your fundraising strategy (see next page).

Once you have finished raising a new round and meeting with tons of investors, the last thing on earth you want to do is meet more (or even the same) investors, but you have no choice except to keep meeting them in order to build your pipeline for now and into the future.

After you've finished with a fundraising round, you have to manage your investors. Following are some of the considerations to keep in mind.

Fundraising Strategy Flowchart

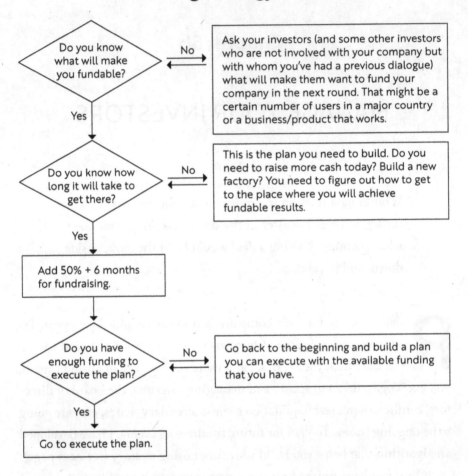

CONFLICTS OF INTEREST

In 90 percent of the start-up journeys I see or am involved with, there will be an alignment of interests between the founders and their investors. You may have different ideas on how to achieve those interests, or you may have to do a lot of ego management (of both you and your investors), but, at the end of the day, you and your investors want the same thing: a successful company and an even more successful exit (for the investors).

Nevertheless, the other 10 percent of the time, there are several areas where conflicts of interest between you and your investors may prove challenging.

1. LIQUIDATION—SHARE PURCHASE EVENT

It doesn't matter if this is an exit, the selling of secondary shares, or bringing on a new investor: no matter what the event, it's very likely that your interests as a founder, common shareholder, and officer of the company may be different than the interests of other shareholders and in particular investors.

It can be confusing. How can it be that, if you're having an up round (raising money at a higher valuation than the previous round), someone can be displeased?

There may be a number of reasons for that.

- Maybe the investor thought they would someday increase their position in the company by investing a few million more and now they can't.
- Maybe they are at the end of their funding term, and raising a lot of money potentially pushes that exit further away in time.
- Maybe they are diluted too much and don't have enough cash to participate in the current round.
- Maybe their new position drops them below the entitlement of any of the preferences (for example, they won't get a seat on the board of directors).
- Maybe the new investors are demanding a "top-up" for the founders and management that dilutes the previous investors even further. Topping-up is when founders, CEO, and management team are getting too diluted and are granted additional equity in a form of ISO or ESOP. A new funding round is always a good opportunity to revisit your expected equity position resulting from the round and the management's and, if needed, hint to the new investor that they might want to consider topping-up.

Resolving these issues is never easy, but raising capital is usually in the best interests of the company! And if worse comes to worst, keep in mind that liquidation is the end of your relationship with that investor.

There are essentially only two ways a relationship between founders and investors can end: They either love each other, or they hate each other, most likely resulting from the founders' and investors' mutual behavior during a conflict of interest. Loving your investors after the journey ends is *not* part of your agenda. Essentially, you lead the company to success and you take care of your employees. That is your mission. If you have a good board of directors (BoD), they will take care of you. In a company I've recently joined as the BoD chairman, I was looking at the cap table and told the lead investor that the CEO was diluted too much and needs to get a top-up. He agreed in general, and tried to push the decision until after everything was settled. I told him that I would not join the BoD if the CEO/founder was not brought to a more reasonable equity position before the round was completed. The investor asked me if this was a "make or break condition," and I said yes. The CEO got that top-up. The newcomer will usually have much more powerful negotiation leverage than existing parties.

2. LIQUIDATION—SECONDARY SHARES

Secondary shares are when you (the founders, the management, and all employees) sell some of your shares to someone else, most likely investors. It results in what's essentially a mini-exit for you specifically and for your team (although it doesn't raise more money for the company).

When you sell secondary shares, you as well as the other founders and management/employees are making money but your existing investors are *not*. This is another example of ego management. How can you resolve this? Try to get the "secondary" event as part of a funding round. Try to get your fundraising to be way oversubscribed. In other words, try to get higher demand where investors want to invest more than the company wants to raise. At this phase, you can tell the new investor that you can only fulfill their desire to buy more if there are secondary shares being part of the deal. Once there is oversubscription on one hand and the new investor realizes that the only way to satisfy it is through secondary shares, then offer your existing investors the option to sell secondary shares as well. Don't worry, they most likely won't and, as a result, you'll get exactly what you want.

3. COMPENSATION

Founders are heavily committed to their journey and mission; they won't leave when the going gets tough, and they won't give up even if they don't get paid. All investors know that. The difference between "pro-founder" investors and other investors is simple—do your investors take advantage of this knowledge?

Compensation should ideally set the company's DNA as one that's generous to its employees. You'll need to push the board to adopt this spirit of generosity, because their initial DNA may be the exact opposite.

4. LIQUIDATION—EXIT

An exit would seem the least likely event to cause a conflict of interest; after all, everyone is making money. Yet, think of the following scenario.

You've raised a seed investment and an A round for a total of $10 million. The most recent valuation was $30 million. So, let's assume the founders' position is about 40 to 50 percent of the equity and the investors have about 40 to 50 percent. Ten percent is set aside for employees. An opportunity comes to sell the company for $50 million. You open your Excel spreadsheet and realize that this would mean about $20+ million for you as the founders. This is a life-changing event for you, and you want to take the deal.

For the A-round investor, however, it's a very mixed bag. The investor thought your company was on track to becoming a unicorn and earning twenty, thirty, or even forty times the investor's money. The proposed exit is only about 25 percent. It is definitely *not* a fund-making exit. So, the investor doesn't like it.

Here's another way this could play out. Let's say the exit is a much sweeter deal—a $200 million acquisition, for example. The investors like it but the buyer says, "Wait a minute, I need the team to remain engaged for four years after the transaction, so we need to allocate 25 percent of the deal for retention of employees and not for the shareholders," i.e., the investors. In this example, you need to think about the transaction and the day after. The investors are only thinking about the transaction. For them, there is no day after.

ALL ABOUT SECONDARY SHARES

You should sell secondary shares whenever you can. We did secondary shares at both Waze and Moovit, as well as other start-ups, and we will keep on doing them at all my companies when it makes sense (i.e., if the price is right, it will result in a dramatic change for the sellers, or there's an over-subscription for the round). For you, personally, if taking home anywhere between a few hundred thousand dollars to a few million means a lot to you, then you should do it.

Selling secondary shares is more common among American companies than those in Europe. There are even secondary marketplaces where shares can be bought and sold.

Secondary shares are not the same as conducting a B or a C round. It's not about issuing new shares. Secondary shares, rather, are critically important to keep founders going and happy. Think of it as a reward for hard work, getting results, and bringing the company to a certain valuation.

Selling secondary shares can also take pressure off the founders to sell the company prematurely. If you've already made a few million dollars by selling secondary shares and along comes a buyer that says they are ready to acquire your company for $250 million, you might be more reluctant to make the deal if you don't need the money.

Selling secondary shares indicates that the company and the founders can go the distance and that they're looking at the big-picture opportunity.

Who should be selling? The answer is everyone. All stakeholders who want to sell secondary shares should. It's particularly valuable for employees, where selling secondary shares can be seen as a reward and a retention builder that makes the employer-employee commitment even stronger.

Another very important reason to do secondary shares is when there is an oversubscription for the round—that is, as mentioned, too many people want "in." This is awesome news and will help to position your company on its way to success. It may also make it easier for you to raise capital, but the main benefit is that it makes your company more attractive to employees.

Occasionally, when selling secondary shares and bringing the opportunity to sell secondary shares to employees as well, they are likely to say no. They believe in the company, or they don't want to signal anything that is not 100 percent belief in it. While you can't tell them what to do, and in fact you are not allowed even to advise them what to do, if this is a company-wide or a multiple-employee opportunity, you should do two things: Tell them you are selling, and then bring a financial advisor/consultant to provide a general presentation or one-on-one consultation to those who want it. We'll discuss secondary shares more in chapter 13.

KEEP INVESTORS UP TO DATE

The best way to manage existing investors is to keep them informed. Send a periodic update every month or two. For existing shareholders, try to ask for their help on specific tasks where they can be useful. You should use the same update for potential investors. All the one hundred investors who previously told you no, keep in touch with them, too.

If the investors ask for more frequent updates or they tend to tie up your time (some of the investors I know simply have nothing to do, so they bug their CEOs), don't let them! You can ignore them, but if that doesn't help, refer them back to the periodic updates you've been sending out.

What should be in your update? Something very simple—just two to three paragraphs showing your progress. You can say: "This quarter we're focusing on product-market fit," or "This month we were written up in this newspaper," or "We have a new management team member."

Keep in mind that probably no one is reading the text of your updates. Investors want to see the progress graphs. Create them in a visually consistent format, so it's clear you're measuring and updating the same data points.

What type of graph is most effective? Those that go up! A time graph—a line or a bar—is better than a pie chart. What if you don't have growth to show? Keep creating the charts and sending them. Investors won't put in more money if you can't show growth, but eventually, they will invest more if you're consistent and can show a steady if slow increase. That way, when your "Eureka!" moment comes, it will be clear to all that you're now finally fundable.

Consistency can be dramatic for investors if you can show it over a long period of time. Consistency creates magic, simply because people can only foresee straight lines. So, if you can show consistent growth over the last three years, most people would believe you can keep on showing this growth moving forward. This has nothing to do with investors; it's simply human nature.

MANAGING POTENTIAL INVESTORS DURING A FUNDING ROUND

Investors are a cautious group. No one wants to be the first to jump, but after the first investor agrees, there may be a lot of follow-on investors interested (sometimes more than you need). Sometimes, an investor will say, "I don't want to lead this round. Maybe others might be interested in chipping in."

On the other hand, if you land a big-name investor like Sequoia, a16z, Kleiner Perkins, etc., then you will quickly see a long list of other investors that will be clamoring to join the round. What do you do then?

- You can increase the size of the round, although this generally doesn't work because your lead investor, assuming it's a big fund with enough cash, will usually want to up their contribution to maintain their position.
- You can divert new investors to a follow-on or spill-over round where you increase the valuation as part of the round extension.

There is a big difference between early- and late-stage investors. Early-stage investors will participate in the seed round and maybe the A round after that, then stop, as they simply don't have enough money allocated to keep on supporting the company. The rule of thumb for early-stage investors is X for their first round and one to two times X allocated for follow-on rounds. So, if the investors start at the seed round with about $3 million, they may have an additional $3 million to $6 million to keep on supporting the company in the future. What that means basically is that, if the valuation will grow significantly, they won't have enough to maintain their position in the company and will therefore get diluted.

HOW LONG DOES IT TAKE TO RAISE MONEY?

Raising money almost always comes with bad timing. You'd rather pour your time into growing the company, not raising money. And if you're not moving forward as you'd hoped, then you're raising capital under very unfavorable terms.

In my experience, plan on it taking six to twelve months to raise a seed round, although it depends on the market and your background. If you just had an exit and have now started a new company, and investors like you, you could raise your seed money in a single day. If you're a first-time entrepreneur, it will take longer. What takes so long? Figuring out the story you need to tell and then telling that story simply takes time. At Waze, we had three term sheets in hand at the beginning of December 2007. We then had three months to close the round. Time tends to work to the advantage of the investor, not you. You would think that everyone wants to move fast, but investors can use delays to see if you're making progress and, if they're not happy, they can renegotiate the terms.

During those three months, you'll generally be locked into a no-shop period. Your investors, on the other hand, can keep doing due diligence on you and your business plan. And they can pull out if they choose to, with no ramifications (for them).

That's why I recommend that you continue to talk to other investors even if you're officially in a no-shop period. You may not be able to receive an actual term sheet from anyone else, but if things do go sideways, you'll have an alternative lined up.

What if your investors find out you're talking with others? I don't see that as a big risk. Tell them it's your responsibility to keep the company alive in case they decide to pull back.

What if you get an offer from another investor during your no-shop phase? You can tell the other investor the truth—that you're in no-shop and it will expire in so many days, and then you will be happy to talk with them further. Or you can simply wait until the no-shop period expires (usually about thirty days), assuming it's a better offer. This actually happened with Waze, not during fundraising but during the mergers and acquisitions (M&A) transaction.

We were under a no-shop with a potential acquirer when the offer from Google came in (it was unsolicited and over email). Google found out about the other offer, and the other potential acquirer allowed the acquisition by Google to go forward. Otherwise, we would have allowed the no-shop term to expire and then reengaged with Google.

At the beginning of the COVID-19 period, I saw many deals renegotiated as travel was impossible and the CEOs' ability to meet new investors was also nearly impossible. Valuations were cut by 30 to 40 percent easily. I saw investors walk away from deals alongside others who stood up to their commitments. During the 2022 crisis, I've seen the same—vanishing investors, term sheets renegotiated, and valuations cut dramatically.

THE FUNDRAISING MUSCLE THAT NEEDS EXERCISE!

You will be meeting investors all the time—before a round, after a round, showing off for your most recent investor, at conferences, and so on. These meetings are the basis for your next funding round. Even if you've just completed a round, keep your executive summary and presentation deck up to date all the time, even if you are not raising funds right now. That way, if an investor asks for something to be sent, you'll be ready.

But the most important thing is to bring the investors to you. Beggars can't be choosers, as the saying goes, so if you want to be a chooser, there is one and only one way to do it: multiple term sheets.

Keep all—and I mean *all* the investors that you've ever been in contact with—informed. Create the habit of sending an update every month (or every other month) to all of them. It should be called "company update," and it is just one page featuring two to three paragraphs and two to three graphs. Those graphs should always be the same (for example, number of users, number of transactions).

For your two to three graphs, pick those that:

- are always growing,
- are higher than the industry,
- show your beauty, and
- show progress over time.

What goes into those paragraphs?

- Company intro in one paragraph (short). For example, "We address the problem of XYZ for Fortune 500 customers." This paragraph doesn't change from one month to another.

- The recent update—again, one paragraph, which could be, "We hired a new VP of sales," or "We've signed three new customers this month." This paragraph *always* changes from one month to another.
- There might be a third paragraph that is an "ask." For example, "We're looking for a CFO. Do you have any good candidates?" Or "We're looking for an introduction to a CIO at a Fortune 500 company."

Now, while this may seem to be generic and far-fetched, the idea is to create demand.

You have no idea what will trigger the demand.

- Maybe it is the progress you're showing.
- Maybe the investor just missed an opportunity with a similar company.
- Maybe the investors realized that they need to deploy more cash.
- Maybe they just have a very good friend who is an awesome candidate for your start-up.

Once you switch from reaching out to requests that are coming to you, not only do you increase the likelihood of a funding round by an order of magnitude, it may be the difference between being perceived as a beggar or a chooser.

It's crucial that investors or prospective investors see consistency. You need that monthly reporting and progress to extend over a long period of time in order for it to work its magic.

MANAGING THE BOARD OF DIRECTORS

The CEO of one of my companies raised capital based on a growth of 3x. Everyone was very excited by this, saying that 300 percent growth is excellent. I've heard Sequoia once say, 2x is nice, 2.5x is good, 3x is excellent, and above that is off-the-chart awesome.

Everyone except for the lead investor.

"Even though 3x growth year over year is nice, it is just not enough," the investor lamented. "We should be doing 4x or even 10x."

"But you invested at 3x," the CEO replied, trying to convince the investor to chill out and be happy.

Many investors tend to be discouraging. It's not on purpose, and it's definitely not you; it's just in part of their habit to be displeased most of the time. And, to an extent, they even have a theory for that.

During the Waze days, we had an impressive period of time where everything seemed to be great, and yet we saw one of our investors very displeased at a board meeting. After the meeting, I spoke with the investor and asked what he thinks about three to four aspects of the company's progress. He was very happy with it, he replied. Then I asked, "If everything is so great, why weren't you pleased at the board of directors' meeting?"

"It's my job to be displeased, this is how I'm pushing the CEO to do more, to make the extra effort," he responded.

"You can get even better results with encouragement rather than discouragement," I challenged him.

"This is working better for me," he insisted. "I'm also using it with my kids."

And I thought: "Poor kids!"

It's true that one of the key roles of members of a board of directors is to get the CEO to drive the company to better results, but somehow, I'm always on the empowering side and not on the discouraging side. Many investors I've seen use different methodologies, however.

There are three rules a CEO should follow when managing a board.

- No surprises. When a member of the board of directors is surprised, he or she feels like an idiot and doesn't like it (no one does), but there is more to it than that. You may have surprised the entire board, but everyone is an individual, and they believe they are the *only* one who was surprised. This now becomes an ego management issue. Prepare each and every board member before the meeting so there are no surprises.
- Lead board members into the decision that you want through a discussion (and with lots of preparation). If you want alternative Y to be chosen, then show three alternatives—xYz—so that Y is the obvious

choice. Not just is the Y in the middle, but it is also highlighted and bold. People tend to choose the middle option out of three options. Or give board members a choice where A is too aggressive, C is too conservative, and B is what you want them to choose. In this way, Goldilocks had it right! (If you have more than three options, make sure the one you want your investors to choose is second from the top or second from the bottom.)

- If board members push back, use the magic words, "What do you suggest?" I've learned that trick from my wife, Noga, who is a life coach. There is nothing like defusing an argument with that question. Not "*But* what do you suggest?" or "*So*, what do you suggest?", just "What do you suggest?"

Manage your board of directors by sending them any materials to review no less than three days—and better, one week—before the meeting.

But the most important thing: Call them up to prepare them.

This may seem to you like you're managing a kindergarten class, but for a second, think about a partner at a VC who is making one to two new investments a year. At that rate, over a five-to-six-year period, the VC partner has somewhere between five to ten boards they are now a part of, in addition to the main role of VC. So, the likelihood that a VC would invest the time necessary to gain deep knowledge about your company and the challenges you face is small.

You might expect board members to come to the meeting prepared, but generally, they're not. You live your company every day. They don't.

You never want to come to a board meeting with a surprise decision to make. Your investors and board members will push back, and then you'll have to schedule another session.

For example, if you have a slide in your presentation saying you're going into the German market and not the Italian market, when you previously said you were doing Italy first, even if you have good reasons, you've surprised the board. They thought you were successful in Italy and now you're not going there. How come? That conversation needs to happen *before* the board meets.

In a recent board meeting, the CEO of one of the companies I invested in presented that the firm would be moving to a bigger office shortly. Not only did I know that before the board meeting, but I also actually told him two months beforehand that the current office was awfully packed.

The other board members were surprised, however. They were not as engaged with the company as I was, and the last time they visited the office was many months earlier. The pushback was way out of proportion, but it was only because they were surprised.

What really irks board members about surprises is the feeling that *they* are the only ones who are out of the loop, that no one is listening to *them*, and that no one cares about *their* point of view. So, of course, they're going to push back!

The main reason you need to brief each board member separately and personally before the meeting is that you can only manage ego on a one-on-one basis. Nobody can (or should) handle ego management in public.

Board meetings can quickly turn into a nightmare. You work your ass off trying to make progress, going through the desert on a roller-coaster journey . . . and then no one appreciates what you've accomplished, at least not if they've come to the meeting unprepared!

Remember the most important thing: Your job is to make the company successful, not to satisfy the board of directors, or your investors—they all are going to be happy when the company succeeds.

REPORT ACCURATELY

Managing a board means always telling the truth. This means only reporting facts as facts and thoughts or hopes as such. You will inevitably be held accountable for what you're reporting to the board.

If your report has a huge pipeline of products in development or you're talking to X, Y, and Z customers or potential business partners, then the expectation is that something will happen out of that. At the next meeting, a board member may ask you what happened with those contacts or with a particular deal that you reported was in the making.

If you say you're in an advanced dialogue with such and such a partner and then at the next meeting you say the same thing, you lose credibility.

Directors and investors want to see progress and they want to see momentum.

Don't bring up anything that has a low likelihood of happening. A long list of prospective customers or potential collaborations—no one cares about the names. Don't mention them. If it's a well-known name, your investors may very well look into it and, at the next meeting, ask what happened. Instead, only mention things that have a high likelihood of resulting in a deal between now and the next meeting. (For that reason, quarterly rather than monthly board meetings are the best.)

CRISIS MANAGEMENT

In the roller-coaster journey that is a start-up, your company will likely be on the verge of dying multiple times. Going up the roller coaster is nice. Going down, you may get too close to the ground and be about to crash. Or maybe your feet (or your entire body) are underwater.

During this time, you will see different behavior from different investors—those who panic and those who support you. You have enough pressure without some of the board members panicking!

During crisis management, it's critical to maintain your relationship with the board. Some board members may be able to get you out of this crisis, maybe by doing an internal funding round, maybe by bringing other investors, and maybe simply by being there for you. You need their support. It's hard enough dealing with a company in crisis, like cutting pay, firing people, or figuring out a new business model in a hurry, without also having to manage panicked board members. You might need to have more frequent calls when you're in a crisis.

What would lead to a crisis in a start-up? Most crises are about money. Some are connected to a lawsuit. Whether it has to do with patent infringement, change in government regulations, discrimination, or sexual harassment, the board will be exposed as well. So, it's a crisis for you and for them.

Pontera raised $3 million in 2013 from Blumberg Capital. A second round was led by Horizons Ventures a year later, in which we raised $7.5 million. That was enough cash to run for a while and to move from an Israel-centric to a US-centric market.

That roller-coaster journey of the company hit us in the face when we needed to raise more capital, even though we hadn't figured out PMF for the US. And yet, we had already shut down the operation in Israel in order to focus our efforts on the US!

When it was time to raise a third round, one of the VCs wanted to do a "severe down round."

"Instead of a $50 million valuation, let's do it at $5 million," they told us.

For Yoav Zurel, the CEO of Pontera, that severe down round represented a similarly severe loss of innocence. The investors smelled blood and weren't reluctant to pounce.

"I'm sorry that this happened to you," I told him. "But I'm also happy. Happy that you learned. Sorry you had to learn the hard way."

While the offer was really aggressive, we were somewhat lucky in that we were able to arrange funding from me and several co-investors that were ready to put in some $3 million at much more favorable terms.

At the time, it was clear who supported the company even when it was difficult and who was there only to support it when everything is fine. Trust me, you want the supporting investors.

How do you know which one is which?

Do your due diligence on your investors and, in particular, speak with other entrepreneurs and CEOs who already separated from those investors (via a liquidation event, either successful or unsuccessful).

That was not the end of it for Pontera, though.

We had to raise another capital round when we were on the verge of figuring out PMF, and another one just at the beginning of the COVID-19 outbreak.

These two rounds were challenging but ended up successful (we didn't die).

Two years later, once we had reached PMF, growth was figured out, and the business model was in place, Pontera was on the path for takeoff with 20x higher valuation than before. Just keep in mind that fundraising roller coaster for any company might change direction a dozen times in the future.

THE SURPRISING BENEFITS OF DOWN ROUNDS

About one-third of all start-ups will have a down round (or at least a flat round) at some point in their fundraising journey. That's not always a negative. Sometimes it can be a necessary evil, a way of cleaning up the capitalization table and weeding out older but now irrelevant investors, the ones who don't support the company.

How does that work?

If a new (or dominant) investor demands a down round, it tends to dilute the previous investors the most. Those previous investors can always put in more money to maintain their position—the term is "pay to play"—but usually they don't. They don't because they don't believe in the company or leadership team anymore.

Let's look at an example.

Say that a company has raised a seed round and an A round and perhaps even a B round, so the cap table looks like this: 30 percent for the founders, 10 percent for the employees, 20 percent for the seed investors, 20 percent for the A investors and 20 percent for the B investors. The valuation for the last round in this example was $50 million.

Unfortunately, the company is not on track yet and thus is unable to raise additional capital or at least not at favorable terms.

Moreover, there is one investor that is saying, "OK, I like the concept and I like the team, but since you have not figured out PMF, it is a seed round at a $5 million pre-money valuation and I'm willing to invest $5 million."

Now, if you do the calculation, the new investor will have about 50 percent of the company following this round, and all the other shareholders will be diluted to half of their holding. However, the new investor is looking at the expected cap table for after the round and realizes that the three founders will be left with only 15 percent, or 5 percent each for a seed-level company. That doesn't make sense, and it's not attractive enough for them to stay on board in their roles, certainly not for the long run.

So, the new investor decides to allocate funds through an ESOP (employee stock option program, as mentioned) for the founders and employees to bring them back to the 40 percent total position they had before the down round.

The new cap table looks like this: 50 percent for the new investor, 40 percent for the founders and employees, and 10 percent for all previous investors. That's a pretty severe dilution from 20 percent beforehand to 3.3 percent afterward, unless the investor decides to "pay to play" to remain relevant.

The best situation, of course, is to have only up rounds, but sometimes during the roller-coaster journey of fundraising, you'll find yourself a beggar, not a chooser, in need of funding while you're wandering the desert.

If a company will need to raise money three, four, five, six, maybe even ten times before an exit event, some of those might be down rounds.

Down rounds don't hurt founders and management as much as you'd think. That's because most investors will try to compensate the founders to keep them incentivized to do their best work. As a rule of thumb, eventually, the founders will be topped up to own up to 10 percent of the company, each. New investors will generally agree to top-up the founders, in particular, as they are not getting diluted in this latest round.

Having no cash, however, means you will die, and it won't affect just you but also be a very painful event for your investors—their investment will be worth zero. If they still believe in you and the company, or they just want to avoid closing a company at this phase, they may find a way to support you through an aggressive down round or pay to play.

WAZE AND MOOVIT'S FUNDRAISING STORIES

In 2010, Waze was just about out of cash. We had raised capital in 2008, but throughout our journey of failures, we discovered that, other than in Israel, we were just not good enough yet. That resulted in our investors not being interested in putting more money into the company.

"You have traction only in Israel, but none in the US," they told us as we were trying to raise $4 million. "You have a nonproven business model, and your valuation is too high."

One of the more successful venture capital funds, in an internal meeting, went even further.

"We wouldn't touch Waze with a ten-foot pole," I overheard one partner saying while I was in the next room writing down some notes.

On the day that Google acquired Waze, Noam Bardin, Waze's CEO, and I discussed whether we should send them an *actual* ten-foot pole . . . we didn't, but we enjoyed considering it!

Lightspeed Venture Partners was another fund that was thinking of investing (a $28 million valuation was the number on the table) but ultimately didn't. On the day of the Google acquisition, they sent us a huge platter of fruit. "Sorry we missed that one!" read the attached note. Shortly afterward, I became a small investor at Lightspeed, and Lightspeed has since become an investor in Pontera.

Moovit CEO Nir Erez managed his company's funding by the book, meaning he would start to look toward the next round of funding the day he'd completed the current round. He built relationships with investors who in the current round said no. To each, he'd ask: "What objectives should we meet so you'll invest in the next round?" He took that input, and where it made sense, he based his funding strategy around it.

What did the investors tell him?

That Moovit needed to show growth, or at least show a strong presence in a number of countries.

Moovit went out and did just that.

Nir took the approach that it will take at least six months to raise capital, so he made sure to always start a fundraising round *a year or more before* he needed the money, to ensure he would have enough of a run rate not to get desperate (as had happened to us at Waze).

He did that consistently and, overall, it worked beautifully.

One investor nearly turned into a disaster, though.

Moovit had received a term sheet from the automaker Ford for Moovit's C round. Nir presented the term sheet to the board of directors and got approval to negotiate the deal and perhaps to try to get better terms.

We had a board meeting in California coming up. And Nir was then supposed to stop in Detroit to get the CEO of Ford to approve the term sheet. Before he got to the board meeting in California, the CEO of Ford withdrew the offer.

The board members of Moovit were very much concerned and offered to reconsider our path. I said, "If Ford would have been sorting out their strategy before the TS [term sheet], you wouldn't even know about it. The same way that you don't know about all other investors' discussions that lead to nothing."

Nir and I were calm.

"We have more than a year of runway. We're not about to run out of cash. We have plenty of time to recover," he told the board.

Nir was, of course, disappointed. But he understood this was just another "no" out of the dozens of noes he'd received previously.

LIQUIDATION EVENT CONFLICT

What happens if an investor opposes a deal? What if there is a clause in their investment agreement that gives them a certain veto right, including the ability to say no to a deal? In this case, the negotiations will turn into a game of chicken, saying, "If you're willing to screw me, guess what, I'm willing to screw you, too."

If you want them to bend, you will need to have a collective resignation letter signed by *all* of the founders and, if possible, all the management, too. Put it on the table in an envelope and say, "This is a resignation letter for all of us. You either say yes or we all leave."

You have to mean it.

It will take the investors a little while to think it through. Some will say that you don't mean it, and of course you will eventually bend, but if you do mean it, it's *they* who will bend.

Regardless of the result, you will hate their guts and they will hate yours. Don't ask them to be a reference for you!

STARTIPS

- Fundraising is an ongoing and repetitive activity.

- Never stop meeting investors and keeping them up to date. Send monthly emails. Include consistent graphs.

- Sell secondary shares when it makes sense (especially for an over-subscribed round and a life-changing event for sellers) to keep the founders satisfied.

- Consider increasing the size of a fundraising round if it looks to be oversubscribed.

- Most of the conflicts of interest that arise between start-ups and their investors have to do with money, rounds, liquidation, and benefits.

- Plan on six to twelve months to raise your first round and the same amount of time for each round afterward.

- Pre-brief your board members so there are no surprises at the board of directors' meeting.

- Goldilocks was right—give board members three choices where one is "just right" and make the "right" one the middle choice.

- Down rounds are more common than you think and much more common than you *want* to think. They can have surprising benefits, such as cleaning up a broken cap table, for example.

- Run due diligence on your investors before they invest. It is like a Catholic marriage afterward. Speak with former CEOs whose start-ups the investor was involved in through a liquidation event, either successful or unsuccessful, so that the business relationship between the investor and the CEO is no longer relevant. Only then can you get an honest opinion, which is the opinion that you need.

Chapter 6

FIRING AND HIRING

Knowing what you know today, would you hire this guy?

One of the biggest challenges for a start-up—and, to be frank, for all companies—is building the right team and the right DNA. This chapter is about how to do it, and, in particular, how to improve in doing it.

Why do start-ups fail?

I've posed that question to many entrepreneurs after their start-ups went under, and about half said, "The team was not right."

"What do you mean the team was not right?" I kept on asking, to which most of them replied, "We had this guy who was not good enough."

The entrepreneurs would then often get into more details like, "I expected my CTO to be able to build a strong engineering organization, and he built a mediocre one."

Another reason for the failure of a start-up that I've heard quite often was, "We had communication issues," which sounds to me more like, "We had ego-management issues." That is, the team was unable to agree and to accept the CEO's leadership.

I then asked the more important question, "*When* did you know that team was not right?" The scary and correct answer was: "Within the first month." All of them said exactly that.

There was even one guy who told me he knew "before we even started."

But if the team was not right, and the CEO knew that within the first month, the problem was not that the team was not right. The problem was that the CEO didn't make the hard decision.

Making easy decisions is easy and making hard decisions is *hard*, and most people don't like to make hard decisions.

So, in a small organization like a start-up, most of the hard decisions will be for the CEO to make. This is where it becomes complicated.

In the early days of a small start-up, nearly everyone is involved with everything. Think of a small team or even a group or a class that you were in and ask yourself the following: "If there was someone who didn't fit, would I know it?" The answer is yes, of course, and it doesn't matter if that someone doesn't fit because they are way underperforming or because that someone is a jerk. Everyone knows, period.

Now, the CEO knew within a month that the team was not right, that there was someone who shouldn't be there. That means that everyone in the team knew that as well.

So, everyone knows, and the CEO doesn't do anything. Guess what crosses the minds of those team members? There is someone who shouldn't be there, and the CEO isn't doing a thing.

There are only two options:

1. The CEO doesn't know, which means the CEO is stupid and this is really not good.
2. The CEO *does* know and still doesn't do anything. That's even worse, as it indicates the CEO lacks leadership and the skills for making hard decisions.

The result, by the way, is always the same—the top-performing people will leave because they don't want to be in a place that lacks the ability to make the right and hard decisions, and they will leave because they have a choice.

Earlier in this book, I wrote that a start-up that doesn't figure out PMF will die. The second reason a start-up may die is because of the team's or, more to the point, the CEO's inability to make hard decisions.

If you're the CEO or a leader in a start-up, or if you're managing people, read the next paragraph, close the book, close your eyes, and think about it. If you can subscribe to this, I've already increased your likelihood of being successful BIG-TIME:

Every time you hire someone, allow yourself thirty days, and then ask the following question: "Knowing what I know today, would I hire this person?" If the answer is no, fire them the next day. Every day this person is still on board you're creating more damage to your team.

If the answer is yes, on the other hand, then give that someone a little raise (in salary or options or anything). You will then establish unbelievable commitment.

Now, if you would say, "I don't know yet," then you're lying. But if you really need another thirty days, take that time and think hard on it.

THE DNA OF YOUR START-UP

When you start your journey, you know it is going to be a journey of failures and that if you figure out PMF, then you will be on the right path and that if you don't, you will die. But when you start your journey, there is an equally important decision to be made: deciding on the DNA of your company. You should define this as soon as you define the problem you're solving and your mission.

All the companies in the world have a DNA—a business culture or a set of values—that defines them. Yours will, too. On the first day, you have a unique opportunity to define it the way you like. Later on, it will be too late to do so.

Going back in time to 1999, three friends of mine started a new company called HumanClick. That start-up was acquired sixteen months later, in the year 2000, by LivePerson (a US-based public company).

For most M&A deals, the buyer is acquiring mainly the people. The heart and the brain are the founders and, therefore, in nearly all M&A transactions, the buyer makes sure that the founders and leadership of the acquired company want to be part of the new journey and sign up for a significant retention package for the next two to three years.

The founders' point of view, however, is very different.

If they commit for three years, in the first year they will do everything in their power to make the integration successful.

In the second year, they will start to search for someone to replace them in their position.

In the third year, they will start to think about their next start-up.

After three years and one day, they will leave to go build their next start-up.

These three friends, the founders of HumanClick, stayed at LivePerson until 2007, exactly when we started Waze. I asked them, "Why? What is it that kept you there for seven years? What's wrong with you guys?"

Their answer amazed me and made me think.

"It was the best working place we ever had," they said.

The next day I went to Ehud and Amir, and I said, "Let's make Waze the best working place we ever had."

They liked the idea and we defined what it would look like. What mattered for us was that: (1) we support employees and drivers, (2) the founders vote as a single person, and (3) we fire fast if someone doesn't fit into our culture.

Waze ended up being a great working place with very low attrition. Only a few people left over the years, and we remained committed to our DNA.

Of the three founders of HumanClick, Tal Goldberg later became the chief engineer at Waze and is now CTO at Kahun (where I'm on the board), Eitan Ron is the CEO at Kahun, and Eyal Halahmi is the CTO at Pontera.

When we started Pontera, we took defining the DNA one step further: we created a "DNA document."

The results are even better than we had at Waze.

Yoav Zurel, the CEO of Pontera, was and is an amazing people manager. Nine years after we launched the company, the level of employee retention is so high that it is hard to imagine Pontera went through multiple roller-coaster journeys.

Think of the best working place you ever had and ask yourself, "Why was it the best place—what made it such?" Then, take those parts and incorporate them into your new start-up's DNA. After all, you will be spending day in and day out working on your new mission, so you'd better love the DNA.

Your DNA must include a section on values (for example, doing good). Occasionally, the values will be associated with the mission, but not always.

How do you decide in cases where there are conflicts or disagreements among founders about things that matter to you and things that will keep mattering to you forever—the values that never change? At the end of the day, you can address conflicts in two ways: Either the CEO decides or there is voting within the founders.

There is no right or wrong, but you can only define it up front and not when conflict arises.

The words "conflict" or "disagreement" should be used very rarely (i.e., once every few years).

Choosing the logo of the company is not important and therefore should be the marketing leader's decision. On the other hand, selling the company could be a major issue, and I would rather have the founders' consensus or at least a majority.

Once you have those in place, you will make them part of your story to investors and candidates, even when they laugh at you or say they don't care. While investors might think it is not important, trust me, this is super important for you and to the success of your company.

When I was hiring people, I used to tell them the HumanClick story and our decision to make Waze the best working place. It meant we aspired to work with people we like to work with, and vice versa. I would explain that because we will be spending most of the hours of the day here, we want the people we hire to want to be here, and in particular, we need them to like working with you, and for you to like working with them. If that is not the case, you will be unhappy, and you don't deserve to be unhappy! If you are not happy here, I will fire you, because you deserve to be happy someplace else.

I later found out that there is a name for this method—the "no asshole rule."

A company's DNA is all about making mistakes, failing fast, firing fast, and transparency.

FIRING AND HIRING

That's the name of this chapter, and no, I didn't get it in reverse; it is more important to fire fast than to hire, that's why the chapter's name has firing first.

While it doesn't sound obvious, firing turns out to be much more important than hiring by far, but we avoid it because firing is hard. It is hard for a few reasons.

Because we are good people (or want to think of ourselves as good people), we tend to want to avoid firing because it may be harmful to the person we fire. It is also hard because we just hired this person and it was a lengthy process, and we don't want to go over it again.

The last point turns out to be the most significant one, in particular when you are following the rule of "Knowing what I know today, would I hire this person?" after just a month since that employee's hiring.

If the answer is no, and you should fire this person, you need to admit that you were wrong in hiring them. This is an opportunity to establish the right DNA, one that says clearly: "It is OK to make mistakes and fix them fast."

If part of your DNA is failing fast, then mistakes or failures are events and not a person, and firing that person fast is a key lesson and demonstration of that value. By contrast, keeping that person for a longer time is a disaster.

The real reason for firing fast is impact.

When I worked at Openwave, the pioneer of mobile internet in the early 2000s, and ran their product marketing, I gathered my team and drew on a whiteboard a normal distribution curve—a bell curve—that represented all the employees in Silicon Valley. Some of the employees were considered great, others less good.

Then I asked my team, "Where do you think Openwave is on this curve?"

There was a consensus: We were a little bit better than average. Not great or awesome, but better than average, which is pretty good.

Next, I asked, "Where do you think *your* team is on the curve?"

All the teams, it turned out, were ranked on the awesome side.

But that created a problem of perception. If all the teams are awesome, then who is less than average? Someone has to be.

Employees Ranking

Shouldn't be here	Mediocre	Good employees	Excellent	Amazing
17%	33%	33%	15%	Top 2%

Generally speaking, in a normal distribution, 2 percent of employees will be amazing, 15 percent will be excellent, 33 percent are good, and 33 percent are less than good. The last group shouldn't even be there.

It's not personal. It's just pure statistics and probability.

You can say that you are actually using two normal distributions—one for performance and one for people you like to work with.

Now comes the most important understanding.

If you want to transition your organization from its current position into a better position, which way will work better—hiring another amazing or excellent person, or firing someone who shouldn't be there?

We know that the top-performing engineer is creating three times higher value than the average, and probably ten times higher value than the bottom-ranked employee. So, assume you only have one choice—hire another excellent employee or fire someone who shouldn't be there.

Let me help you out here.

Remember that everyone knows if there is someone who should not be there. This is why firing that someone is *more* impactful than hiring another excellent staffer. Because everyone knows, if you fire that person, the trust in the organization and its leadership increases, and therefore the commitment to the company increases. The result is that everyone will perform better.

In some cases, I hear the concern, "What if I'm wrong? What if I fire this person and the organization is not happy with it?"

Guess what? You are usually the last one to know that someone doesn't fit and, therefore, if you fire them, the organization is actually going to be happier.

But hey, if you don't trust me on that, go and ask some people (peers in particular, but also direct managers) this very simple question: "On a scale of one to ten, how sorry would you be if that person leaves?"

Now, you may want to ask that differently with some other people involved or as an open question: "Which person, if he or she leaves, will make you really sorry, and which person, if he or she is no longer in the company, would you not miss?"

In most cases, when you need to make a decision, you know which is the right one but you are looking for confirmation.

Your team will provide you with what you need.

WHO TO FIRE? SOCIOMETRIC EXAMS

Firing is critical and doing it fast is even more important, but how do you know whom to fire? How do you know who should not remain in an organization?

It's simple: You ask the people.

When you are accepted into the Israeli Defense Forces officers training course, there is one part that is very unique: the sociometric exams. In these exams, your peers rank you (and others); those who fall to the bottom are dismissed. But more often than not, the top-performing candidates will be selected by their peers.

Think about it: There is nothing more powerful or predictable than speaking with those you are working with. They know best if they want you on their team. They know you better than anyone else, and they know the combination of performance, likeability, and whether or not they can trust you, in particular under pressure.

Feedback from peers is the most powerful tool in your hiring arsenal. They know better, but there is one thing to remember if you ask for peers' point of view: You have to take what they say into account. If they tell you that John Doe shouldn't be there, that should be the last day of John Doe. Otherwise, they won't trust you and your top-performing people will leave even faster.

You may ask, so now I need to prepare a long survey with many questions? Not really.

There are very few questions you need to ask, and they will eventually repeat themselves, but you're looking for a straight answer.

Here is a flavor of the sorts of questions to ask to figure out which are your key employees and which staff members shouldn't be there.

1. If there is a new team being built and you get to be on that team, who would you like to join you? Who would you like to lead the team?

2. If there is a team like that being created and you are about to lead it, who would you *not* pick to join you?

3. If you were promoted to a senior role and you got to guide your replacement, and the replacement asked, "Is there someone who should not be here?" what would be your answer?

4. There is one follow-up question: Once you have sorted between the keepers and the "get-rid of" candidates, ask your team, "On a scale of one to ten, how sad would you be if X would leave (X being a key person)?" Then, add another key person's name and then one or two people from the bottom of the list. If you want this to be more focused, use a scale of zero or one. If you want the question to be open-ended without any names, ask, "Who are the top people that you will be sorry if they leave?" and "Who are those that you wouldn't care that much if they leave?"

That's it—four questions and you've got the picture.

The challenge is very simple, but if you ask the question, you *must* act accordingly. So, if you think someone is a top performer and it turns out that they are such an asshole that people don't want to work with them, that they steal the credit from others and don't recognize others' efforts, you will have no choice but to fire that person.

This method, though the strongest there is, is not widely implemented. Many organizations are simply afraid to find out that they are not as great as they want to think are. This is an organization's ego-management issue.

Another reason this method is not widely used is simple. As mentioned, if you ask employees, you have to implement their insights and the action items raised, meaning act accordingly. Otherwise, you lose credibility and leadership. For some organizations, it is too hard, and so they prefer to avoid even asking!

The good news is that if you fire an asshole or an underperforming person, everyone will recognize that—for the good.

Running a sociometric exam involving team members can ferret out the jerks much earlier. Many workplaces will say they have a "no assholes" policy, but the reality is, you don't know when you hire someone what they'll really be like. Asking an employee's peers is the fastest way to find out.

How often should you run your sociometric exams? Do it every six months. And whoever is ranked lowest, fire them immediately.

Remember, if you don't get rid of the people who shouldn't be there, the amazing ones are going to leave sooner or later. The difference between an awesome organization and an average one is that the awesome one reaches its target by getting rid of those who shouldn't be there. That is enough to make all the difference.

Asking staff about their colleagues doesn't have to be limited to just lower-level employees. You can ask about the top executives, too. So, if many people start saying that such and such VP is not doing a good job, then you should start asking the same question: Why is this person not doing a good job?

How do you know if your organization is awesome, good, or less than average? There are two metrics: the biased and the scary.

- The biased is NPS—net promoter score—which is a simple question and a simple number. "How likely would you recommend your best friend to join the company?" using a number between -1 (never) to 1 (already did). (Substitute "your team" or "your department" for "your company," as appropriate.)
- The other method is measuring attrition, both within the company and compared to industry standards for your company's area of expertise. So, you may have a 20 percent attrition rate, which seems awful, but if the industry standard is 30 percent, then yours is actually pretty good.

NPS is biased but indicative. Attrition is real but lags.

How, as a CEO, can you make sure your organization fits your desired DNA?

Speak to people regularly. If your organization is small and in its early days, speak with new employees after one month, and to all employees every three months, in a one-on-one dialogue.

DECISION-MAKING

Making hard decisions is hard. This is the reason we need confirmation and tools to make those. Below are some of those tools; use the ones that work best for you.

When I was young, I asked my dad for advice. I told him that I have two alternatives and I'm not sure which one to choose, so he reached into his pocket to pluck out a coin and said, "I'm going to flip this coin, and before the coin drops, you are going to make the decision." That essentially forced me to decide based on what I already knew, and to use the coin drop as the confirmation.

It worked. The coin dropped, and I had made the decision.

One of my CEOs told me his method. He asks himself the following question: "Assume there is a new CEO in my place and that CEO knows exactly what I know. What decision will the new CEO make?" This approach disconnects the decision-making process from the past and from the emotions in order to make the right decision *now*.

I heard another version of the coin flip.

You say, "If it is heads, I'm going to do X and if it's tails, I'm going to do Y." You flip the coin. Now, if you like the results then do it, if not, do the opposite.

For firing people, it is easier: "Knowing what I know today, would I hire this person?"

Here's another tool that turned out to be very powerful: "What will you do in your next company? If you know, then do it *today*."

Many years ago, one of my team leaders came to me and said, "I'm not happy with one of my team members; he is not doing this and this and this, and I don't know what to do."

So, I asked him, "Are you coming to me for my point of view or for confirmation to fire him? If it's for confirmation, feel free to let him go."

The team leader was not ready to fire him, though.

"Maybe we tell him that we are not happy, and he has to change X, Y, and Z," the team leader suggested.

I asked him if he hadn't already had this dialogue with the guy and he said yes, he had.

So I told him, "You're looking for confirmation, which could happen in two different ways. One, you give him a probation period, in which you're actually waiting for him to fail and then you would feel OK to fire him. Or two, I'm giving you the confirmation right now that you can feel OK to fire him."

HIRING

Provided that you realize how important firing is, it's now time to think about hiring.

There are three parts to hiring: when to hire, who to hire, and how to hire.

WHEN TO HIRE

Many companies hire too early.

Let's say that you hire a salesperson before you reach product-market fit. What do you want her to do? Sell a premature product?

The most likely scenario is that she will try to be successful, and you will end up with displeased customers. And that is the case when you hire right. Otherwise, she won't be able to sell, and that will impact your PMF, mainly because the inability to sell will be redirected into product requirements.

The best time to hire is when you know what the new hire is going to do in the next ninety days. Can you define the objectives or deliverables for such a new hire? If you're not sure, ask for another person's point of view—a consultant, perhaps, or another CEO.

WHO TO HIRE

Once you determine that you do need to hire, look for a generalist in the early days and a specialist later on. In both cases, you are looking for staff who you don't need to tell what to do. You want to tell them what it is that you are trying to achieve, their objective, or what *not* to do. You're looking to hire someone who can deliver the expected results and, at the same time, someone who fits into the DNA of the company.

There are good, bad, and ugly aspects of your potential hires.

Good: They can figure out what to do based on understanding their goals. Other people think they are great, and you can see them as a potential replacement for their boss, should the boss decide to leave.

Bad: People who are drama queens and victims suck the energy out of the organization rather than create one. A third "bad" type is the nonconformist, the troublemaker. These people are very hard for an organization to swallow even though they might create huge value.

Ugly: Other team members don't want to work with them.

HOW TO HIRE

In the chapter about fundraising, we discussed how a first impression is made in a matter of seconds. It's the same when you go on a date; it takes just a second to decide if you like the date or not.

It is the same with a candidate to hire. It takes seconds to establish the first impression, and then the natural tendency of the hiring manager is to look for confirmation.

If this is the case, then interviewing is misleading. While most organizations will engage in multiple interviews, there is a better way. If you will eventually seek feedback from peers from about a month after hiring a person, why not seek that feedback *before* you hire?

Interview the candidate's references rather than the candidate. Even better than that, reach out to someone you know you can trust, perhaps someone within your organization who worked with the candidate before or who knows the candidate well. Seek out this point of view.

The dialogue with a reference should either start or end with this familiar question: "Knowing what you know today, would you hire this person?"

The biggest challenge in a future employee's interview is your state of mind. You are looking to hire for a particular position, so you have a task to complete, and that is to hire.

In many cases if you are in growth mode, you will need to hire a bunch of people. Hiring is very time-consuming and interviewing requires a lot of attention. To use the "first date" analogy, the candidate is on a first date, but so are you, and there is a lot of pressure on you to "close the deal."

The result is the same, whether you are in a bearish or bullish hiring market.

In a candidate-centric market, you are competing against many other companies to hire, and the natural tendency is once you find a candidate that you like after the first impression, you start to oversell the candidate on the position and the company. All that pressure to "close the deal" will reflect on you as a hiring manager. So, you are biased toward your first impression.

If it is an employer-centric market, you actually have so many candidates per position that the result is the same—you want to "close the deal" so you do not want to waste your time to meet so many candidates!

RECOGNIZING YOUR BIAS

Once you realize how you are biased, how can you change that? How can you become neutral?

The general practice is rather simple. Here are a few rules:

- Take your first impression and try to prove otherwise. So, if your first impression is that the candidate fits, try to challenge that, and prove that he or she doesn't fit.
- Do a deep-dive interview. A pro would know what they have done and, in particular, why they have done it. And this is exactly what you

are trying to find out. If the candidate is a pro, you can dive deep into what they've done in the past; if not, it is going to be a rather shallow interview. Therefore, you should lead the interview into talking about areas where the candidate feels they're at their best, perhaps the last project or something that the candidate is really proud of. Only then start to go deep. Ask what they did and then *why*. Once they explain, peel another layer off the onion and go deeper still. Ask a "what-if" or another "why" question and go yet another step deeper. Keep on going deep until you get the answer "I don't know" or " I didn't think about it." Now, if this is on the first or second peel of the onion and the candidate doesn't really know, you can go deep into multiple layers. If the candidate has a depth of understanding, they are a real pro.

- Don't be afraid to be challenging. Most candidates want to work at a great place and a great place hires great people. Therefore, the more challenging the interview is, the more the candidate will get the impression that this working place hires only great people!

Remember that a great hiring manager will have a hit ratio of about 80 percent and a miss ratio of about 20 percent. Even Golden State Warriors basketball star Steph Curry doesn't score 80 percent from three-point range.

A good hiring person will have a 70 percent hit ratio. While the difference may seem huge, the reality is that it isn't. This is because we solve the misses by firing fast. So, if one company is hiring at an 80 percent hit ratio and another company is at 70 percent, if both hire ten new hires in the next six months, the first one will need to let go of two people and the second company will need to let go of three—not such a big difference.

Some years back in one of my start-ups, we had a less than average engineer leading iPhone development. While the Android version was already out and working, the iPhone version was late. I asked the CEO what was wrong. He told me the engineer was not great. I kept on digging.

"What's not great?" I asked.

It turned out that, if he knew then what he knows now, he wouldn't have hired him. So, I told him point-blank: "Fire him."

The CEO pushed back. "He is our only iPhone developer. If we fire him, we won't have anyone to work on the iPhone version."

"For how long have we known that he is not great?" I asked. ("Not great" is a polite way of saying "mediocre.")

"From about a month after he started, which was six months ago," the CEO replied.

I kept on digging. "And what's happened so far?"

"I didn't find the right time to do that, and we haven't hired a replacement yet," the CEO said.

So, I summarized. "For six months, you knew that this person doesn't fit, and the only reason you haven't fired him is that he is the only iPhone developer?"

"Yes," the CEO said, and then I continued.

"I think it is the other way around: You didn't hire a replacement because this guy was filling up the position. If you fire him, you will need to search for a replacement immediately."

The CEO fired the guy the next day and, a week later, there was a new iPhone developer in place, much better than the previous one.

Great leaders hire people they think are better than themselves. Average leaders don't; they're afraid of hiring smarter or better people, and the result is that they build average teams or even less than average teams and then that becomes the DNA of the company. And there is more to it. The organization becomes mediocre, and is set up to be unsuccessful.

Average teams attract less than average people and distract great people. The team members reflect the quality of the leader.

Powerful and great teams lead to amazing leaders and vice versa.

When great people leave, it is time to train all managers and replace that specific leader.

THE CEO

In fundraising, at least in the early phases, we've established the understanding that an investor is going to put his or her money into a company *only* if the investor likes the CEO and the story the CEO tells. In a later phase, the CEO is measured by the execution and delivery of the results. So, we are essentially looking at two capabilities: telling a story (salesmanship) and execution.

But there is more to it.

When we started Refundit, the CEO, Ziv, didn't come from the high-tech industry. He was running a green bio-ag technology company. While we were looking to raise capital, I met a VC in Israel and told them about Refundit. They liked the concept and met Ziv, but they decided not to invest.

As I had a pretty good relationship with the managing director of the VC, I asked him why.

"The CEO is not from the industry," he complained.

I strode up to the whiteboard. "Tell me the things that you're looking for in a great CEO," I said.

Together we generated this list:

- someone who never gives up
- someone the team will follow
- someone who listens to the company's customers
- someone who is not afraid to make the hard decisions
- someone who can build strong teams
- someone who reports accurately (not a BSer)

It took us about ten minutes to compile the list. Then I asked him, "Where exactly is 'coming from the industry' on the list?"

In fact, in order to disrupt, leaders probably *shouldn't* come from "the industry."

- When we started Waze, none of the founders or team had experience in the navigation/traffic space except for some consulting that I did at Telmap.
- When we started Pontera, no one came from the financial industry.
- For Moovit, Nir and Roy (the founders who carried the company from day zero to the exit) had no experience in public transportation or mobility.
- The same was true at Refundit, Fibo, FairFly, and SeeTree—their CEOs did not come from the industry nor were they high-tech people.

The point is: You don't need people "from the industry." You need people who understand the problem and who can listen to customers.

There are even advantages to not hiring someone with industry experience.

If someone has been in the industry for decades, it will be harder for that person to change his or her perspective. But someone from outside the industry doesn't yet have a point of view and may be in a much better position to disrupt!

As most of the hard decisions will end up being made by the CEO, it turns out that the CEO may be very lonely. She or he may not be in a position to consult with their investors (they may panic if you would tell them you have issues with the CTO), nor their team members, who may panic as well. Then who is the trusted advisor for the CEO? Very simply, other CEOs. Theirs is the best point of view you can ask for, and they have no agenda. You may have a mentor as well, but nothing compares to the support and advice of other CEOs.

THE HARVARD STUDY

In 2017, the *Harvard Business Review* published the results of a ten-year study called "The CEO Genome Project." In the report, the researchers delineated four behaviors they say set successful leaders apart. Boards should focus on these behaviors in the selection process. The best CEOs tick more than one of the four boxes.

1. Make decisions with speed and conviction.
2. Engage for impact. You need to balance stakeholder priorities with a focus on delivering business results. Get people on board around value creation.
3. Adapt proactively to changes and make new decisions if circumstances change.
4. Deliver reliably. Over-exceeding expectations by too much creates more uncertainty than value.

To be clear, there's no perfect mix of the four behaviors that will work for every CEO. Consider that 100 percent of the low-performing CEOs in the Harvard study scored high on integrity and 97 percent scored high on work ethic.

But there is nothing "exotic about the key ingredients," the Harvard researchers conclude. It's all about "decisiveness, the ability to engage stakeholders, adaptability, and reliability."

One caveat: If you look at the most successful CEOs of recent years, you'll see that none of them fit the study's conclusions. CEOs like Jeff Bezos, Steve Jobs, Larry Ellison, and Travis Kalanick are one of a kind.

TRAINING THE MANAGERS

People join companies because they like the position and the terms. They often don't know what their manager is like, at least not really. In most cases, they don't do due diligence.

And yet, **most employees leave because of their manager**. Maybe the manager didn't appreciate them, didn't recognize their contribution, or would take all the glory for a job the employee did. If this is the case, all is not lost. You can build the right DNA by *training the manager*. Or by replacing managers whose key employees leave.

Training starts with what's important for the company as a whole. You want to make sure that all the leaders in the company use that understanding to manage their people accordingly.

When staff leaves, it can have a domino effect. All of a sudden, a respected and high-quality team member is leaving. A month later, another person leaves. It starts to look like everyone is running away!

It's not about new opportunities, but rather that the existing one is not meeting the employees' expectations. This attitude can be summarized as: "I like what I'm doing, I like my title, my mission, and my compensation, but I don't like being here!"

If one of your managers is not good, replace that one and train the others! This applies to all levels of management. Bring in a management coach or run a series of seminars. Just set the expectation that it may not help that particular manager, but it can help the rest of the managers.

Training is not just for managers, of course. Training is critical for new hires as well. In some ways, training is even more important than hiring. It's challenging from two aspects.

You hire someone and expect them to start delivering value, but they don't know the company, the organization, or the material yet. So, the first one to three months is the time to invest in training to counteract the (unrealistic) expectations from the hiring manager that they will deliver value immediately.

If, after one to three months, the new employee lacks knowledge, you as the manager may conclude that they shouldn't be there. While I generally advocate firing fast, in these cases, that might be the wrong decision. It might be an indication of lack of training, and therefore it may suggest that the manager is the one who needs to be fired!

A hiring organization needs to make sure they have training in place. If you are about to grow your start-up from fifty to two hundred people within a year, you as the CEO don't need to interview all the candidates anymore. Once you cross one hundred people on staff, you won't even know all of the team members working for the company.

That might be a challenge for you as the CEO, but it is a bigger challenge for everyone else. Teams of five people may become twenty within a short time frame. Managers who were just OK running a one-man show or a three-person team may not be immediately great at managing twenty.

The biggest challenge, though, is to maintain the DNA of your company. To do that, think of training those 150 new people even before you hire them, and build the training as you hire.

I once heard the following story.

The CEO and CFO of a company were having lunch one day. The CFO said to the CEO, "I'm concerned that we're investing so much in training our employees, and then they would leave."

The CEO replied, "I'm more concerned that we will *not* invest in training, and they will *stay!*"

THE FOUNDING TEAM

What if you need to fire a founder? In general, I'd rather have a team with two to four members than a single founder. The journey is hard, particularly at the beginning, and for as long as you are in the middle of the desert, you really want to have with you more than one believer.

But founding teams can be a challenge, in particular when you experience hardship and have no traction. When you start the journey with multiple founders, you often don't know if you are all on the same page—of belief, of being in love, of risk-taking, or of perseverance. You will find out eventually if you are aligned, and it's awesome if you are, but if you aren't, it can be a nightmare, because now you have a founder that doesn't fit.

You may want to say that this is not going to happen to you, or that you trust your cofounders, so you would never need to separate from a cofounder. And hopefully, you're right.

But what if you're not?

At Waze, we started as three cofounders, and then we recruited Noam Bardin as CEO after a year. In 2013, we sold the company—all four of us.

At Moovit, we separated from a founder within a year or so of starting the company and ended up with just Nir Erez and Roy Bick. However, separation was on good terms and they stayed friends.

At Pontera, we started as four and we are still four (after about nine years).

At FairFly, we started with four and we are down to three.

At Engie, we started with four, went down to three, and then again to two.

At SeeTree, we started as three and we are down to two now.

I think you get the point: half of the start-ups I'm involved with experienced founders' separation for multiple reasons.

The biggest challenge has to do with ego management. The board of directors cannot fire a founder in the early days, and potentially not the CEO either (this is dependent on the founders' agreement).

In addition, no one within the start-up will tell the CEO they should fire one of the founders. People are likely to say nothing about it, and yet, if you have a founder that doesn't fit, you're the CEO and you don't do anything—you have a deeper problem than any other member of the team.

It plays the other way around, as well. If the CEO doesn't fit and the other founders are not doing anything about it, it is even worse.

So, what do you do when you need to part ways with a founder? It's very simple: separate the discussion into three parts.

- **Equity**—assuming there is a vesting schedule.
- **Legal**—what the articles of association say.
- **Executive position**—Can we have a "nonexecutive founder"?

Regardless of what you do, expect no further relationship with the founder who's leaving. Even if you were friends, chances are you won't remain that way.

Equity is the first issue. If there is a vesting schedule, once you separate, the vesting for the departing founder will stop; that represents a major financial blow to the departing founder.

At the same time, the vesting was put in place in order to compensate those who are carrying the hard work uphill throughout the journey, not for those who don't.

In the early days of my career, I would push my founders to have a vesting schedule that was shorter rather than longer. It was only in recent years that I found a CEO who said, "I wish we had a *longer* vesting period." So, four years is better than three years in that sense. The likelihood that a founder will depart within the first few years is high and, if they do, you want to have enough equity going back into the pool to allow you to bring on new executives if needed.

The legal part is simple: You do exactly as it is written in this book or in the articles of association, in the founders' agreement, or the investment agreement—do exactly as it says.

One of the alternative solutions I've seen over time is to create a non-executive position. If one of the founders is valuable in some areas but is creating damage when at the office, find a non-executive position for that founder *away* from the office. You may still want his or her perspective or even the founder's presence at the board of directors' meetings.

It looks like a magic solution—I can keep the founder, but at a distance—but it raises possible ego management issues if that founder feels his or her ego was hurt. You may need to make a complete separation later on.

Let me summarize this part for you.

- If a founder is due to leave—whether that's you or another founder—when thinking of the founders' agreement or vesting schedule for founders' shares, take the perspective of the founder who stays. It helps in thinking of the situation correctly.
- When I speak with CEOs who have had another founder depart, I hear a very consistent answer: "I did it too late and I wish the vesting schedule was longer."
- Today is the first day of the rest of your life. You have to think about the future, not the past. And the future is better without that founder.

When you think of what to put into the founders' agreement from the perspective of the founder who stays, there are four critical elements to keep in mind:

- a long vesting period,
- a process to decide on separation,
- a multiple-person veto (that is, no single person can prevent moving forward),
- a generous attitude to any partner that leaves.

TEAMING UP

Occasionally, people ask me where to find a cofounder. This is very challenging and, while I don't know how to answer such a question, in most cases, it would be to look for people who you've worked with before or know personally.

Then, the key question is not who to choose, but rather who would choose *you*. Obviously this will be very different if you are a serial entrepreneur and have led different companies to success. In such a case, you would have people following you, and you can choose from a larger pool.

But if it is your first start-up, think of the following story. It may sound inconsequential, but I assure you, it is very relevant.

The first country to adopt Refundit's model was Belgium. It's not one of the largest countries in Europe and there are only a limited number of tourists.

Once we completed the second funding round, at the first board meeting, one of the investors asked, "Why Belgium?"

"Think about your first date in high school," I told him. "Not who did you want to date, but the actual first date—the person who said yes."

That's it! Belgium was simply the first one to say yes.

It may be the same with finding your founding partners. You're already in love, so you are looking for founders who would fall in love with the same problem that you fell in love with. That will be the starting point.

However, if you are looking to construct the team, think of the following:

- **Complementarity**—Three engineers are good but you will still need other capabilities to balance the team. The same is true if your starting team is three marketers or three salespeople.
- **Egolessness**—It is clear that the mission is more important than the individual, and it is imperative that everyone accepts the CEO's leadership (final word).
- **Clear planning**—It is clear what everyone is doing in the next ninety days and thereafter. So, a start-up with a CEO, a COO, and a president as the founding team is not a good indication, not in terms of who is doing what and not in terms of it being egoless.
- **Alignment of interests (the mission) and commitment**—If someone is part-time because they have a day job, and this is going to be the case for a long period, it is not going to work.

Let me share several stories that will give you some additional perspective.

In one of the start-ups I was involved with, there were two founders, one with 95 percent equity and one with 5 percent equity. In the beginning, both of them were happy, but over time, when they realized that this was way out of the standard, there was a lot of mistrust between them, which ended up with separation. The start-up was ultimately unsuccessful.

I would rather have at the starting point fully equal, or at least all in the same order of magnitude.

At another start-up in which I was involved, there were three founders. During the early days, they seemed to support the CEO, but what I learned later is that they didn't trust him from the very beginning. A while later, they claimed they didn't believe in his leadership either. It turned out that the other founders were driven by ego, and the CEO was the only egoless person in the equation.

That start-up was unsuccessful as well.

At Waze, rather early in the journey, we decided to bring on a CEO to replace me; we did so in the second year of the company. Noam Bardin became the CEO and stayed after the exit to Google until 2021, when he finally departed.

During the search for a CEO, we met many candidates. One of the most critical considerations for us was to recruit someone who believed in our vision of "the best place of work we ever had" and who would subscribe to that, enjoying the value of it and not trying to change it. Noam was like that.

We eventually said yes to Noam and no to another candidate, which turned out to be much better for that candidate, Naftali Bennett, as well. He turned to politics and became the minister of education and, later on, Israel's thirteenth prime minister.

He is a good leader.

Choosing Noam turned out to be very successful for Waze, and for Israel as well.

STARTIPS

- Firing is by far more important than hiring.

- For every person who is hired, after one and then three months, ask the question: "Knowing what I know today, would I hire this person?"

- If everyone knows that someone at the company is not right and the CEO does nothing, it means either the CEO doesn't know or that the CEO *does* know but is not doing anything. In both cases, top-performing staff will leave.

- Interviewing provides limited insights. References are more important. Speak to people who used to work with a potential employee.

- Only other CEOs can help combat CEO loneliness.

- Ninety percent of attrition is because of the direct manager. People join companies but they leave people.

- Founders' vesting is about protecting those who stay, not those who leave.

- The magic key for decision-making is asking, "Knowing what I know today, would I do something different?" and then, if so, asking, "Can I start doing things differently right now?"

Chapter 7

UNDERSTAND THE USER—YOU ARE ONLY A SAMPLE OF ONE

Simplicity is the ultimate sophistication.

—Leonardo da Vinci

Steve Wozniak, cofounder of Apple, and I were seated at the same table during a pre-convention dinner in Latin America several years ago. I wanted to take a selfie of the two of us, so I took out my iPhone. I framed the picture, then reached my finger to the volume button on the side of the phone.

"Finally!" Wozniak said. "You're the first person I've ever seen who's using the camera the way I believe it should be used, like a camera!"

The truth is, neither tap nor click was right or wrong—you can, of course, take a picture either way. Rather, the story demonstrates the importance of understanding that not all users are the same, nor will they use your product in the same way.

For example, we were sure that the "right" way to use Waze was to input a destination and then leave it running on your car's dashboard. As it turned out, about 20 percent of users open the app but don't tell it where to go. They just want to be alerted to hazards and jams along the way. Another 10 percent open the app, find the best route, and then close it for the rest of the trip.

Sometime around 2015 or 2016, I was speaking at a conference in Chile. We used taxis to take us from one place to another while in the country.

Chile was at the time one of the fastest-growing Waze countries in the world. Just about every driver in the country was using our app. They still are today.

On the third taxi ride, I noticed that the drivers were using Waze differently than I would use it. Instead of entering a destination and following the navigation guidance, they simply had Waze on and, every couple of minutes, they moved the map around to see what was coming.

As my Spanish was limited, I discussed what I saw with a Spanish-speaking friend. He asked the driver on our next ride. The driver told us this is how it is being used in Chile. The driver was so excited to explain how to use Waze and that this is how it is meant to be, and he didn't even know who I was.

We are accustomed to doing things in a certain way, but others have their own ways. There is no right or wrong, simply different ways. The challenge, when thinking of users, is that our nature is to think of ourselves as the perfect example—yet we are just a sample of one.

It is nearly impossible for us to think of a different way to do things. That's what this chapter is all about—understanding that there are other types of users, how to capture their ways of thinking, and, in particular, understanding the huge gap between first-time users and returning ones. As the creators of the product, we are not first-time users and, therefore, it's nearly impossible for us to think of the first-time user, even though most of the users we will have in the next few years are first-timers!

THE FIRST TIME

When was the last time that you read an instruction manual? In most cases, there isn't even one.

When was the last time that you actually stopped to read the guidelines for a new version of an app?

How do you learn how to use an app for the first time? Think of the last app that you installed. What did you know about it beforehand? How did you discover how to use it? How many of the features do you use?

The most important part is that you may be very different than other users.

To understand users, you have to start with the humble approach—you're an amazing sample of ONE person.

But there is much more to it.

In your current or most recent relationship, do you remember your first kiss? Of course you do! It was an amazing one, an explosion of senses and emotions; you cannot experience a first kiss all over again. You may experience amazing kisses and an awesome and ever-improving relationship, but the first kiss is a one-time event.

It's the same with first-time users. No one can recreate the first-time user-experience for the second time, which means that it becomes very hard for you and your team to think of the experience of the next user.

Recent statistics from the website BuildFire (September 2021) reveal that the average American will check his or her phone every twelve minutes. That amounts to five times an hour, maybe eighty times a day, or more than two thousand times a month. What is it that you are doing during these two thousand times? How many apps do you actually use? How many do you have?

The average American has eighty apps installed on their phone. Out of them, about 10 percent are used daily. Actually, it's just nine apps. There are another thirty apps that are opened on a monthly basis.

Most of the apps you download are never used!

Try this: Look at your phone's main screen and swipe two to three times into one of the screens full of apps that you don't use often. Now try to answer the following questions.

- Say there are some twenty to thirty apps there. Do you even know what each one of those apps is doing?
- When was the last time you used half of those apps?

Surprisingly, the answer for many people is: "I have no idea what this app is." For those that *do* know, you probably won't be able to remember the last time you used the app.

So, in terms of *not* using, all users are the same, but in terms of *how* we use our apps—there are great differences.

USERS ARE DIFFERENT

I started Waze because I hate traffic jams.

Facebook started because of the frustrations of one college student, Mark Zuckerberg.

In many cases, we start with a sample of one person's passion. Then we use other people's feedback to understand the perception of the problem. But there is a huge leapfrog from understanding the perception of the problem to understanding the users. That difference relies on a large number of users.

When you're telling stories, examples are key (they are authentic and emotional). When dealing with a large number of users, there is one thing to remember: normal distribution.

Users are different; they don't all fall into the same group or category. In fact, there are three relevant categories of users: innovators, early adopters, and the early majority. *The biggest challenge is that a user from one category can't even realize that there are other users that are not like them.*

These users might be in different categories with regard to different types of activities. Most people would be a notch up when it deals with their hobby or main line of business. Say you're a handyman. Not only do you know which tools exist and you have a toolbox that you're really proud of, you actually know how to use those tools.

User Segmentation

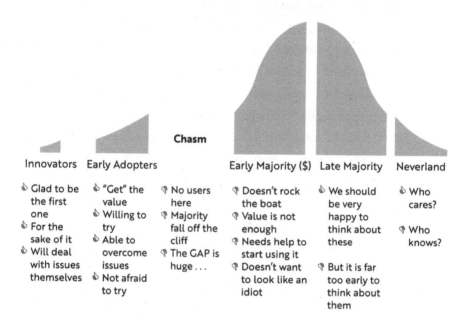

Innovators	Early Adopters		Early Majority ($)	Late Majority	Neverland
🖒 Glad to be the first one 🖒 For the sake of it 🖒 Will deal with issues themselves	🖒 "Get" the value 🖒 Willing to try 🖒 Able to overcome issues 🖒 Not afraid to try	🖓 No users here 🖓 Majority fall off the cliff 🖓 The GAP is huge . . .	🖓 Doesn't rock the boat 🖓 Value is not enough 🖓 Needs help to start using it 🖓 Doesn't want to look like an idiot	🖒 We should be very happy to think about these 🖓 But it is far too early to think about them	🖒 Who cares? 🖓 Who knows?

But most people are not like you. So, while using a jigsaw, you know exactly which blade to use for what, when dealing with an app to scan a document, you might be completely helpless.

It is important to understand the four different types of user categories:

1. **Innovators** will try anything just because it's new. They will deal with any issues like special settings and will even try something where the value is unclear, but because it is new, there might be something there.

2. **Early adopters** will use an app **even if** it is new. Most people are afraid of changes, but **early adopters don't mind them**. They are not afraid to try new things, and they will overcome most of the issues, if there are any. As soon as they understand the value for them, they will give the app a try.

3. **The early majority** (which includes me, I admit) are **afraid to try new things**. They don't like changes. In fact, their state of mind is: "Don't rock the boat." Your app's value proposition is not enough; they will need someone to guide them and help them start using the app. They hate to ask for help since they don't want to look like an idiot. Therefore, they need more hand-holding. This category represents your biggest challenge for two main reasons. Without these users, you are not going to become the market leader because it is the largest relevant group, and it is the hardest to understand as most likely you, your product, and your developers are not part of this group.

4. **The late majority** will use something only if they **must**. For example, if a user's aging Nokia phone died and a new one from the same brand is no longer sold, they must try a new model. You should always be thinking of this category of users, even though they are not relevant at the beginning of your start-up journey.

The gap between early adopters and the early majority is so huge and complex to cross, it is like a meeting between people from two different planets. The states of mind of those users are so entirely different that you cannot understand each unless you watch them and speak with them.

But there is more to it.

When you start your journey, and you want to become a market leader, you imagine that your value proposition is relevant to everyone, and you imagine those people as a large portion of the population.

But when you start your journey, most of your users are actually innovators or early adopters. So, you gather your product feedback from those users and your product becomes good enough for them.

And then you get to the chasm, when you think your product is ready. This is where many users will fall off the cliff. You already believe you have figured out product-market fit and then, all of a sudden, it turns out that you haven't.

There is ONE and only one bridge for crossing this chasm: *SIMPLICITY.*

Say that you're the kind of person who can easily approach someone attractive in a bar. You're full of self-confidence, but you have a friend who wouldn't dare to do that. You don't get what the big deal is for your friend, while your friend can't even imagine what crosses your mind when you approach that special someone.

That's the gap between users: **We cannot even understand how other users from a different group think, feel, or act.**

But let me help you out here to better understand user behavior. Think of the last five apps that you've downloaded and ask yourself the following questions:

1. Why did I download it?
2. How did I hear about it?
3. What did I do after I downloaded it?
4. When something didn't work or was unclear, what did I do?
5. Am I still using it and if so, why?
6. Did I check the settings for the app? Why?
7. When there is a new version of one of the apps I use every day (say Waze, Netflix, Facebook, or WhatsApp), did I like it more or less on the first day I used the new version of it?

Now go and ask ten different types of people those questions.

Self-exploration is an *innovator* or *early adopter* behavior, while "someone told me about the app" is an *early majority's* profile.

"I thought it was valuable" is an *early adopter* answer, while "I had no other option" (like using the Tesla app or your bank's mobile app) is an *early majority's* answer.

Next, ask, "What did you do after downloading?" Going to find more information (i.e., you looked on YouTube for a video tutorial) is an *innovator's* act.

"I started the app" is an *early adopter's* answer. "Nothing" is an *early majority's* reply and, no, the fact that "a friend told me to download this app because it can do X, Y, and Z, and now I've downloaded it," doesn't say whether you overcame your concerns about something new and were able to make a change.

The most common behavior of the *early majority* users who have downloaded the app is to do nothing. It's a state of mind: "My life was good before I downloaded the app, and it will remain the same if I do nothing."

The same is true when something doesn't work.

Innovators and early adopters will go back to YouTube or Google to find out what to do or to try to overcome the issue. The early majority, on the other hand, will churn.

Think of an app's settings. If you are an early adopter or an innovator, you will get there pretty quickly, but it is *not* for the early majority, unless they *have* to do that.

It's exactly the opposite when a new version comes out. While early adopters and innovators are all excited, the early majority hates it. It means a change for them, and they hate change.

If you are reading this book, you are likely an innovator or an early adopter user, but you have to think of the early majority, otherwise, you won't become a market leader. To think about that category means understanding the group's basic behaviors.

- They will quit faster than you think.
- Simple = less.
- There is only one way for you to understand them: Watch them and ask them why they are doing this or that and not that or this.
- They will *not* figure out by themselves how to use your app or what it should be doing.

To learn, you have to watch and speak with all your users, not just with the early adopters who will usually tell you that you're great. "You," by the way, means everyone in your start-up: the CEO, the product lead, developers—they all should be watching and then speaking with users.

B2B VERSUS B2C

OK, so we've realized that there are major differences between innovators and early adopters on one hand and the early majority on the other. What about B2B start-ups—are there any differences between businesses? Do these users belong to different types as well?

Of course they do.

Think of your first B2B customers or design partners. They are innovators or at least early adopters. The early majority would ask for reference customers and would be willing to wait until "others" will use your product.

That's exactly the same behavior as we saw with consumers. The early adopters and innovators are willing to try something new and the early majority is not. The "don't rock the boat" state of mind is what drives the early majority.

And what about users within the B2B customer's organization? What if you are selling a productivity tool to the client and expect staff within the buying organization to use it?

Well, if the buying organization doesn't force the decision throughout the entire company, the people within an organization behave pretty much the same way as individual users do.

- Some of them are innovators, and they will be the first ones to use it.
- Some are early adopters, and they will try it as soon as they realize the value.
- Most are the early majority (as well as late majority users). They won't even try unless someone guides them.

In some cases, you can accelerate the adoption, but in many other cases, these organizations simply have a cadence of their own, and it may take a couple of years for an organization to fully adopt, or to adapt to, a level that they are ready or willing to mandate the wide use of such a product.

The good news is that larger organizations tend to "force" more than smaller ones.

What about gender groups? Are these different groups of users?

In some cases, of course, they are. In other cases, they are not, but let me show you a few places where there are major differences that you may not have even been aware of.

GENDER DIFFERENCES

By this point, it should be clear that I'm passionate about mobility and, with more than two billion people using Waze, Moovit, and Zoomcar (an Indian car-sharing marketplace company, like Airbnb for cars, of which I am chairman) combined, I would say I do understand mobility users pretty well.

My main claim is that given multiple mobility alternatives, people will choose their means of transportation (mobility) based on three major criteria: convenience, speed of arrival, and cost.

Is there a difference between what criteria are important to men versus women? Well, nearly all females riding public transportation have felt unsafe multiple times in their life. Maybe someone was standing too close, someone said something, and in many cases the experience was even worse.

So, where is personal safety in this order of criteria? If you're a male product manager, you probably didn't even think about it!

Now, I deliberately chose as an example a service that has no inherent difference between males and females. Obviously, if this is a gender-specific value proposition, everyone understands that it is harder to capture the user's sensibility if you are not a user (i.e., the target gender). But this situation will pose a true challenge for product lead. If the claim is for "one product fits all," then gender differentiation needs to be carefully examined.

THE IMPACT OF GEOGRAPHY

Is there a difference between users in the US and those in India? Or Israelis versus Brazilians? Of course there is. The following two stories demonstrate the impact of geography.

In one, the nature of the beast is different, so the perceived problem is different.

On the other, the perceived problem is the same but there are still many differences between users.

Mego is a perfect example.

No one likes to wait in line or waste their time. Mego brought your Amazon package from the post office to you—when and where you wanted it.

As explained briefly in chapter 1, this problem was pretty bad in Israel, as the post office wouldn't even try to deliver the package to you; they would simply tell you that there is a package and you should go to the post office to pick it up.

Now, while getting a package is awesome, the process of going to the post office in the middle of the day, with no parking available and a long line of people, is not what you were hoping for. But that was the situation in Israel.

In the US, this was never an issue. The postal or delivery services will deliver the package to your doorstep if you live in a single-family house or smaller multiunit building or to the doorman in a high-rise building.

Now, that's an obvious difference between users based on geography—the problem exists in one region and does not exist in the other. But is there a difference in users' states of mind between geographies when the problem exists in both?

Of course there is!

Think of two drivers who are early majority Waze users, one in Brazil and one in Germany.

No doubt drivers in both countries don't like traffic jams, and they have downloaded Waze because someone told them it would help in avoiding backups on the roads and, eventually, arriving on time.

Waze is a "social+" app. Social+ means that there is an increased value of using the app when others are using it as well, to a level that it won't even work if there aren't other users. The participation of users is mandatory in order to create value for everyone. In many places around the globe, the speed traps and police-report functionality in Waze are the app's second most valuable feature. For some drivers, it's the most important aspect.

It turned out that there is a major difference between Germany and Brazil. Germans are significantly less active when it comes to reporting police traps compared with Brazil. The result was that you couldn't rely on Waze to avoid speed traps in Germany.

Why should you care about this geo-based behavior? You must understand users in different geographies in order to know where to go in your GTM (go-to-market) global plan. A cultural gap should define your GTM plan and your product.

Think of the following geographic differences:

- How good is good enough?
- Social and social+ behavior
- Gig and the sharing economy
- Trust in general and trust in government or brands
- Safety and perception of safety
- Inclusion
- Small or large in terms of population
- Wealth (GDP per capita will be the best way to compare that)

REGULAR USE

The most important part of getting inside the heads of your users is to understand those who left your app very fast.

In 2006, I was a consultant to Telmap, but before I joined them, a friend who knows me well and was working there told me, "I know you're early majority. I need you to try our app on a phone, and I need it to be with no help at all. So, I'm not telling you anything about how to use it. Here is a test phone and I would appreciate it if you can provide me with feedback next week."

While I don't like changes, the cause was significant enough for me to say yes. Helping a friend is always a good cause.

After three days he called me up and said, "I've noticed that you haven't used the app at all."

"You're right," I replied. "I really wanted to, but you gave me a new phone with the app, and I have no idea how to find the app."

That's the state of mind of an early majority user—if it is just a little complex, we simply give up.

Think of simplicity and start by looking at those nine apps per day that you use on a regular basis. Take a moment to count how many apps you used today. Make a list of them and then, for each one, write down how many features you have used today in those apps.

Not only will you discover that you are using very few apps daily, but the number of features you're using is even smaller—only about three to five features per app, and sometimes even less.

Here are some examples of apps that I'm using daily:

- The local news app. I use this app every day and I only use one feature: browsing news.
- While driving, I use three apps: Tesla to turn on the AC before I get to the car; Waze where I'm using two or three features (looking for a recently used destination or saved destination and then navigating there, and occasionally reporting things on the road or acknowledging the report of someone else); the third app is the one that opens the gate to the parking garage when leaving or entering my building. On a side note, Tesla does not support Waze and as a result I've decided to sell my Tesla and get a car that does.
- Google—two features. I search, and then I click on the link that I think is the right one.
- My banking app. I don't use this daily, but when I do, there are a lot of features within the app I find useful.

- Google Maps. When I need to go somewhere by bike, which is my main means of mobility, I want to check the route and the distance/duration so I can plan accordingly. Sometimes, I may want to ride on a certain road and the duration of the ride is not the main issue in choosing the route. (Riding my bike along Tel Aviv's beach route is amazing, for example, but is not necessarily the most direct way to get to my destination.)
- I do use a few more apps on a daily basis—mail, calendar, social media, and messaging, but that's about it . . . and very few features on a regular basis.

KEEP IT SIMPLE

But wait a minute: If we only using three to five features every day, why in heaven do we need all the other (and many) features?

The answer is simple: we *don't*.

The first rule of complexity is **more = less**. More features means more complexity, and therefore it's harder for users to adapt and likely results in less active users.

The second rule is that the complexity level of the consumer-facing side of the app plus the back-end server side is a zero-sum game. If you want the app to be simple, the back-end must be complex and perform a lot of work behind the scenes in order to keep the user side simple.

Going back to features, I'd like to share some Waze features that you didn't even know exist; in fact, most likely you would say, "I didn't even know that the app can do that."

At the same time, you might think, "Wait a minute, I've been using this app for a long while and, not only did I not know that such and such functionality exists, I was doing just fine without it!"

One such "hidden" feature of Waze is that you can choose the avatar for your car. Not just an arrow but a long list of different avatars.

"Why in heaven do I care?" you might ask.

Well, if you can choose your vehicle type, in general, it doesn't matter if you are driving a passenger car, but if you are a taxi driver, then it can matter very much since taxis can drive in public transport lanes.

A custom avatar can also be helpful if you're riding a two-wheeler, which in many places don't get stuck in traffic, so the fastest route for you may be different than for those driving cars.

Another lesser-known Waze feature: You can connect it to your calendar. Now, you will probably say, "Well, up until now it wasn't connected and everything is just fine," but think about the advantages. You can get an alert notifying you when to leave based on where you are now, the location of your upcoming meeting, and the time estimated to drive there. As soon as you invoke the app, it knows where to go.

One of the most useful features of Waze involves its notifications for when it's time to leave. If you know you need to go someplace later in the day, you can start the app, plug in the destination, and then, rather than tap *go*, select the best time to leave. Waze will tell you how long it will take to get there, and remind you when to leave based on the time you wish to arrive and current traffic conditions.

If I wanted to keep it simple, though, why are there so many features that are used so infrequently?

There are two main reasons for it. One is that many of those features were created during the product-market fit journey in the search for a killer feature that would work and make the app a success. Afterward, once you do find the real deal—the feature that makes the difference—you usually just hide the other features in the settings or advanced settings sections, simply because, while they do have users, there are not many. At the same time, we don't want to remove those features and upset the users who do use them. The second reason is that features in general do increase the addressable market, so without a taxi avatar, a taxi driver wouldn't be using Waze.

Should we want to keep it even simpler and remove those features, the best time to get rid of a feature is on the version *following* the introduction of that feature—once you realize that it doesn't make a huge difference and not a lot of your customers are using it, that is.

Another app that I'm using, not on a daily basis, but perhaps a few times a month, is Moovit, the world-leading public transportation app. You'll recall that I was the first member of the board of directors of Moovit from before they even started, and while I find this app relatively easy to use, it turned out that Waze is much simpler, because there aren't a lot of alternatives.

In public transportation, though, the alternatives are much more complex. As a result, the user experience is a little bit more complex, too. In particular, picking the right option for the infrequent user is hard.

If Waze were to tell you to choose between Highway 101 and Interstate 280 in the San Francisco Bay Area, most likely you would know what to do, regardless of the turn-by-turn navigation.

But with public transportation, the difference between "walk 7 minutes + BART + walk another 12 minutes for 57 minutes altogether" versus "walk 5 minutes then BUS, then walk 9 minutes for 72 minutes in total"— well, it's unclear for the user which one is better.

On top of that, you need to add in the cost of public transportation. And there are other concerns. Perhaps you have a monthly pass for one bus service but not another. Or this is the timing if you leave your home right now, but in five minutes everything changes because that bus has already left.

In the early days of Moovit, we realized that the app was complex, in particular for infrequent riders of public transportation, but also for new users. We had to separate between first-time users who are frequent riders of public transportation and the infrequent riders.

A major part of the complexity had to do with the fact that the app is de facto multimodal: even if you're only riding the bus, there is still walking from your starting point to the first bus station, and at the end of the bus journey, there's another stride to your destination.

That was where we saw different behavior between the frequent riders and the infrequent ones.

The frequent riders knew where the bus station was, and they turned off the app once they got on the bus in some cases (and certainly when they got off the bus).

The infrequent users kept the app on until getting closer to reaching their destination.

This insight was critical to determining the different types of riders so we could target them better through the app. The flow for the first-time use, the second, the third, and then later uses had to be different in order to increase the conversion rate. The churn after using the app three times was very low. But we can only convert you if you're a frequent rider, that is, if you're a commuter.

While Moovit is the best public transportation app in the world, it still doesn't overcome the complexity of public transportation.

- Which is better for a certain user? Less walking and more switching buses? Less walking and a longer ride? Switching trains for a faster arrival?
- Does cost influence decision-making? Does the user have a monthly metro card or do they pay per ride?

UNDERLYING ASSUMPTIONS

I'm writing this book with the help of two women: Adi Barill, who is my PR & brand manager, this book's partner, rainmaker, and co-editor, and my wife, Noga Peer Levine, who is a life coach. In our discussion about maps and user experience, each of us presented different use cases for Google Maps while in pedestrian mode.

Say that you just got out of the subway station and your destination is about four blocks away. How do you know where to go? In which direction should you start walking?

Here are three answers from exactly three people.

- The early adopter said she uses Google Maps' augmented reality feature that shows you exactly which direction is which on the phone's screen and therefore she can start walking in the exact right direction.
- The early majority user said she will start to walk in any direction and then will follow herself on the map. If the map shows her going in the right direction, she continues; if it is the other direction, she simply turns around and walks the other way.
- And me, as an early majority as well, I had no idea about the virtual reality feature.

So, you drop your product on a new user. I've deliberately used that term—"drop"—because you have no clue how this user came on board and if this user is an early adopter or in the early majority and what their impression will be.

What are your underlying assumptions about this user? This user may have heard about your app through your marketing activity or maybe from a friend. They may know what the product is supposed to do or they might not. This is where you need to think of the users and going back to basics.

1. No one is going to read anything, so it is not as if you can provide users with seven screens of guidance. If you're not sure that this is the case, think of the last ten apps you've downloaded. In how many of them did you read the guidance screens rather than swiping through them as fast as you could?

2. It's unclear if your users know what the app does, and therefore they are going to be reluctant to provide any information. Would you provide your phone number or access to your calendar for an app if you don't even know what it does (or what it will do with your data)? Of course not!

3. Users from the majority groups don't like changes; this "no change" state of mind for a new user is to simply not use your product. But what about existing users—what does the new version mean to them? It's a change, and they don't like it either!

MAPPING THE STREETS TURN BY TURN

In the early days of Waze, the map was nowhere near completion, even in Israel. So, there were a lot of roads, intersections, and definitely turn restrictions and driving directions that were not yet accurate. As the founder and, like most of the other employees, every time we ran into a situation where there was an incomplete map, we would drive around to let the system "learn."

Now, to put things into perspective, it was like driving home, figuring out that a road or a street is not on the map, and deviating from the journey home to drive up that street and then back, and then up and back again, and just one more time, because the system needed three rides to confirm a road.

And then, throughout this street, we would make every possible turn. So, if there is an intersection, that means twelve turns (to the right, to the left, and straight, from each direction) and then each of those turns had to be repeated three times.

All told, it would take about half an hour of going back and forth for a quarter-mile street with one intersection in the middle that was not on the map.

It's not that we had to do it—the crowdsourcing would take care of it over time—but the joy of creation was certainly a major driver. Once we'd finished, the map would be updated overnight, and tomorrow that street would be on the map for everyone to see.

BATTLING FRUSTRATION

I get frustrated when I fail to do something online. I feel like an idiot or helpless, and it is usually because of the app or its designers misunderstanding the user.

What do you answer to a security question asking your state's nickname when you went to school? Well, there isn't one for Israel.

Or you are filling out a tax form and it asks for your home phone number? Well, I don't have one of those either.

Or you're asked for a name and I write Uri, and the form tells me it is too short.

We run into similar situations every day and we all get frustrated. I tell myself this is what happens when the product lead is distant from the user, or this is what happens when the product lead didn't watch enough new users. The attitude of product leads who say "We know better than the users" simply doesn't work.

I recently tried to file a lawsuit in small claims court in Israel. It turned out that you can do it online. I wrote everything in a Word document and then tried to upload it digitally. After an hour and a half, I gave up and hand delivered my lawsuit physically to the court.

With Waze, I was watching users all the time and the general guideline was for everyone at the company to watch users.

Think of a staff member in R&D who is building the product and, all of a sudden, someone is using a feature in a different way than the programmer intended or pictured in the design process. Or maybe the user doesn't even understand what's expected from him.

If you want people to use your product, there are no shortcuts. You will need to *watch* the users.

DIFFERENT USE CASES THAN EXPECTED

When we built Waze, we realized that drivers may report different things along the way. That included traffic jams, speed traps, and road hazards, of course, but we didn't know *everything* that drivers would come to report.

So, one of the open-ended options we had was a "map-chat" where you can chat and upload pictures of anything. That report would stay on the map for approximately fifteen minutes unless someone responded to it.

We had some ideas about common use cases but nothing prepared us for what we witnessed.

During events, ticket-speculator sellers and illegal dealers would use this feature to say, "I have two tickets for sale," upload a picture of the tickets, and Waze would place them correctly on the map.

Or someone would post "I have good stuff to sell," and, as soon as the transaction was over, they would report that the map-chat was no longer there, move to a new location, and do it all over again.

Neither was exactly what we had anticipated as use cases, but keep in mind that, when you're creating features, there are many different kinds of users who will find much more creative ways of using them.

THINK OF THE NEW USER

In the early months after the release of your product, most of your users will be new. For them, what seems obvious or simple for us as the app's creators is *not* the case—they are *new.*

While using your app, you know exactly what you're doing. The assumption that a new user knows what you know is wrong.

More likely, they know very little if anything at all.

The identity and characteristics of your users change over time, in two dimensions. First, your users in the early days are more likely to be innovative or early adopters. The other dimension is also critical: Your users today are largely new users. Once successful, your users are recurring users that already know how to use the product.

- Today, it is likely that they will be early adopters and new users.
- Tomorrow, they will be early majority and new users.
- In the future, it's all about returning users.

The "time difference" between today and tomorrow is about two to three years, and between today and the future is about four to five years.

The challenge is that when you start your journey, you imagine the early majority users, and you say to yourself, "My app is for John and Jane Doe; anyone can use it." You start your app development journey with the early majority in mind, but the first users are innovators or early adopters at best, with nearly no early majority at all.

The early majority users need the early adopters to guide them, to tell them it is OK to use the app and to help them to make that leap of faith.

The gap between the users you dream of and the ones that you actually have is critical throughout the journey, because while your product looks to be at product-market fit, it is PMF for early adopters. It is still not a fit for the early majority.

Once you start to get early majority users, you will need to go back into the process of making the app good enough for them.

The early adopters will have much higher conversion and retention rates, so the metrics might get biased. Therefore, you should do two things with early adopters:

- Measure them separately. Have separate cohort measurements. If you're not sure how to distinguish them, keep first-year users completely separate from the rest.
- Always bring in early majority users as soon as possible to gather feedback. Recall that they are not going to show up by themselves; you will need to encourage them to try your product.

STARTIPS

- To understand users, start by internalizing that you are just a sample of one and other users are not like you.

- Imagine your first kiss with your loved one. You can only have a first-time experience *ONCE*. Most of your users are first-timers and you cannot understand that use case for them. So . . .

- Watch the first-time users. As we agree that no one can experience a first-time experience twice, the only way for you to get a sense of it is to watch those who have never used your product before.

- There are three main categories of users: innovators, early adopters, and the early majority.

- Users are afraid of change, and early majority users, in particular, don't like changes. Before using your service, they were just fine, and if they will not use it, they will still be just fine. If something doesn't work for them, they will abandon the product.

- Users don't know what they are missing. People might be using the product differently, not using a key feature, or not using the product at all. You will need to find a way to reach out to show them features they haven't discovered.

- No one reads anything. Not manuals, not app blurbs, not messages.

- Don't rock the boat; people are afraid of change.

Chapter 8

FIGURE OUT PRODUCT-MARKET FIT OR DIE

> Simple can be harder than complex: You have to work hard
> to get your thinking clean to make it simple. But it's worth
> it in the end because once you get there, you can move
> mountains.
>
> —Steve Jobs

The most critical part of all start-up journeys is figuring out product-market fit (PMF). The good news is that if you figure this out, you're on the path to success and your likelihood of being successful is way north of 50 percent. If you don't figure out PMF, though, you will die.

This chapter is about figuring out PMF and the critical tools to measure it and improve it until you get all the way there. It's also about realizing that this is an iterative process, a journey, and, surprisingly, another journey of failures.

There are graveyards filled with start-ups that didn't figure out product-market fit. And yet, most of those start-ups that failed didn't realize that was the case; they were suffering from a self-belief that they *did* figure it out.

You never hear of companies that didn't figure out PMF—most of them simply die (hopefully peacefully), but for a second, think of those that did get PMF right.

Think of all the apps that you're using every day—Google, Waze, WhatsApp, Facebook, Messenger, Uber, Netflix, the whole suite of Microsoft products—and ask yourself how you're using those differently today than the *first* time you used them.

The answer is very simple: There is no difference. You search on Google today the same way that you searched the first time (even if it was more than two decades ago). You use Waze or Uber today the same way you did the first time you used it. You chat on WhatsApp just as you've done since the beginning.

Once you figure out PMF, you have figured out the value proposition, so your product will not change anymore. The back-end may change, the business model will be crafted, and scalability capabilities will require tons of development, but the value creation remains the same.

How long did it take all these amazing companies to get there? How long does it take, in general, to figure out PMF?

For Waze, it lasted from 2007 until the end of 2010, about three and a half years. For Microsoft, it took longer—five years. Microsoft did that a long time ago when they realized they would be building the operating system and not the computers (that was IBM's job). Microsoft figured out PMF in 1980, but the company started in 1975.

For Netflix, it took even more time—ten years. The Netflix that we all know started in 2008 but it only recently began to have real competition. Keep in mind that Netflix actually launched in 1998; it took them a full decade to figure out PMF, even though they had a different PMF before!

THE ROAD TO PMF

Product-market fit is all about **value creation**. If you create value, you will succeed. If you create great value for many people, you will be *very* successful. If you don't create value, you will die. Unsurprisingly, getting to PMF is yet another journey of failures, with many iterations until you get it right (or, rather, good enough).

This entire book is about increasing your likelihood of being successful by sharing my experiences, but if there is one chapter that will help you the most, this is the one. If I can shorten your time to figuring out PMF, I've done my share in helping you to increase your likelihood of success.

Why are there so many start-ups that think they figured out PMF but, in reality, didn't? I hear the following a lot:

"We are selling our product and we even have paying customers. So, how can you tell us we haven't figured out product-market fit?"

"The answer is very simple," I tell them. "Users will come or businesses will sign up if you're telling a PMF *story*, but they will stay only if your product *delivers* the story to them."

Essentially, the only metric is if users are staying—in other words, retention. If they are coming back, you have figured out PMF.

There are, of course, some differences between consumer apps (B2C) and business-to-business services (B2B), but the essence remains the same. If users are coming back, it means you're creating value.

In B2C, this is pure retention, which means we calculate how many of those who first used the product this month will return to it three months down the road.

In B2B, it is about the customer buying more, which means renewing their annual contract or expanding its engagement and coverage. B2B is about the same customer buying more, not a new customer buying for the first time.

MEASURING PRODUCT-MARKET FIT

Most of the start-ups I've seen believe they have figured out product-market fit, but they haven't. PMF is hard to sense and, therefore, it needs to be measured.

In this case, if possible, I would drag the CEO who believes they've achieved PMF (and where I say they haven't) with me to see an identical twin start-up that is exactly in the same place that they are.

I imagine here the CEO would tell me, "Hey, they haven't reached PMF!"

What is it that blurs our mirror, that is obvious when we see it elsewhere, but is unclear when we look at ourselves?

Isn't it always like that? Don't we always seem to know better what's good for others, but we have a much harder time implementing it for ourselves?

It is hard to sense PMF *for us*, yet someone else might sense it easily. In fact, if you want to have a reality check, bring another CEO or a friend to spend a few hours with you to answer that question.

Our perception is much more accurate when looking at something fresh than looking at our own products, services, or companies. That "someone else" will do one thing very easily—they will ask about the conversion, retention, and frequency-of-use numbers.

We have to measure in order to avoid misleading ourselves. We mislead ourselves because of a few main reasons:

1. You hear the feedback from prospective users, leading you to confirm that the nature of the beast (the problem) and the conceptual solution are correct.

2. You already took into consideration the next fix or version that you know is coming and so, in your mind, you are 100 percent sure that this change will make the difference. You think of the future version of the product as if it has already delivered the results.

3. You mainly listen to active and retained users who confirm your point of view, and you do not listen to those who "churned" (left your platform or product).

The good news is that there are clear measures that will tell you if you are at PMF or not, and the even better news is that there is a process that will bring you there.

The metrics are very simple. There are only two of them:

- **Conversion**—measures the percentage of first-time users who were able to obtain value from the product (i.e., use the main function of the service/app).
- **Retention**—the percentage of users who kept on using the product over time.

There are a few other metrics that will eventually tell you similar things. MAU (monthly active users) is one and NPS (net promotion score) is another. NPS reflects the percentage of people who would recommend (or not recommend) your app/system.

With both these measures, you will get a similar POV, but if you are looking for the number of users or the app's score on the various app stores, they can be misleading. They show either the efficiency of the marketing machine in the case of MAU, or how happy the retained users are in the case of NPS.

App store score and the number of users don't help you improve your product. Your journey to PMF is about increasing the conversion and retention numbers and not just measuring them.

A little while ago, I received an email from an entrepreneur saying that his company had figured out PMF and they were seeking my help. As I'm very busy and not in the position to make new investments at the moment, I told him, "If you are seeking my point of view, please send me your cohort table (a cohort table shows the attrition/retention of users over time) and tell me what it is that you need from me. If you are looking for funding, I'm not investing this year."

He sent me an email back saying that they didn't have a lot of users because they hadn't invested in marketing yet. To which I replied, "I didn't ask how many users you have or don't have. You said you figured out PMF, so I want to see the cohort graphs."

It turned out that they hadn't measured cohort or retention. Then, I asked him, "How do you know you've figured out PMF?"

It turned out that he was trying to raise capital and he thought he should be telling potential investors that he had reached PMF to increase the likelihood of getting funded. I was the first one that responded, "Show me the numbers."

PMF is not about a gut feeling. It is about numbers.

RIDING THE FUNNEL

How do you get to high retention? There are two main things to consider:

- the funnel of users
- first-time users

See the figure below. At the top of the funnel is the total addressable market—that is, *all* the users. At the bottom of the funnel are "retained users"—those users who are coming back.

The PMF Model Funnel

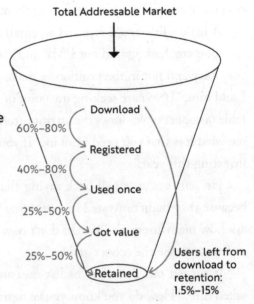

In between are several phases of user adoption. To an extent, you should think of a single first-time user and what it takes for them to get from downloading the app (or going into the landing page) to get to the value. For many services, the phases are similar: registration, understanding what to do and what to expect, and then, eventually, getting value.

Remember what we discussed in chapter 7—that not all users are born equal, and that you are an excellent example of only ONE user. You are facing, by and large, first-time users, and their experience is what you need to have in your mind.

In this funnel, every step is a barrier—a roadblock—and only some of the users will get through it. If they don't, you might think they are missing something, but they aren't. Their life was good until now, and they will remain unchanged afterward. It is *you* who has just lost a user!

That's the right way to look at the funnel. While you are measuring all the users, you are considering the thought process of a *single user.*

This rule is very simple: Users get stuck at various roadblocks during the flow of the service. For example, if your service requires registration, then the phase of registration becomes a gate or a roadblock because there will be users who simply don't register.

If registration is mandatory at this phase, then you just lost that particular user. If there are many of those types of users, then this barrier becomes very significant.

In many cases, I would recommend postponing registration until after some value is obtained. If you require additional interactions before getting to the expected value, each interaction is a gate, for which you have one critical measure—the percentage of users who fail to get through this gate.

There are three main types of barriers from the user's perspective:

- understanding what your app or service does
- getting to the value
- deciding if there is there enough value in it

BREAKING DOWN BARRIERS

Now, the funnel of users is a method, but to make the most out of it, you need to master two things:

- **The metrics**—This is basically an accurate and consistent measurement of each one of the gates over time. This is how you know where to focus your efforts to improve, and determine whether or not you are improving.
- **The learning**—In order to understand why this is a barrier (you know it is because you just measured it), you need to speak to users who failed at this gate and ask them one very simple question: *Why?* There is no one else in the world who can tell you that. Active or retained users don't have an issue with this particular gate and therefore they don't know how to answer the question. You or your product lead don't know either; after all, if you had known, it wouldn't be a gate. So, all of a sudden, when you are in the iterations of PMF, the most important person in the world is the one who failed. Only that person can reveal to you the secret: the *why*. Because this learning is critical, I would say that everyone in the organization must understand the issues and, in particular, understand the users. If everyone is not feasible, I would start with CEO, CTO, product manager, and the rest of the management team, followed by those in product development.

The rest is easier: Release a new version that addresses a single gate issue, then measure again and again until it is good enough or until you cannot move the needle for a while.

In most cases, you will find out that there are only a few (maybe three or four) gates, and the metric will show you which one is the most dramatic. I've seen two main methods here:

- one by one according to the flow of the application or service (first one first)
- one by one according to the severity, so that you're dealing with the most severe gate in terms of how many users fail at this point

In the end, the value to users will be affected by all the gates. Which one is the better method? I would say severity, simply because you are more likely to see results faster.

While we were iterating Waze, we were constantly trying to figure out PMF. The biggest leapfrog we made was when we completely changed the routing algorithm.

In general, all navigation/routing algorithms in the world work the same way—they search for the starting point and endpoint on the map and then try to connect all road segments and intersections either via the shortest or the fastest route. The underlying assumption of this algorithm is that the map is fairly complete and accurate, so if you are allowed to turn left at an intersection, the map data will know that. But Waze's map data was incomplete, and we didn't have that information for all roads and intersections. In fact, we had the data completed for just a fraction of the roads and intersections.

Then we decided to change the algorithm and rather than say, "It is allowed only if we know it is allowed," the rule now was, "It is allowed unless we know it is *not* allowed."

That made an overnight impact. All of a sudden, nearly all routes seemed reasonable, although, in some cases, we told drivers they could turn even though it was a "no turn" intersection. So, we then needed a couple more iterations but, still, it was the most significant leapfrog in Waze's journey to becoming "good enough."

As a general rule, I've taught my kids that it is better to say sorry than to ask for permission—you simply try more and dare more this way. The journey to PMF is similar: Don't be afraid to piss off your users; you will make faster progress towards PMF that way.

Productwise, you have four ways to deal with a barrier:

1. **Remove it or move the gate to a later stage in the user experience**. Users are much more willing to register, for example, after they see the value and hopefully understand why registration is needed.
2. **Simplify it**. Let's say registration requires four steps. You can either have all of the steps appear on a single page or have a progress bar,

but having four screens *without* a progress bar means that the user faces the unknown until they are done. And there is nothing like uncertainty to push users away.

3. **Copy (and microcopy).** "Better" frequently is "fewer." If you think because you have seven pages of guidelines therefore users should understand, let me ask you the following: When you get a new version of a product, and there are seven swipes you need to do in order to continue, what do you do? I will tell you what most people are doing: If this product is mandatory for you, simply swipe swiftly seven times without reading a word. If, however, you are a new user and this is your first time using the app, and it is not a mandatory app, most likely you will give up.

4. **Make use of visual language**. This point has a lesser impact but is still very important. Product designers can influence decision-making through interface design that directs the user. For instance, critical information and call-for-action buttons should be designed to emphasize the preferred action you want your users to take, such as registering or completing a purchase. If you have a yes and no button both in the same color, or the yes button is in green and the no button has no color at all, most users will choose yes. Choices of color, size of text, and placement of buttons are very valuable for increasing conversion and getting better results.

WATCH WHAT YOUR USERS DO

I've described two practices so far: the funnel of users and new users. Measuring the experience of the latter is a much more complex method, simply because, as explained earlier, no one can experience their first time with your product or app for the second time.

So, what do you do?

You **watch** the new users, and the more the merrier. You can have different types of users working through the system for the first time. You use the opportunity to tell people about what you're doing and, if they are ready, you simply watch them use your product for the first time. You say nothing—no hints, no guidance, no nothing.

Then you ask the users: "Why did you do this or that?" You can hold focus groups to try the product, complete with pizza and beer (or margaritas and nachos). You watch them and then facilitate discussion.

One of the conclusions you're likely to reach is that your product is too loaded with features and that less is actually more. Fewer features mean better usability.

Who should be speaking with users? And who should be watching new users?

Start with the CEO and then add everyone in the start-up. You need to have that sense of listening to users as a key part of your company's DNA—everyone needs to speak with and watch them.

INSTANT VALIDATION OR INSTANT GRATIFICATION

Once an early majority is starting to use a product, initially they are very suspicious; for them, the shift to a new product has a toll to be paid, and the proof of value should be rather instantaneous.

If you recommend to me a new travel site that says, "I can find you better deals," I want to see the better deals compared to the other travel site I typically use. If the two are the same, it means there's no value in the new product.

When we started Waze, we had to deal with map inaccuracy. The first thing people did was look for their own homes. If Waze passed that test, they went on to look for their work address.

Once we figured out that part of the data, the next set of users consisted of more or less ordinary drivers, a mix of early adopters and early majority drivers. The map data was fairly accurate by now, so Waze could easily pass the first two validations, but the real validation was *on the road*—how well would the app report traffic and other "events"?

The rationale was easy: If the system reports something and it's there—"Wow, there's a traffic jam and it was reported accurately by the system!"—then I can trust Waze.

But what if there is a traffic jam and it is not reported? Or the other way around, what if the system reports a traffic jam, and it is no longer there?

This is where we had to do a few more product iterations until we figured it out. Drivers needed to get instant confirmation of their experience.

So, say you are stuck in traffic, and we didn't know about it beforehand. Within seconds, your app will show there is a traffic jam there. In that way, we maintain our credibility.

It works the other way around as well. If the system thought there was a traffic jam in a particular location, and you were driving at sixty miles per hour, obviously the road is clear, so Waze instantly removes the traffic jam marks on your app.

This instant validation was critical in establishing credibility.

Most consumer apps have what's known as the "three uses" rule: *If someone uses the product three times, they are very likely to remain engaged, so conversion happens within three uses.*

Make sure these three uses end up being both credible and valuable.

LESS IS MORE

When we first launched Zeek, we ran into exactly this issue. Zeek was a marketplace for store credit and gift cards, so if you had a store credit at Home Depot for $100, and you had nothing you wanted to buy there, you could sell it in the Zeek marketplace. You'd get a price that was lower than face value, but it would be in cash, from someone interested in buying products from that store.

Having a store credit that you're not going to use is leaving money on the table. And we've established how much I hate leaving money on the table!

The product lead at Zeek said that the product was going to be very simple, with only four features:

- Post a gift card for sale (seller side)
- Search for a gift card to buy (buyer side)
- Buy a gift card (buyer side)
- Keep all your gift cards in a digital wallet

When the product lead presented the feature set, I said, "Wait a minute, why do we need the wallet feature? If we are a marketplace, then you are either a buyer or a seller. There are very few people who actually have multiple gift cards that need them to be managed."

The product lead was insistent. He claimed that he would definitely use it.

After we deployed the product, we started to look into conversion, retention, and what people were actually doing. We saw that only 15 percent of all our customers entered the wallet feature and, of those, only 2 percent used any of its features. So, essentially 0.3 percent cared.

For the buyer side, we actually had nice traction. About 60 percent entered the marketplace to search for something.

We had a long discussion in which I pushed them to remove the wallet feature, saying that, not only was it not being used, the fact it was even there was confusing for some people and might impact our conversion.

We decided to follow the rule of the first-time user and held dialogue sessions with dozens of users who entered the wallet but didn't do anything afterward.

We asked them why. The consistent answer was very simple.

"I didn't know what it was, and once realized, I didn't have anything to put in the wallet, so I didn't know what to do next."

When we told them they didn't actually need the wallet to buy or sell, their reaction was: "Oh, I didn't know that."

We removed the wallet in the next version and the percentage of buyers searching for something leaped.

It required more iterations to become good enough.

In a marketplace, the challenge is usually to provide enough inventory. Once you reach a balanced supply and demand in the marketplace, you are at PMF.

The essence of simplicity and "less is more," however, is critical for conversion.

I want you to think of Waze, or for the sake of the discussion, nearly every product you are using regularly, and ask yourself: How many features have I used today? Yesterday? You will likely identify very few, less than five most likely.

Then, look at the feature set of that product and ask yourself: "What if a feature were removed from the product? Would I even notice?"

Imagine if Waze removed its avatar features. Would you stop using Waze because of that? Would you care? (If you're a taxi driver, the avatar feature allows Waze to take you through public transportation lanes, so if it was taken off, you might have stopped using Waze.)

Now, think of the features that, if they were removed, would stop you from using Waze. These *are* the critical features.

A critical feature is one that:

- dramatically improves usage, conversion, or retention
- enables a new total addressable market (e.g., language or support of the iPhone in addition to Android)
- results in a lot of people complaining if you remove it

Each one of the features developed needs to comply with one (or more) of the three bullets above, and you need to measure it. If the feature doesn't comply, you simply don't need it, and it will be a waste of time to build it before you figure out PMF.

In fact, it would be a waste of time *after* you've figured it out as well.

REMOVING FEATURES

One of the best ways to figure out if a feature is needed is to remove it and see if people scream.

This is exactly what we did at Waze.

One of the features in the Waze app is the speedometer, the circle that shows you your current speed. Today, this feature also shows you if you exceed the speed limit, but back in the day, it was simply a plain vanilla speedometer that showed you how fast you were going.

One day, the product lead said that we could remove the feature because there is already a speedometer on the car's dashboard that is doing exactly the same thing. Ehud and I didn't like that idea, but we had a very good VP of product, so we gave her the freedom to lead the process.

We removed the feature and . . . people started to scream.

"There is a bug in the new version, I can't see the speedometer! What happened?" was a typical response.

It turned out, by the way, that 90 percent of the complaints were from men who were using the feature or believed they were using it.

There were two more iterations. The next one, the day after, to bring it back quickly, and then another one of compromise, which made the speed-ometer an option you could disable in the settings.

When you add something to the settings, the main question is: "What's the default?" Let me demonstrate that to you, but I will need your active participation.

Here's a very simple questionnaire:

- Did you know that you can remove the speedometer in Waze?
- Did you remove the speedometer?

Please email your response to fallinlove@urilevine.com and I will share with you the results (that is, how many people know the feature is there and how many people have changed it).

While you are looking into this feature, let me tell you a secret: You can also change *when* the speed limit alert appears. You can find that function in the same place in settings where you can remove the speedometer: Settings → Map display → Speedometer.

Like everything else we've discussed in this chapter, the product road map is a list of experiments that you conduct until you find the one thing that does work and then you move into the next phase of building your start-up.

WAZE VERSION 3.5

There were dozens of versions of the Waze app until we got it right. While Waze was actually good enough in many markets, we were looking for a breakthrough in growth and for a feature to increase word of mouth and virality.

We laid out the framework for version 3.5, which was supposed to create virality—to influence non-Waze users to download the app. The main feature of this version was the meetup place. Essentially, if you want to pick someone up, Waze will send them a live location with an ETA that updates in real time.

So, for example, if you want to pick up a friend to drive to an event together, you would send them the pickup note, and that friend would be able to see where you are and your ETA. It's similar to the Uber passenger app that allows you to see where your driver is and when he or she is scheduled to arrive.

We thought that this feature would be used frequently and, as a result, many of the people who would be receiving the pickup or meetup note would download Waze.

Well, we were wrong!

While the story was really good, and the use case examples made sense, the reality was that most of the meetups or pickups were sent by parents to their kids, and the kids didn't drive and therefore didn't download or use Waze!

The funny part is that, when I explained why this feature was a breakthrough, I used this exact parent-child example.

My younger son at the time was about ten years old, and one day I went to pick him up from after-school basketball practice. With Waze and the accurate ETA, I was there exactly two minutes before his practice ended. I waited in the car.

Five minutes later he called me asking where I was.

"Waiting for you at the gate," I replied.

"You're not there," he said, looking toward the gate.

It turns out we had ended up at different gates of the school. Eventually, we figured it out through the phone call. But a light bulb went on in my head: if we only had the meetup/pickup feature at the time, that wouldn't have happened.

Even though this feature could reduce some frustration for kids and their parents, it didn't deliver the expected results for us (more users). The feature is still there, but to put things into perspective, I've used this feature exactly three times in my life.

YOU'VE REACHED PMF? GREAT. NOW, START ALL OVER AGAIN.

"Wait a minute," you say. "If we've figured out PMF, why in heaven do we start all over again?"

There are a few possible reasons.

One is that the PMF is not large enough.

Another is that the PMF became irrelevant, or perhaps some regulation has changed. With Pontera we experienced all of those.

We started Pontera in Israel, intending to create transparency in financial fees, in particular with a few long-term savings instruments. We believed that people did not know how much they were paying and therefore were paying too much, so if we told them how much they were paying, it would lead to the obvious decision on their side.

But it wasn't enough.

We then told them how much they were paying compared to other people like them on what we called the "sucker meter," sort of a rip-off meter, and advised them what to do to lower their fees. We pissed them off by showing how they were getting ripped off, but still, they took no action.

Only when we told them "Click here to lower your fees" did it start to work. When users clicked there, the system sent a letter to the financial institution on behalf of the user with all the data, asking for a discount on their behalf.

Once we figured out PMF in Israel, we moved into the growth phase in our home market and, at the same time, we decided it was time to focus on the US, which is about one hundred times bigger than Israel.

It took a while to convert the product into one that would work in the United States—mainly with 401(k) plans. The nature of the beast is very different in the US compared with Israel; the problem we were trying to solve in our home country had no merit in the US.

While we were struggling to figure out PMF, we also realized that we have to focus, and that growing in Israel and figuring out PMF in the US would be impossible to handle concurrently. This led to the painful decision to drop the Israeli market altogether.

R&D redeveloped the product to fit the American financial market, creating unique technology, but the real struggle was that American consumers had no perception of the problem.

While we were struggling, an opportunity came from a completely different place.

The Obama administration had set a new rule—the DOL (Department of Labor) fiduciary rule, a new regulation, which states that financial advisors (FAs) who want to advise on retirement—401(k)—plans have to assume fiduciary responsibility for their clients.

In other words, if I'm an FA and I want to tell you to switch your 401(k) into my plan or even into an IRA, I can only do that if my plan is better. Yet, there is no way for me to know if it is better if I don't know what you have in your existing plan; I simply don't have access to it.

The result was immediate. Financial advisors and financial investment (FI) firms needed Pontera's platform to comply with the new rule. That felt like winning the lottery or running with a sudden and very strong tailwind.

We reached PMF overnight and started to sell FI firms a license to our platform.

And then . . . Obama was replaced by a new president—Donald Trump—and his administration didn't support the DOL rule. It was practically banned! Well, to be precise, the new administration didn't appeal when the court ruled against the DOL fiduciary rule.

The extremes of this roller coaster—on one hand, the administration is helping us with a tailwind, and on the other, the next goes and changes it all over again—put us in a situation where we had a very unique and complex technology that no one else could provide, but with no further demand for it.

We had to reinvent ourselves once again.

This is where we lost the support of the investors, and I was left as the only one to support the company.

We had multiple dialogues with financial advisors and financial investment firms; we realized that there was still hope and we might be up for something unique—to enable financial advisors to provide advice on 401(k) (and other held-away accounts) to their customers.

That turned out to be a win-win-win for the client, the financial advisor, and for us. It enabled the FA to provide their customers with better service, not just on their brokerage accounts but also on their retirement accounts, thereby increasing their "retire richer" goal.

We launched the new product in the summer of 2018, and since then, we've seen rapid growth and, in particular, *zero* churns over the last three years.

The Pontera journey entailed figuring out PMF three times. The current PMF is so significant that I doubt we will need another one, but I had the same feeling before, and was proven wrong.

"GOOD ENOUGH" MAY BE "NOT GOOD ENOUGH" IN SOME MARKETS

I was speaking at a geographical information system (GIS) conference around 2012, when Waze was already "good enough" in many places, and while explaining the concept of crowdsourcing and how the map is created, I noted that Waze is available just about everywhere but that it is not yet *successful* everywhere.

"Did you say there is Waze everywhere?" one of the wise guys from the audience asked me.

"Yes," I replied.

"Is there Waze in Antarctica?" he challenged me.

To which I said I didn't know.

During the break, however, I connected to the system and found out that there were twenty-seven Wazers in Antarctica.

What in heaven are they doing there? There are no roads, and obviously no traffic jams or speed traps.

I reached out and asked them exactly that.

It turned out that, because Waze is tracing the GPS and creating "pseudo routes," they were able to use that capability to create roads on the map that allowed them to navigate back and forth from base camp to various research sites. (Keep in mind that, if you're in the South Pole, the compass won't work: north is everywhere!)

While Waze is awesome in many countries, it still sucked and probably will remain at this level forever in some other countries.

Take Japan, for example.

In most countries, the house numbering plan has a geographical order.

In Israel, for example, there are odd numbers on one side of the street and even numbers on the other side, running sequentially.

In the UK, numbers start on one side of the street and come back on the other side.

In the US, every block is within one hundred numbers.

Those geographical models enabled us to get to the level of "good enough" relatively fast. We could take you close enough, which was the definition of "good enough."

Imagine a street in Israel with about three hundred houses. On one side, we will have numbers 1, 3, 5 . . . 299. On the other side will be the numbers 2, 4, 6 . . . 300.

Now, imagine that we only have about ten house numbers that were edited by the community of active users. We can place those houses in their exact location and recalculate the estimated location of all the rest of the houses. That will make it good enough for more than 90 percent of the cases. So, with 3 percent data, we can get to a 90 percent good-enough level.

In Japan, though (and South Korea, as well), the house numbering system is much older, and it is in *chronological* order. So, the oldest house in the neighborhood is house number 1, and the second oldest one is house number 2, which could be anywhere.

In this case, the 3 percent data will bring you exactly to 3 percent "good enough." The result was that Waze is not good enough there.

Furthermore, nearly all the cars in Japan come with a built-in navigation system, and the only entity that has the exact location of all house numbers is the Japanese postal service.

We didn't even have a chance.

WHAT IS A "GOOD ENOUGH" FEATURE?

We tried to build gamification into Waze—various ways for users to collect points while using the app. For example, if you place a report on a car crash, helping the rest of the drivers to avoid dangerous situations, you get points. In the early days, when you drove someplace that no one had ever driven before, your avatar would change into a steamroller, and you "paved" the road as you drove. And, in particular, if we wanted you to drive in a place where very few had driven before, we placed goodies on the map, so that if you drove there, you'd run over the goodies and gain even more points.

It was cool and delivered some increased usage and retention results, but it didn't deliver a leapfrog result.

Many entrepreneurs think of adopting a gamification model and are surprised and disappointed when they discover that it often doesn't work.

Recall that, between 2009 and 2010, Waze was not good enough and we were trying many things to reach this goal. The challenge was that the first-time user dropout rate was very, very high—some 80 percent of users in the US would try it *only* once or twice. We needed them to use it more, not just with the hope of getting to a "good enough" level, but in particular because Waze gathers information as you drive, so every ride counts.

If we could change the 80 percent of users who tried the app once or twice into just one more time, we would increase the data collection dramatically.

We were looking for ways to make that leapfrog, realizing that the real issue was that our map and traffic data was not good enough. We tried to tell users that the system is learning, and that they should give it another try. That worked a little, but gamification was a major thing.

Gamification worked for some of the users but being the first one to drive on a road is rather rare. So, we decided that we wanted to encourage the map completion task through gamification.

We created a Pac-Man-like game on the map.

If you had driven in an area where we needed more data, the avatar would change into a Pac-Waze-Man, and the road would be full of dots for the Pac-Waze to collect (eat).

Many people have asked me if drivers were deviating from their most direct routes home to collect those points. What were the points worth? And, oh, yes, *they* would never do that.

Those people were right: Most users didn't care about gamification. But those who did, cared a lot.

So, rather than getting just one more drive, we got from about 10 to 20 percent of the users ten to twenty more drives. That seems like a lot, but it wasn't enough to make it. Even with gamification, Waze was still not good enough.

The feature was good enough, but the product wasn't yet.

DATA IS KING

How do you know when good is good enough? Look at the data.

We have a very limited ability to see the average, or the aggregated numbers, we are extrapolating. Take Waze for example and think of the key metrics:

- MAU—What percentage of all Waze users have used it in the last month?
- Average use per month per user—How many drives are completed with Waze per active user?
- Ninety-day retention—How many of the users who have used Waze for the first time in January used it also in the following April?

Now, please try to guess those numbers.

As I often do in presentations and in one-on-one meetings, I ask people what they think the numbers are. Usually, this is what I hear:

- MAU close to 100 percent—After all, why would someone have Waze installed and not use it?
- Sessions per month—I actually have seen someone counting. Here's what they came up with: Home to office and back is forty times a month + gym + grocery + pick up kids from school. The total was eighty times a month. Throw in some other trips that weren't logged, and the grand total would be around one hundred times a month. For someone living in the US suburbs, this is about the number of times the car is being started per month.
- Ninety-day retention—Same as with MAU. Why on earth would anyone *stop* using Waze? This number must be close to 100 percent, too, right?

Sorry, but you missed it by a mile!

Waze was downloaded about a billion times, but there were only about 150–250 million active users.

Wait a minute, do you also count those who downloaded Waze on their iPhone and then upgraded to a new iPhone and now have two versions of Waze? Well actually, maybe, depending on the phone.

Do you count users who downloaded the app once but never used it or someone that is not driving, but using Waze to figure out a taxi ride when traveling abroad?

Yes, we count this, too. A download is a download and active is active.

The reality is that the MAU number as a percentage will be decreasing over time, as more and more users who are not the target audience for commuting download the app and use it infrequently.

How frequently is it being used? Is it close to 100 times a month?

No way near.

It was about seven to eight times a month. And retention reached about 40 percent and declined over time to about 30 percent.

When Waze was acquired, retention was around 35 percent, MAU was about 27 percent, and the sessions per user per month were at six to nine, depending on the country.

So, just putting things into perspective, if you want to think about a daily use case, expect five to ten use cases per month and a retention rate of give or take 30 percent at best. This may sound like very little when thinking of a daily use app, but it is the same with your weather app, even though you might think you check it every day. In reality, it, too, is only about six to nine times a month.

If your app is tied to a monthly bill payment, around the first of the month, it issues payment orders to all of your monthly bills. And that's it. But you can change that if you use notifications correctly.

For example, if you send users a text, "Time to pay the electric bill—click here to pay," you are much more likely to increase the usage.

Here's the rule of thumb about conversion: It takes three times to convert, so a user, after using your app or service three times, is much more likely to remain active versus those who have tried only once or twice.

That's your key. Find those users, reach out to them, and convince them to convert. What you want to measure is the time lapse between the first, the second, and the third time, and reach out to those who are late in their third usage.

But by far the most important thing, as I have mentioned before, is to always *listen to* and *watch* the users, so you can understand their issues around converting and, later, to keep on using those insights.

Going back to basics, your journey to figuring out PMF is to start with any level of readiness and improve on two main issues: conversion and retention. How do you do that? Simply watch new users and ask those who fail *why*.

So, to an extent, the only metric you need is the funnel efficiency, and the only road map is what makes it better.

You approach each barrier separately and make the needed corrective action to remove it.

When watching users, keep in mind that there are no "wrong users"; most likely the product's copy needs to explain how to use the app or service in a simpler manner.

STARTIPS

- To reach PMF, use the funnel of the user as your key way of measuring, removing, or improving one barrier at a time.

- While you want to believe your customers know how to navigate the system, most of your users are new. They are clueless and don't read anything these days.

- The only way to reexperience first-time use is to watch new users.

- You can only learn by watching new users and asking those who failed at a barrier: "Why? What happened?"

- Rule of thumb: Users convert on the third use.

- You'll be surprised, but daily use is more like seven times a month and those who keep on using your product forever make up just 30 percent retention after three months.

- Prepare for dozens of iterations to remove the barriers and improve conversion and retention.

Chapter 9

MAKING MONEY

> Management is doing things right. Leadership is doing the right things.
>
> —Peter Drucker, management consultant
> and bestselling author

Building your business model means figuring out how to make money. What is it that your customers are going to pay for, and how much? Not surprisingly, this is going to be yet another journey of failures.

A business plan refers to how much of that business model you're going to sell and when. What will be the company's expected revenues and expenses over a certain number of months and years? In that respect, a business plan is essentially a "forecasted long-term P&L."

All the business plans I've seen always forecast making initial revenues in year two. This number increases by 5–10x in year three, then the company becomes profitable in year four, and finally hits the $100 million mark in year five. If your plan is different, I'll be surprised. The reality will always be much harder and will take longer.

This chapter is about how to define and build a business model and how to derive a business plan out of it. While we want to think about this as our own choice, often it will be dictated by the market: What makes sense, what's the link between the value you create and the reward you can expect, what are some common golden rules and ratios?

While we already established the "operate in phases" approach, and that before reaching PMF there is nothing that you should do, there are two exceptions.

- If you expect your customers to pay for your app or product, PMF is measured by the renewal of payment by the customer. So, figuring out the business model happens concurrently with the PMF.
- You will need a business model and a business plan to raise money, even for a seed round.

An entrepreneur came to me recently and said, "I'm building this product and, as it includes hardware, I've built the business model and plan as follows: I've calculated the COGS (cost of goods sold). I doubled that amount, and then I will try to sell that in the market."

"You've got it backward," I told him. "You should start at the end with how much people are willing to pay. Then ask yourself, 'Can we become profitable if this is the market price?' If the answer is yes, go and build your product. If the answer is no, don't even start."

He explained to me that, in his model, he is going to be profitable, and in mine, maybe not.

"At the end of the day, you cannot charge more than the willingness of customers to pay," I responded. "You either have a business model under this constraint or you don't have a product. The price is determined by the market."

When it was time to raise a seed round for Waze, I knew that I needed to tell a story of a business model and I needed a business plan. So, I created one.

In that initial plan, I was basically saying, "Today, the mapmakers are selling maps and earning about $1 billion per annum. The market is growing and the mapmakers are selling traffic information on top of that. My cost of making maps and generating traffic information, by contrast, is nearly zero compared to theirs. So, I'm going to sell this data at a price that is 25 percent of the current market. They cannot compete at this price because they will be losing money."

While this business model resonated with the first investors, when we were looking to raise our B round, we struggled, as we hadn't made enough progress on the PMF journey (i.e., we were not "good enough"). But while we knew what to do with PMF, selling data (Waze's business model at the time) was much more complicated, and we were having trouble moving forward.

The main reason the product was not good enough was because the data was not good enough and, therefore, selling the "not good enough" data was nearly impossible.

One time, we overheard one of the leading VCs, who had previously told us no, say, "These guys have no clue what they are doing. They don't even have a business model!"

Very few investors will put money into a company that doesn't have a business model. Just keep in mind that "they don't have a business model" is the most common reason for VCs to justify to themselves why they are not investing.

However, if you figure out how to create a lot of value for a lot of customers, you will figure out a business model to monetize the value you created. But telling this to an investor can be very challenging.

A business model must be simple and reflect what customers are buying and how much they are paying for it.

CREATING VALUE

When you're building your business model, assume that, at the beginning, the users you expect to pay will be reluctant to do so. Yet, this is the most critical input—making sure you're creating enough value that they are willing to pay for it.

The next phase is to figure out *how* they are going to pay you and, finally, *how much*.

Once you've got all that figured out in your model, you will need three more pieces:

- **A business model story**—a simple explanation of how you will make money. That story needs to be simple and comparable to other successful companies' business models so that it will be easy for the customer to accept . . . and also for investors to digest.
- **A formula**—to make sure that the LTV (lifetime value) of your product is significant. The final sum—LTV minus COGS divided by CAC (customer acquisition cost)—must be large enough so you can become profitable (three times is generally good enough).

$$\frac{LTV\text{-}COGS}{CAC} > 3$$

That one is a bit tricky, but here's an example to make it easier: Say you are building an education/learning app with a subscription business model of $5 a month. Now, you already know from the PMF journey that, on average, your users are staying for four months. So, your LTV is four months times $5 = $20. If your user acquisition cost is $50, you will be losing money. If it is $5, you are in good shape and you should invest heavily in user acquisition.

- **Time**—assume it will take about three years to tune the first two pieces. It usually does and, in many cases, you don't even know the LTV until you get there.

The question of "how much" your customers will be willing to pay is a very interesting one; the real answer depends on the value you create.

- If you create a value of X, you should be getting something in the range of 10 to 25 percent of X.
- If X is just a one-time event (a paid download, for example), then you should be getting a one-time fee of 10 to 25 percent of X.
- If the value of X is created constantly, however, you should be getting that amount annually (or periodically).

But wait a minute: How do you know how much X is?

Well, that's what your journey is all about. It's about creating value, so you should be able to measure it. And once you figure it out, *all* your sales pitches to customers should be exactly like that: "We create X value for you, by doing X, Y, and Z."

How do you know if it is 10 or 25 percent?

This really depends on the competitiveness of your offer. If you are the only one who can do something, aim higher!

What if there is a higher willingness to pay so that, essentially, there is a gap between the perceived value and the real value, where the customer thinks your value is 2x, but you know it is only 1x?

While it seems like taking more money "because we can" is the right strategy, the better long-term strategy is to start with what you believe is the true, fair market price.

There are two main reasons to keep to a fair market price strategy:

1. You don't want your customers to find out you've ripped them off, as they will be pissed and will switch to someone else as soon as they can.
2. A market with very high margins attracts competition, and the competition will bring the price down to a level where it is unclear whether you will be able to maintain it. Some will tell you that you should strive to become a monopoly so that you can charge more and be more profitable. This is true *only* if you can defend the monopoly position. Otherwise, you invite competition faster, and your defensible position may be harder to maintain.

There is another, more philosophical reason.

While the essence of a business is to make maximum profit for its shareholders over time, your start-up is more than just a business. It is your dream, and it is part of you and your DNA. It is up to you if you choose to maximize profits or if you try to maximize the value to your customers or the world.

MONEY UP FRONT?

It is very attractive to take money up front, particularly if hardware is involved.

Let's say, for example, that you provide a health-monitoring app and, in addition to the app, there is a sensing bracelet that monitors motion, heartbeat, and other biological inputs.

Now, because the bracelet is separate hardware and you're selling it in a box, you may think that people would be willing to pay for it. And you are right; they will. But how to price it?

Say that you figure out that people are willing to pay $120 for the bracelet. Is $120 in advance better than a monthly subscription of $10 with an annual commitment and the bracelet for free?

Which one is better?

Well, I could argue that cash in hand is better because, with proper cash flow, you will not need to raise as much money for operations.

Or I could argue that a subscription model is better because of recurring revenues and higher LTV.

In 90 percent of cases, I prefer the subscription: higher LTV plus recurring revenues means the company is measured by annual revenue rate (ARR) and not revenues.

- ARR is the last month's revenues times twelve.
- Revenues, on the other hand, look at what happened over the last twelve months.

So, if you're growing, ARR is going to be the higher number.

But for me, the most important reason I favor subscriptions is that it forces you to deal with PMF sooner rather than later. For a one-time sale, by the time you figure out that there is insufficient value, it may be too late.

There is an accounting definition for ARR—"the annual rate of return of all annual contracts"—so if your company's business model is a monthly subscription, and the subscriber can cancel his subscription anytime, the accounting ARR is 0.

To be frank, you don't really need to care about this one until you have a CFO.

AR (annualized revenue) is used by companies that don't have annual contracts. Although, in essence, it is similar to ARR (the last month's revenues times twelve), from an accounting perspective, the key thing is that it does not require an annual contract. So, a monthly Netflix subscription that I can cancel at any time is measured by AR and not ARR.

DIFFERENT TYPES OF BUSINESS MODELS

While you might think there is an indefinite number of business cases, and your company is so unique that you must have a new and unique business model, the reality is it is much simpler to use an existing business model than to build your own.

There are a few that come to mind, and they may apply to different companies and different value propositions.

We already established that price is a derivative of the value that's created; now you just need to decide how to price your product, which essentially depends on what you offer.

1. CONSUMER APP

There are three business models for consumer apps.

- **Paid app**—These come in different flavors and colors (e.g., one-time acquisition fee, in-app purchases), which basically say that you create value for the user and the user pays for it, either one time or occasionally (most games are like this), via subscription (Netflix, NBA, your local newspaper) or pay per use (Uber, Fibo, Refundit). This model might have another flavor, freemium, which is where the basic package is free and a higher-value package has a premium fee associated with it (Spotify). If your users are willing to pay, this usually generates the highest expected revenues.

- **Selling data**—This is where you sell to a third party the data derivative of the app. When you have a winner and a free app, which means a lot of users and, in particular, high frequency of use, this model allows you to sell the data to third parties and charge them according to a B2B model. When Waze started, that was our model—the app was free but the data derivative was the map and traffic information, which we proposed to sell. Moovit's business is also partially built on this: The company sells data to public transportation authorities, planners, operators, etc. If a transportation planner wants to decide how many times a day a bus needs to run between points A and B or where to place the stations, knowing the demand (which Moovit provides) can help the transportation executive do that planning much more efficiently.

- **Advertising**—This model applies *only* if you have a lot of users, high frequency of use, and high duration of use or intent. For most startups, this is going to be the longest desert, mainly because you need to figure out PMF, and then growth, and only then you can validate your model, as you need the basic relevance for the content advertiser (that is, many users).

2. CONSUMER APP WITH HARDWARE

What if you have a consumer app and a piece of hardware associated with it—say, a tracking device or, in the case of Engie, an on-board diagnostics (OBD) port connected to the car computer? Well, this one becomes a bit trickier because, if you carry the cost of the hardware, you may bleed cash as you grow.

Your options are simple: Subsidize the device in return for a longer subscription or charge for the device either cost or cost plus. In general, if you are unclear about which one you prefer, try both and see which works. This is known as A/B testing. In it, group A gets one model, group B gets a different model, and you monitor the reception of each of the two groups.

You will need a lot of A/B testing to determine not just the model, but also the price. A/B testing can happen concurrently (both groups at the same time) or over time (this week I'm trying A and next week B).

Unless most of the value is in the device, subsidizing it with a longer subscription is a better idea. Doing so increases the likelihood of higher engagement and an ARR business model.

Think of Verizon, T-Mobile, or AT&T. They subsidize a new iPhone in return for a two-year subscription commitment. If it makes sense for them, it most likely will make sense for everyone else.

The key question is how to deal with cash flow if you're growing.

Say that your device costs $100 and you can sell it for $200. Or you can use a subscription model of $25 a month with an annual commitment. It is rather clear that $25 × 12 = $300, which is more than $200, but there is a risk that a subscriber may cancel the subscription and you will subsequently lose money.

Think of your printer or your espresso machine. The devices themselves are not that expensive—they may even be subsidized—but the ink or coffee is where most of the money is being made.

You can, of course, take that model one step further and make the printer *completely* free, as long as the customer signs a two-year commitment for paper and ink.

On the other hand, charging $200 up front is harder than offering a monthly subscription of $25 a month. And, of course, there is the issue of cash flow.

With a subscription, you make the $100 expense way before you even have a subscriber, and then it will be recovered only after four months of the subscription period. As a result, you may need to fund those devices for six to eight months (prepaying the cost of the device at month X, get the device shipped at X + 2, sign-up subscription at X + 4, plus four months until you recover the cost of the device).

By itself, this may not be an issue, but if you're enjoying 4x growth year over year, which is awesome, and you're signing up 10,000 subscribers the first year, your funding of the hardware is about $100 \times 8/12 \times 10,000 =$ $670,000. The year afterward, it is a $2.7 million—you will need that cash.

To summarize: If you have the cash, subsidizing the device for a longer subscription is a way better model. In terms of value creation for your company, recurring revenues are always much better.

3. B2B SAAS—SOFTWARE AS A SERVICE

Probably the most common and preferred business model in B2B is SaaS, which means you provide your app/system/solution/platform or whatever as a turnkey service and you charge monthly or annual fees.

There are many flavors of these periodic fees. It could simply be a monthly flat fee, a fee per seat, a price per user within the customer, per usage, or value.

All of these options are good. The most important thing in this model is the recurrence; once the customer is satisfied with the value you bring, the churn will be very low, and these revenues will continue nearly forever.

The revenue growth, therefore, is exponential—everything we had last year *plus* all the new revenue.

But which is better? Flat fee? Per seat? Per usage? Per value?

At first, you don't know, and it doesn't really matter. Over time, you calibrate your sales pitch and model accordingly. You are looking for something simple, with a short sales cycle, and that maximizes your long-term revenues/profitability (which in many cases means maximizing the linkage between the value you create and the reward that you get).

4. B2B HARDWARE

What if you're selling hardware, like servers, computers, cars, devices, or even a power plant? Usually, you would say its price has to connect to the COGS (cost of goods sold), but it still needs to be associated with the value you create and the competitiveness of the market.

Say that you have a physical cybersecurity gateway that monitors all traffic in and out so that nothing malicious enters your network (and that this is a really nice piece of hardware!). If the hardware's COGS is X, should you price it at 2X in order to have enough margin to become profitable? No! This is totally the wrong point of view.

The price is determined by the market and the willingness of customers to pay. Then you look at the cost and ask yourself, "Can I build a sustainable business if this is the price and these are my costs? Does the model even make a difference?"

Well, just imagine that you've ended up with price X (the amount customers are willing to pay) and this keeps your lights on. But what about services like support and maintenance? These represent recurring revenues.

In general, if you have to recover the cost of the hardware, then try to build a business model that includes hardware plus annuities—those components that need to be added on an annual basis like support, maintenance, insurance, and upgrades.

But don't discount these; these are your future. If you need to negotiate, give your customers a longer free trial period but not a discount on the price that will last. If you don't have to recover the cost immediately, try to convert the model into a SaaS model so that, rather than selling hardware, you are renting out the service to customers.

5. B2B HARDWARE + SAAS

This should be obvious by now: If you can bear the cost of the hardware, convert it into SaaS.

MAKE MONEY OR SAVE MONEY?

Most of the B2B business models will translate into one of two options:

- Our product helps you save money.
- Our product helps you make money.

Which one is better?

At the end of the day, you can tell a different story to support the same product, so which one should you tell?

There might be more flavors, such as saving time, increasing efficiency, etc. But try to nail them down into these two: make money or save money. Your sales pitch will be easier and your sales cycle will be shorter.

Remember how my dad told me there is only one justification for a revolution—"if it is a successful one"? That applies here also. Out of the two options, use the one that works!

But assume you can choose either. Which one is better?

The saving-money value proposition is easier to sell and also easier to prove, and you can easily adjust the business model to fit. You may get a relatively higher share of the savings, but it is limited by the total spent.

So, for example, imagine that your platform optimizes business data connectivity and reduces customers' costs by 30 percent with no work required on their part. You should love this value proposition. It is simple, clear, and a no-brainer to engage.

You then ask for 25 percent of the savings and the customer agrees. So, if the customer's data connectivity spend is $1 million a year and you can save 30 percent of that, meaning $300,000 gross, then you charge the client $75,000. The client's net saving is now $225,000.

That's it; that's the maximum you can get. Your ceiling is the total spend.

In an organization that spends a million dollars a year on data connectivity, the savings of $225,000 doesn't move the needle. It is going to be a decision by someone in the finance department, not the CFO, but one or two levels below.

To put this into a consumer perspective: If my current mobile and internet bills are less than $30 a month and you offer me a way to save $10, well, even though I hate waste, as an early majority user, I will be reluctant to change anything for so little. My concern is that it will be too much of a hassle for too little money.

What about making money?

Here, the sky is the limit. So, for the same offering, if you can tell customers that they can utilize their underutilized capacity and make money based on that, well, that is much more appealing to most potential clients.

In addition, in B2B, you're selling to a different part of the organization—the part that has much higher budgets to spend. The challenge, however, is that it's a longer sales cycle and will take a longer time to demonstrate the value.

Think of a company that optimizes ads and promos. This company can tell you that, with us, you can save 50 percent of your marketing costs or, with us, you can double the impact of your marketing spend.

If you can choose which story to tell—making money or saving money—always opt for making money. Since the state of mind of saving money is that the floor is the maximum you can do, but in making money, the sky is the limit, customers will feel more empowered with this value proposition.

Very early in my career, when I was a software developer at Comverse and then a product manager, I met the VP of sales for the Americas at the company, who told me, "In B2B, to be successful, you can be only two things—an arms dealer or a drug dealer." He then explained how the arms dealer will sell weapons to both you and your enemy, so you will need to buy more. The drug dealer, similarly, sells products to which his or her customers become addicted so they cannot stop buying more.

WHY DOES THE BUSINESS MODEL JOURNEY SEEM EASY?

The journey seems easy because of the initial confirmations that you get from some customers who provide you with the false feeling that your model works.

In the early days of Waze, we landed a fairly large deal with Apple. Apple had licensed our map in Israel to use with its Apple Maps product.

We regarded that as confirmation of our model, the willingness of customers to pay, and a proof of concept for the business plan and the size of
the market.

In 2011, we had small traffic data deals in Israel and a couple of mega-
million pipeline deals in Chile and Colombia, so it looked right.

But it wasn't.

When the model is right, customers will come to you. In that sense, this
journey is very similar to the PMF journey: Paying customers need to convert fast, the sales cycles need to be shortened from deal to deal, and there
should be just one or two sales pitches to convert a customer.

The answer of "Yes, I want this, and yes, I'm willing to pay" should
come up rather early in the discussion with a customer, either on the first or
second call.

It was a long while before we realized that the long sales cycle wasn't
working for us. The slow pace of dialogue with governmental authorities
versus the consumer social+ app was too much of a gap.

We went looking for a different business model.

We held many internal discussions about the right model. There was
even a strong voice suggesting that drivers would pay to use the Waze app.

Now, in reality, if I would ask one hundred Waze users today if they
are willing to pay, many would say yes. But back then, while the willingness to pay was already established in some regions, our main concern was
reaching critical mass in several major markets, and we were afraid that
if potential users found out that Waze is a free app at the beginning and
then, later on, they were asked to pay, it would be harder for us to reach
critical mass.

I also had the point of view that a business model that charged users
would eventually lose to a free model (like Google Maps) and therefore
would not be sustainable. There was even a claim that we were unsuccessful
in Germany *because* Waze was free and that Germans don't think free is
good enough.

That might have seemed like another reason to charge users, but the reality is that we were simply not good enough there compared to the alternatives (such as dedicated in-car navigation systems).

It took a couple of years of trial and error until we landed on the right business model—advertising.

THE RIGHT MODEL

How do you know when you've found the right model? Well, you won't until you try it. Beforehand you can argue in favor of multiple business models, but the right model will be the one that works.

In our internal discussions at Waze, we came up with the idea of advertisements. We convinced ourselves that, since we had a lot of users, with high frequency of use and a long duration of use, the advertisement model was the right one for us and, in many cases, it even adds value for Waze drivers.

We tried to figure out the willingness of customers to pay for advertising on Waze and, even though it looked like too small a market at the beginning, we knew the rule of 10X, so if at the beginning your business model seems like it's generating X, eventually it is likely to get to 10X.

We had two missions for our journey into the advertisement business model.

- On the product side, we needed to understand what's available in the market and what we need to build.
- The more important journey was: let's validate the model, try to engage some customers, and deliver something fast, so we can gather feedback as soon as possible.

We built something rather quickly, realizing that we would later need to integrate an ad server and many other technology components for a complete system.

We launched the first advertising model for Waze in Israel. It was a combination of three promotional elements: a splash screen (what you see on your display when you first open the app), POS (point of sale) on the map (e.g., a gas station or a café), and search results.

The first brand to use the system was Eldan, one of the largest rental car agencies in Israel. Eldan is also a very large dealership (it sells those leased cars after their two- or three-year lease period is up), with twenty-seven branches across Israel.

Highlighting those locations on the maps with branded pins and search results seemed like a lot of value for Eldan. At the time, Waze was already very successful in Israel, so we expected the exposure to be significant.

We didn't anticipate what came next.

The next morning, I received an email from the chief of staff of the CEO of Avis.

"The CEO would like to know how come Eldan is on the map and Avis isn't?" the email read. That was the trigger that told us we were doing something right, that people care. Those customers were coming to us.

But it wasn't enough for us. We reached out to users to try to figure out if we were overwhelming them.

It turned out that we were not.

In 2012, we got the model right in Israel and started to think about promoting it globally, which essentially only happened in 2013. Even today, when I speak with users, they ask me, "How does Waze make money?" and I tell them Waze sells ads, many will say, "But I don't see any advertisements on the app." Occasionally I would hear people saying, "But there are so few of them. How can you make money with so few ads?"

From there it was yet another PMF journey—on one hand, building the advertisement product and, at the same time, trying to sell it in the market. Our thesis was that any POS company should be able to promote their business on the map through a branded pin, and therefore, this is a long-tail play and all we needed to do was build the tools and they will come.

That turned out to be completely wrong!

At that point, we thought we should integrate ad servers and use their capabilities to sense locations to provide a location-based ad server.

That turned out to be wrong as well.

The location-based ad server was wrong because of the behavior of the users. If you are in a city and searching for the nearest Starbucks, the closest one two blocks away in any direction will do. But when you're driving and looking for a gas station, if the nearest one is one hundred feet *behind* you, it is more frustrating than it is helpful.

Drivers don't care about how far away it is; they care about *how long this "off-the-route detour" will take*. So, we built our own ad server that focused on drivers, destinations, and directions. It allowed us to publish relevant ads to drivers based on their routes and not on their locations.

We also realized that drivers don't see or like pop-ups unless they are stuck in traffic and at a complete stop, and then they care much less.

But the most important learning we had was that the advertisers needed help in buying media. That was something we were unable to provide.

We teamed up with a number of companies that sell ads in different regions to use our media in addition to other media those companies were selling. The self-fulfillment advertisement model, while remaining in place, ended up being a smaller part of the business.

THE BUSINESS MODEL JOURNEY NEVER ENDS

When you're in the PMF phase, once you figure out the product, it doesn't change anymore. That's not the same for the business model journey. Once you find something that works, you should try to grow it.

It is also possible there is another business model that is even better and bigger.

Moovit started to think of a business model after figuring out growth, which was about five years into the company's existence. The first discussion was whether Waze's business model would be the right one for Moovit, too.

Waze worked and turned out to be very successful, so why not duplicate it? But Moovit lacked one key element of the Waze use case—duration of use.

While most of Waze's users are driving while the app is running and displayed on the screen, the Moovit use case is different—users open the app to determine where their bus is and when it's coming. Once the bus shows up, the app runs in the background until a reminder that it's time to get off the bus is triggered and pops up.

During the ride itself, users are on their phones for many other things, from reading emails to watching Netflix or browsing social media. Therefore, the opportunity for an advertisement business model is limited.

However, it turns out that the data collected by Moovit is very valuable for transportation planners, municipalities, public transportation operators, etc. In fact, in many cases, these organizations are *paying* today for the data, but in a very costly and inefficient way.

Just imagine the origin-destination surveys that provide the public transportation planner with information about where people are coming from and where they are going. What today requires tons of manual surveys becomes an overnight task when using Moovit data or even a very simple question: For people who board the bus at station X, where do they disembark?

Yet, what seems obvious is not always so.

FairFly's value proposition is very simple: We save you money on your travel expenses. The business model was a simple derivative of that—pay us a part of the savings.

But many customers said, "This model means unknown expenses in the next month and we are trying to keep our budget accurate. Can we pay a regular monthly fee instead?"

While most customers prefer to tie the business model to the value and pay per saving, others favor a flat-fee model. So, essentially, we had the same company, the same value proposition, and two different business models. That's not completely unusual; most cellular providers in Europe sell both subscriptions and prepaid (pay-as-you-use) plans.

NOT AN EASY JOURNEY

Building a start-up is not easy, you know that, and getting to PMF is really hard. But figuring out a business model is, in some respects, even harder.

Sales are the hardest part of all. The reason this part is hard is because of the long gap between the validation of one thesis and another.

Say that you are a B2B start-up and your business model is a monthly SaaS subscription. Your customer likes the story and says, "Let's give it a try. Can you do a pilot or a trial here?"

You want to believe that "this is it," but there is still a long journey ahead of you. The trial may take a few months and may require numerous product iterations until it delivers actual value to the customer. *Only* then do the negotiations start.

From first engagement into a deal may take many months, and yet we know that only a renewal is the "done deal" part. After the first customer, you expect the second and third customers to be exactly the same, but it turns out that they are not.

They might have different requirements and nuances and, in particular, they might have different perceptions of the value and, therefore, may require another business model. As a result, you have very few customers and more than one business model!

The business model journey ends when a few things come together: the story, the value, and the renewal.

- If the **story** is simple, most customers will say it is interesting and relevant for them. It also means that salespeople can tell that story to prospective customers and they will see similar responses.
- **Value** means your product delivers the perceived value that you described in your story.
- **Renewal** is when a customer renews his or her annual deal. This is the clearest indication that you are delivering value and customers are willing to pay. It is the ultimate validation of your product and business model.

SALES CYCLE

One of the reasons the validation intervals (iterations) are so long has nothing to do with you. Sales cycles are long for many industries.

Over the years, when I've spoken with entrepreneurs, I've heard a common point of view: "Ohhh, you don't understand. In my industry, the sales cycles are awfully long."

They're not wrong.

If you think mobile carriers' sales cycles are long, try selling to carmakers.

If you think that medical devices have a long sales cycle, think about selling to insurance companies.

Forget insurance companies; those are easy. Try selling to the agriculture industry—that's, without a doubt, a long sales cycle. You came up with a magic fertilizer that increases yield by 25 percent year over year and tell that to a few farmers. First, they laugh at you, but then you convince them with your story, and they say, "You know what, let's give it a try. You see that tree on the corner? Go for it."

And guess what? It does work! Six months later, there is 25 percent more yield on that tree.

Then you ask the grower, "Are you ready to buy now?"

"Well, so far," the grower says, "we've tried it in the autumn. Now, let's try it in the spring."

Another six months go by and the farmers are still not ready. Now they want to see it in action on another group of trees. It may be a three-to-four-year journey until they will say, "Next year, we are going to use that instead of the old stuff."

Everyone believes their sales cycles are long, and they are all right. Very few things can accelerate sale cycles. Fear, and in particular panic, and competition are among them. Just think about what happened to the sales of Pfizer with the panic and concern around vaccinations for COVID-19. That kind of fear is hard to manufacture.

Competition in the customers' market is easier to create. In your sales plan, you should try to engage most of the industry so you will have references and, in particular, so you can accelerate the sales cycle of everyone because their competitors are already in dialogue. FOMO (Fear Of Missing Out) works for businesses as well.

VALUE IS CLEAR WHEN THE CUSTOMERS RENEW

Just as you learned about PMF—that you're not there until customers renew—the same applies to the business model. Renewal means that there is value and that the business model is right. While it is possible there is a better business model, or even the same one but with a higher price tag, those calibrations can and should happen when you have more customers.

The key takeaway, however, is very different. While you have a never-ending journey to calibrate the business model, customer satisfaction is critical to reaching the renewals. Therefore, when you start your customer sales, you should focus your efforts on three elements:

- The success of the customers. You may want to hire staff dedicated to customer success or even assign the product leader to it.
- Measuring everything so you know how to align the product or the story or the sales toolkit.
- Avoiding the temptation to sell more and more before you see renewals. Otherwise, it could lead to a crisis with multiple customers, and you want to contain that crisis to fewer customers. This point is probably the most critical one of the three I listed here.

At this phase, *the function of customer success is even more important than bringing in new customers*. Once you see renewals of about 80 to 90 percent, this is the time to start building up the sales organization.

BUILDING YOUR BUSINESS PLAN

Think of the business plan as a five-year Excel table that shows for each year (and possibly each quarter in the first couple of years) the business story that

Period	Q1	Q2	Q3	Q4	Q5	Q6	Q7	Q8	Q9	Q10
New users	1,000	2,000	3,000	4,000	10,000	20,000	30,000	40,000	60,000	90,000
In Q churn %	60%	55%	50%	45%	40%	40%	40%	40%	40%	40%
Net adds	400	900	1,500	2,200	6,000	12,000	18,000	24,000	36,000	54,000
Churn % after first Q	25%	25%	25%	25%	25%	25%	25%	25%	25%	25%
Total users	400	1,200	2,400	4,000	9,000	18,750	32,063	48,047	72,035	108,026
Conversion to paid	10%	12%	14%	16%	18%	20%	22%	24%	26%	28%
Paying users	40	144	336	640	1,620	3,750	7,054	11,531	18,729	30,247
ARPU	$5.00	$6.00	$7.00	$8.00	$9.00	$10.00	$12.00	$15.00	$15.00	$15.00
Revenues	$200	$864	$2,352	$5,120	$14,580	$37,500	$84,645	$172,969	$280,937	$453,711
AR (Annualized Revenues)	$800	$3,456	$9,408	$20,480	$58,320	$150,000	$338,580	$691,875	$1,123,748	$1,814,843

you want to tell. As I noted earlier, it is essentially a forecasted P&L but starts with the objectives, such as the number of customers, users, or countries/metropolitan areas of deployment.

Say that you have built a video game. You start with basic assumptions about how many new users you will have every quarter and how much churn you expect to experience.

Then you have the "convert-to-pay" ratio and the average revenue per user (ARPU) for the period. This simplistic model will deal with the revenue stream for the next five years.

This top-line business plan shows that, eventually, five years down the road, you will have about 1.3 million active users and about a $2 million a month run rate of revenues.

Is that a good plan?

Well, this is a video game, the churn is high and, therefore, you will need to bring many more users in order to have a better plan.

Just a note on how to read the business plan shown above and on the next page: it is a quarter-by-quarter plan, so Q1 is when you start; it runs until Q20, which is five years down the road.

Q11	Q12	Q13	Q14	Q15	Q16	Q17	Q18	Q19	Q20
120,000	150,000	200,000	250,000	300,000	350,000	500,000	600,000	700,000	800,000
40%	40%	40%	40%	40%	40%	40%	40%	40%	40%
72,000	90,000	120,000	150,000	180,000	210,000	300,000	360,000	420,000	480,000
25%	25%	25%	25%	25%	25%	25%	25%	25%	25%
153,020	204,765	273,574	355,180	446,385	544,789	708,592	891,444	1,088,583	1,296,437
30%	30%	30%	30%	30%	30%	30%	30%	30%	30%
45,906	61,429	82,072	106,554	133,916	163,437	212,577	267,433	326,575	388,931
$15.00	$15.00	$15.00	$15.00	$15.00	$15.00	$15.00	$15.00	$15.00	$15.00
$688,589	$921,442	$1,231,081	$1,598,311	$2,008,733	$2,451,550	$3,188,662	$4,011,497	$4,898,623	$5,833,967
$2,754,356	$3,685,767	$4,924,325	$6,393,244	$8,034,933	$9,806,200	$12,754,650	$16,045,987	$19,594,491	$23,335,868

The next line is new users. How many new users will you acquire through your marketing efforts on a quarterly basis? This will be a very low number at the beginning but, in five years, you will bring in close to a million new users per quarter.

Your challenge starts on the next line: "in-quarter churn."

How many of those new users will churn during that same quarter? Remember, churn is the opposite of retention. While initially this will be at 60 percent, over time, you will get better, and this number will become only 40 percent.

The following line is the "calculated net adds"—that is, how many new users (minus any churned ones) were added at the end of the quarter?

Next comes the churn rate after the first quarter. The churn numbers are relatively high because of the underlying assumption that this is a game and, therefore, it has inherently high churn rates.

The bottom line of this exercise is the total number of active users, which reaches about 1.3 million after five years. Now, if you don't bring new users in Q21, since the churn is 25 percent per quarter, you will be left with less than a million active users. Your marketing machine will need to bring more and more new users every quarter to grow.

The second part of the exercise is the top line (revenue) model, which basically says: not all the users are going to be paying users, and there is sort of a conversion from active users into paying users (a freemium model). Here, each one of the paying users will contribute an average amount (which again increases over time) of dollars per quarter.

Is this a good business model? Or a bad one?

The duality of the business model can be frustrating. If you present this business model in order to raise money for a seed or A round, you are not fundable. You are not aiming high enough or the opportunity is not large enough. As a result, it's clear that you are not going to be a unicorn in five years. Therefore, you are not attractive.

However, if you get funded and this is a *de facto performance*, you will have an amazing and successful journey. You're probably going to be profitable after five years with $2 million in monthly revenue and 2.5x growth in Annualized Revenues (AR) year over year.

That's a very, very good company.

At this pace, if your lifetime value (LTV) over customer acquisition cost (CAC) is greater than three, you can get funded easily in order to continue and accelerate the growth. While it looks pretty bad, if you can get to 2.5x growth from year four to year five, that's still impressive.

While the Excel sheet can present and calculate everything, your model assumptions should be the ones that make sense. An investor would look at the assumptions and at the bottom line and decide if he or she likes it; you should do the same. Look at the assumptions and then at the bottom line (results in five years) and decide if it's worth your journey (efforts, alternative cost, sacrifice, etc.).

QUALIFY AND QUANTIFY THE VALUE

How do you know how much value you are creating? In reality, you don't! You keep on trying and you speak with customers or users to find out. The process is the same as your search for PMF or for any part of your journey where you have underlying assumptions (the thesis) and then you try to validate it with *real* customers. The same dialogue that helps you understand what features customers are using and why is the one that helps you to qualify and quantify the value.

BUILDING THE SALES ORGANIZATION

It takes time to build a successful sales organization—a sales machine that brings predictable results. There are a few keys to sales success: product maturity, the sales story itself, and the readiness of the sales toolkit.

Here's what happens with most start-ups.

Initially, all the first five deals or so are made by the CEO or one of the founders and, once it seems like the process is repeating itself—the value proposition or the pricing, for example—you may feel like you are ready to scale the sales organization. You bring in a VP of sales and expect them to sell.

That's a mistake.

A sales organization is a smooth machine that streamlines the sales process. There are four to five critical functions in this organization, and if they don't play like an orchestra, it won't work. The role of the VP of sales is to be the conductor of the orchestra.

The functions are:

- **Pipeline feeder**—this role is to feed the sales machine and to make sure you bring enough leads for the sales machine to handle. So, essentially, if you think the salesperson can handle one hundred leads a year, the pipeline manager is responsible to feed one hundred qualified leads per salesperson per year.
- **Sales**—these people are taking qualified leads and, through the sales process, they try to close deals.
- **Sales support**—their role is to support the salespeople with the different requirements from customers (e.g., data, technical discussion, integration, etc.).

- **Customer success**—perhaps the most important part of the sales process. Their aim is to make sure the customer is engaged with the product and is using it. This role is the feeder of future growth from this customer.
- **Sales ops (operations)**—streamlining the entire process, providing the tools and the practice to manage the process.

If it is time to build a sales org, make sure that you can build *all* of these functions. If you hire a VP of sales, that person needs to focus on building the organization and is not supposed to be selling.

If you are not sure yet that you're ready, and you just want to make sure the sales pitch is ready, bringing on a single salesperson today will miss the point. That person doesn't have the feed, nor the follow-up or support required to close deals.

～～～

There are four key takeaways from this chapter:

1. Figuring out a business model is yet another journey of failures—and a long one—but this journey, in particular, is more frustrating because of the large amount of time between iterations.
2. At the end of the day, once you create value, your derivative of this value should be anywhere between 10 and 25 percent.
3. In order to accelerate this journey, start by quantifying and qualifying the value you create. Then, adjust the business model and price level to its 10 to 25 percent derivative.
4. If you have a choice in your business model, choose the one with recurring revenues.

STARTIPS

- 10x over time—while your initial price may not add up, over time this number will increase by an order of magnitude once you figure out the right model.

- No one can do it for you. If you think for a second that someone else can figure out the business model and business plan for you, think again. You must qualify the first five to ten deals yourself.

- Sales cycles are not up to you. While you can create and build the sales organization and make it a rather smooth machine, the buying cycles are not up to you, and therefore you have to align with those cycles rather than try to change them.

- LTV/CAC > 3. The proven lifetime value of a customer needs to be at least three times higher than the customer acquisition cost, otherwise you don't have a sustainable business model.

- Price is determined in the market, and not by the company. The cost, however, is determined by the company, and the market doesn't care about it.

Chapter 10

HOW TO GET TO A BILLION USERS

Figuring out growth is a home run—the hardest journey of all.

P eople tend to ask, "What's the big deal? I will build it and they will come." Or: "What's the big deal? One article in the *New York Times* and I'm done." Or: "What's the big deal? With a Facebook ads campaign, I can get as many users as I want."

Well, growth *is* a big deal. It is the hardest journey, and very few are successful in figuring it out big-time. This chapter is about how to figure out growth, the role of marketing, word of mouth vs. viral, and the go-to-market plan.

TIM COOK DAY

Apple launched its Maps app on September 19, 2012. It was by all accounts a fiasco.

Their app was simply not good enough, and it led to one of the most remarkable public mea culpas in tech history.

Just nine days after its launch, Tim Cook, Apple's CEO, issued a stunning apology message to users, writing that Maps "fell short," and that users should try an alternative.

Among his recommendations was Waze.

At the time, Waze was already doing well in terms of PMF, and as a result, we had somewhere between 50,000 and 100,000 new daily users worldwide, which translated to about two million new users a month.

We like to call the day that Apple's CEO advised users to give Waze a try "Tim Cook Day." After Cook's announcement, the number of Waze users leaped by 100 percent compared to the top day beforehand. That resulted in some 160,000 new users.

The higher-user-numbers impact lasted for a week and then decayed, so 100 percent more users on the first day compared to a regular day, 70 percent more on the second day, and approximately 10 percent more new users per day a week later.

And yet, the significance—while it looks impressive—was worth only about a 10 percent increase in users for the entire month of September. That record of downloads per day lasted about a year, and when it was finally broken, the daily average number of new users had more than doubled.

～

Growth is not about a single event. It is about consistency in the results and the ability to demonstrate growth over time. Your GTM (go-to-market) plan will need to deliver replicable results and increase efficiency over time. It is not about a two-page-spread article in the *New York Times* that brings many customers one time. It is about a plan that will bring repetitive results.

HOW FAST SHOULD YOU GROW?

The more relevant question is, "How fast *can* you grow?"

At the end of 2010, Waze had about 2.3 million users globally. Noam Bardin, the CEO, and I were preparing for a board of directors meeting. We needed to set the target for the end of the year.

Noam asked me how many users we would have by the end of the year.

"Ten million," I said.

"Where in heaven are we going to get those?" he responded.

"Two to three million in Latin America, two to three million in Europe, and two to three million in the US and some other places," I explained.

"OK, but how in heaven are we going to *get* them?" Noam pressed on.

I had lots of ideas. "But in reality, I don't know," I admitted. "I just know that the market is there and we will try different approaches until we figure it out. In particular, I know that we need to show 5x growth to be on the takeoff track."

We ended the year with 10.6 million users. We ended 2012 with 33 million and about five months later, when Google acquired us, we had a little north of 50 million users.

The table below summarizes these numbers.

Date	Number of Wazers	Y2Y multiplier
Jan 2009	34,417 (all in Israel)	
Jan 2010	538,077 (still all in Israel)	15x
Jan 2011	2.6 million (nearly half in Israel)	5x
Jan 2012	11.9 million (global—we figured out PMF)	4.5x
Jan 2013	36.6 million	3.1x
June 2013	50.9 million	2.2x

The growth factor from year zero to year one is indefinite. The reality is that no one looks at growth for those years, but the ratio of growth year to year (Y2Y) afterward is critical to understand—it provides the feedback that lets you know if you've figured out growth, and it provides the real essence of a start-up on track to become a market leader.

If you look at established, profitable, big companies, their Y2Y growth in business is 10 percent, which is pretty fair. Higher is good. Smaller is less good.

If you're a start-up, until you get to the level of an established, profitable, big company, you should demonstrate a very different pace of growth.

Once you start, you will be expected to grow 10x, 5x, 4x, 3x, and 2x in the next five years. To put things in perspective, let's say that when you start (year zero) you have 50,000 users. A year later, you are expected to end up with a total of 500,000. At the end of this five-year period, you should have $10 \times 5 \times 4 \times 3 \times 2 \times 50,000 = 60$ million users—this is what unicorn growth looks like.

If you're a B2B business and you're selling $1 million in the first year, in the next year you will need to be at 5x that, and then 3–4x, and then 3x, and then 2–3x, and then 2x. So, $1 million in year zero will look like $180 million to $360 million five years later.

We said earlier that PMF is the most critical as well as the first part of the journey, and that if you fail at it, you will die.

Getting the business model right is usually the longest journey, as the validation process is slow. But the GTM or growth journey is actually the hardest. The number of failures in this phase is going to be much greater.

WHEN SHOULD YOU START YOUR GTM JOURNEY?

If you are a B2C start-up, then you should start your go-to-market journey as soon as you figure out PMF, but not before. The reason is very simple: If your product is not there yet, your churn is going to be high (and retention will be low). So, if you bring new users, most (if not all of them) will leave.

Just imagine a colander that you need to fill with water. To be successful, you need to either move really fast, or seal the holes before you fill it with water.

Sealing the "drainer" holes is PMF.

In B2B, however, PMF and business model are not that separate. Growth will start once you figure out the business model *and* PMF.

While the metric is different, the journey is mostly the same—to prove that you can grow efficiently (businesswise) and become a significant player in the market. The main difference between B2C and B2B is the definition of "efficient."

If you're a free app and you haven't figured out the business model yet, then acquiring users at zero cost (or a price very close to zero) makes sense. Acquiring users at a hefty price doesn't.

If you're a B2B product or paid B2C and you know that your users are spending $X on the first day and overall $3X in the next year or so, then acquiring users at less than $X makes sense, but acquiring them at more than $3X doesn't, since your entire GTM journey is to improve the efficiency.

Even if, on the first day, your customer acquisition cost doesn't make sense, at the end of the journey it will have to make sense.

WOM (WORD OF MOUTH) AND VIRAL—THE HOLY GRAIL OF MARKETING

Let me start by defining these two terms, as I've seen many people become confused by them.

"Viral" is the simpler of the two. I cannot use the product unless you're using it, too. If I were the only person on the planet with Messenger or WhatsApp, these apps wouldn't really help me, and therefore, in order to use them, I would need to invite other people to use the apps, as well.

It is clear that a successful product with virality enjoys huge growth, and the winner takes it all. Keep in mind that there might be different winners in various markets, so Uber in the US, DiDi in China, and Grab in other parts of Asia. Or Messenger in the US, WhatsApp elsewhere, for example.

Word of mouth (WOM) is way different.

If I would ask one hundred people how they heard about Waze, 90 percent are likely to answer "someone told me." That's word of mouth.

You can try the same thing with Uber, Netflix, Facebook, and most of the apps you use daily. If you are creating a consumer-focused app and your total addressable market is large, at the end of the day, you will win if you figure out WOM.

Unfortunately, WOM is only relevant for apps that are used with high frequency.

Let me explain why.

As we learned in chapter 4, if your product is used more than a few times a month on average (say, even ten times a month but not every day), then WOM is your path, simply because people have more opportunities to tell someone else.

Now, imagine that only 10 percent of your users will ever tell someone else about your product after they use it, and then 10 percent of those who are told will eventually become users.

Let's say you already have a million users. If 10 percent of them tell someone else, that is 100,000 people. If only 10 percent of those become users, that's 10,000 new (organic) users.

Now, if your app's frequency of use is once a year, this is *only* 10,000 users per annum (nothing to write home about; in fact, you would probably have a pretty high churn rate).

If your app is used once a month, though, this is 100,000 new users over a year—not as bad but, again, not enough.

But if your app is used daily or even just ten times a month (as with Waze), and your users have a positive experience that prompts them to tell their friends, the compound effect will be 3x the number of users at the end of the year without any spend on user acquisition.

Forget about churn for a second. I want you to realize the impact of frequency of use on organic growth. We'll stick with the above assumption that only 10 percent of users will tell someone about your product and, of those users, only 10 percent will start to use it—so 1 percent, essentially.

Frequency of Use	January users	December users	X factor
Yearly	1,000,000	1,010,000	1%
Monthly	1,000,000	1,126,825	12%
Weekly	1,000,000	1,677,688	67%
10 times a month	1,000,000	3,138,428	3x
Daily	1,000,000	37,783,434	37x

For Waze, the most effective tool in our go-to-market arsenal was word of mouth. There's nothing like being in a car with a friend and seeing an app running on the dashboard to make you ask, "What's that?"

What does WOM look like in real life? Like a hockey stick—exponential growth.

Look at the graphs of Moovit and Waze on page 290. While the numbers are different and the metrics are not identical—at Waze, it counts people who have downloaded the app and used it, and at Moovit, it's someone who has used the service through an app or the web—the shape of the curve is exactly the same.

It's the same for WhatsApp, Facebook, and all of the most successful consumer apps in the world. Once WOM kicks in, exponential growth kicks off.

It took Moovit 436 days to reach the first million users, 107 days to reach the second million, and about 19 *hours* to reach the last million before the company was acquired.

WOM is a derivative of frequency of use.

High frequency of use means you will end up with WOM marketing.

All other GTM activities that take place beforehand are a means to get to critical mass to enable WOM.

It may take you a few years to get to critical mass, but once you're there, *all of your growth* is going to be WOM.

When looking at the table above, let's say you have a frequency of use of ten times a month. In this case, the WOM or organic growth is about 3.13x year over year. That's 10x in two years and 100x in four years.

Moovit Total Users (K)

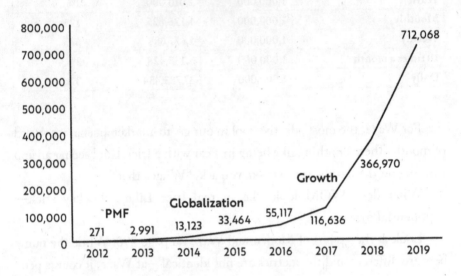

Waze Total Users

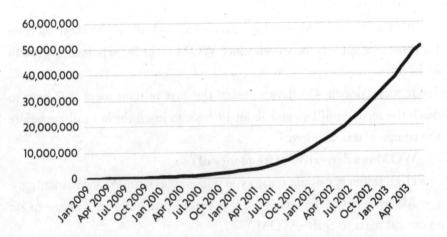

If you start with a few million users, 100x is a few hundreds of millions—certainly a market-leader position. If, however, you start with just 1,000 users, 100 times that number is still a very low number. To get to the first few million users, you will need the entire marketing machine to bring them.

WE GOT IT ALL WRONG

Let's reorder everything and realign our start-up strategy.

If your product has a high frequency of use, then start with PMF, go to growth, and only then try to figure out the business model.

If not, then start with PMF, then figure out the business model, then growth.

The reason is rather simple: If you can show high growth, that will increase dramatically the valuation of your company, will allow you to raise a lot of capital, and then enable you to figure out the business model.

However, if you don't have a high frequency of use, it means that your user acquisition will be costly, and therefore you will need to show that you have a business model to support it.

Frequency of use *defines* your start-up strategy and, of course, your *GTM strategy*.

MARKETING 101

Finally, we can start discussing the role of marketing.

I have witnessed many start-ups over the years that, when they begin to think about marketing, generate complete confusion around the role of this important function. It's therefore very unclear how to build, hire, and measure marketing.

Let me start with what I've heard founders expect from marketing:

- "I want a double spread in the *New York Times*"—so PR is the key role.
- "I want them to buy users on Facebook"—which means the job is all about user acquisition.
- "I want to streamline the look and feel of the company and to sharpen the message"—which means marketing is about positioning.
- "I want marketing to provide tools to the salespeople"—which means marketing is about sales tools.

The bottom line is that nearly all CEOs have one point of view on the role of marketing—promotion. But marketing is so much more, and if you engage the marketing team early, they will create the market-product-price strategy, and only after that, the promotion of it in the market.

Marketing's job is to *create a system for accelerating the PMF journey.* There are two phases:

1. Learning the needs in order to define the product and the market (who are the users and where are they) and fixing the price, which is a derivative of the users' willingness to pay.

2. Promotion, which is by and large intended to bring users/customers to use the product.

A key question is: How early do you engage the head of marketing?

Do you need to hire someone early who can do inbound marketing, someone probably very experienced, well rounded, and who understands the users, the product, and the market?

Or do you need a completely different person at a later stage in the company, someone who understands promotion, outbound marketing, and the different tools of promotion? This person simply takes the market-product-price—which is so important for the early marketing hire—for granted.

These are two very different types of people. The first type is rather rare; not many people can do product-market-price.

The second type is more common. So, if you are going to say, "I'm looking for a VP of marketing or a chief marketing officer (CMO)," which one do you want? The first or the second type?

It's more likely you will get most of the résumés from type-two candidates, those focused on promotion. Yet, if you hire a type-two professional to do product-market-price, that person is likely to fail.

The other way around has a low likelihood of success as well, as the type-one person is much more capable of doing just the part of promotion and most likely they won't like the job.

So, now that you know what marketing can do for you, it is up to you to decide if you want to bring marketing in-house early (for the PMF part where the mission is to get there faster) or later (when the mission is to accelerate growth).

PROMOTION—MARKETING OR BUSINESS DEVELOPMENT?

Most start-ups will engage in marketing when it is time to bring in customers or users, but I've seen many companies that need to choose between marketing and business development (BD) capabilities to bring those customers.

I define marketing as "bringing users one at a time." BD is about bringing *groups* of users. So, on one hand, I will do PR, online and offline marketing, referral programs, etc. On the other hand, wearing my BD hat, I will approach groups, employers, and teams to engage *their* customers or users.

The most important conclusion is simple: If you don't know how to bring your users, NO ONE else will know either. Regardless, whether you end up with direct user acquisition (marketing) or indirect (BD), you will need to *start* by bringing them directly.

In general, think about the following ratios:

- If your sales pitch is right, at the end of the sales cycle, your close-win ratio will be somewhere between 25 and 75 percent.
- In your fundraising journey, your close-win would be between 1 and 2 percent.
- In BD, the ratio is way better than fundraising, but way lower than sales, somewhere between 5 and 10 percent.

If, for example, you have a tax-free shopping app like Refundit that simplifies everything for people to get their money back while traveling, and you think you can go to travel agencies (online or physical), or airlines, or any travel industry entity and tell them, "Let's cooperate; why don't you promote our app to your customers?" about 5 to 10 percent will say yes. Even then it will take time to deploy, and the results may be disappointing.

Let me share with you some stories that will provide perspective.

LOCATION WORLD

Waze's partner in Latin America, Location World, was, to an extent, our boots on the ground. They followed our guidelines on GTM activities, plus they added some of their own. That's nearly the only model that works—you write the GTM cookbook that someone on the ground will follow, and they will do their own localization and adjustments. At the end of the day, Location World was responsible for all GTM activities in LATAM except Brazil, and we have tried dozens of approaches. To a certain extent, they have helped us to write the cookbook of GTM.

TELEFÓNICA

Telefónica is a Spanish mobile operator that became global and is a market leader in Latin America. Location World engaged them as a distribution partner in multiple countries in Latin America and promoted Waze over their media, including a special data tariff (i.e., free) for using Waze, etc.

It took about six months to get them on board. There were many conversations between Location World and Telefónica. I even had to travel to a number of different places in Latin America a couple of times to get them going.

At the time, Telefónica had more than a third of the mobile users in the region, and they had committed to ATL (above-the-line) spending, which is where advertising is deployed around a wider target audience such as television or radio. Contrast that with BTL (below-the-line) spending, where advertising targets a specific group of potential customers.

Telefónica planned to use all kinds of media and not just theirs to promote Waze. We expected a 20 to 30 percent increase in growth in the countries where the campaign was planned to be launched.

The results were rather disappointing—a 2 to 3 percent increase, that's it.

Business development GTM activities require a lot of patience. Many of these GTM activities won't deliver any results at all. Many others will deliver some results. Only a very few will deliver significant results.

The problem is that you don't know which is which before you start. Therefore, I recommend that you start with BD GTM. Even once you have some GTM traction and you know what works and what doesn't, don't expect your marketing team to pull a rabbit out of a hat—they are marketeers, not magicians!

HUTCHISON

In 2012, Waze had raised funds from Horizon Ventures and Kleiner Perkins. Horizon is the investment arm of Li Ka-shing, a very well known businessperson in Hong Kong and the owner of Hutchison, which in turn owns the mobile operator 3. The latter at the time had a valuable footprint in some countries in Europe, including Italy.

Horizon told us they could help and made a very warm introduction to 3 Italy. We had started a dialogue with them, and they told us, "We know how to promote your app. We will do an SMS campaign and send it to all relevant users. We usually see awesome results with that."

It took about three more months until they launched the campaign.

At that time, our growth in Italy was pretty good—about 3,000 to 5,000 new users a day, which adds up to approximately 100,000 to 150,000 users a month.

The day of the campaign was amazing, bringing in about 100,000 new users. The next day was about 60,000 users and the following day was about

40,000 until it got back to 3,000 to 5,000 a day after about a week. The grand total: around 250,000 new users.

These were amazing results, equal to about two months of organic growth. It was much more than we had expected.

We took this model to other mobile operators, including TIM (Telecom Italia Mobile), Vodafone Italy, and a dozen other operators in different countries. I also spoke with the Hutchison 3 operators in Austria, the UK, and other countries; none of them agreed to do an SMS campaign like 3 Italy had done.

That was truly frustrating because we found something that works with very little effort on our side, and we were unable to engage other mobile operators.

I went back to 3 Italy and suggested that we do it again. This was about six months later and Waze was now growing at a faster rate.

It took three more months to launch the campaign, and the results this time were just about 50,000 new users altogether, which equals only about a week of growth.

What's my point? Even when something works, you can't be certain it will work again or that it will work the same way somewhere else.

TIM BRASIL

While in my dialogues with TIM Brasil, Waze was unable to get any distribution capabilities (it was too early for them); when Moovit showed up, we told the guys at TIM, "Hey, you missed the opportunity to do something great with Waze—don't miss it again!"

Omar Téllez, a friend and, at the time, the rainmaker president of Moovit Latin America, orchestrated the deal, which led to amazing results. A year after the campaign was launched, one-quarter of all Moovit users were in Brazil. That campaign led to about 15 million users over the course of a year.

While out of the one billion users Moovit has today, this number is not a lot, out of the 50 million the company had back then, it was a phenomenal number.

Yet Moovit, like Waze, was unable to replicate that success in other places.

ABC MEETS CARMAGEDDON

The ABC television network was one of the key triggers for Waze taking off in the US. Close to the Fourth of July weekend in 2011, there was major construction scheduled for the I-405 highway in Los Angeles. The road was due to be completely shut down and demolished. The media called it "Carmageddon" and, a couple of months before the shutdown, ABC reached out to us, saying we were the only ones who could report real-time traffic, including reports from the ground.

ABC liked our Carmageddon weekend reports, so we continued to work together. Throughout 2011 we went to other local ABC stations and became their traffic reporting tool. The station was very pleased, as they in effect had better traffic reports than their competitors. We were very pleased, too, because we got free promotion and recognition by a major brand name.

What did we get out of it besides brand recognition?

Waze provided the traffic reports for ABC in Detroit (and in many other cities as well). If you asked me how many new users we got after the 11 PM news broadcast in Detroit, the answer is probably small—just about one hundred.

That doesn't sound like a lot, but remember, the traffic reports were aired three times a day, thirty days a month, and in fifty different cities. And that turned out to be significant.

DATA ACQUISITION

Remember the "flywheel" of Waze? The more users there are, the more the data is improved. Better data increase retention and usage, and therefore bring more users. So, in addition to business development trying to bring users, we had many BD deals trying to bring more data (in particular GPS data from fleet-management companies and base maps from mapmakers).

That turned out to be an easier deal because they had the data, and it was rather easy for them to engage.

It was also risk free. My general offer to fleet-management companies was simple: Give me your GPS data in real time and I will provide you with traffic data in real time.

That worked in some cases. In others, the companies said, "Our data is valuable and others are buying it, so pay us."

We ended up paying ten to twenty cents per vehicle per month. So, a fleet management company that had 50,000 active vehicles got a $5,000 to $10,000 check every month.

Once we got to the level that our traffic was good enough without them, we revisited the deals and ended up with one of three end-game results:

1. The partner agreed to the model of raw data for traffic data exchange.
2. The partner opted to give us a 50 percent discount.
3. The partner decided to terminate the agreement.

The traffic data acquisition model was a springboard for us. We needed it to improve our traffic data at the beginning, but once we got enough users, we didn't need it anymore. Now, this is important: In every part of the journey, you may need different assets and therefore different BD deals. Those that bring users are the hardest.

FIFTY OTHER WAYS IT DIDN'T WORK

I was traveling a lot for Waze, trying to engage those partners for users and data. I could have had a trip with five, six, or even seven meetings with several potential partners and eventually return with nothing.

Sometimes I would get something, but it would yield so little that it wasn't even worth it. Jackpots were rare, but when they did happen, they covered all the misses. Think about BD as scoring from half-court in a basketball game.

There are three ways to look at such "opportunities."

- If you don't try, you are not going to make it.
- If you score, you win.
- You always think the next one is going to be the winner.

Should you decide to try the BD path to bring users, there are two major alternatives:

- Many deals that bring a few users each.
- A few deals that bring many users each.

Always strive for the second one—that's what will truly move the needle.

START-UPS CANNOT HELP EACH OTHER!

Start-ups are all looking for the same thing and, therefore, they don't have much to share. In many cases, you meet another CEO, and it turns out that you are both aiming for the same addressable market. You establish a trusted relationship with the other CEO and you want him to help you to get users. But the other CEO is looking at you and thinking the same way—that you can help *them* get users as well.

Guess what: You don't have enough users in a way that you can promote that other CEO and vice versa. No matter how much you try, you simply have no way to help them, and they don't have the assets to help you.

So don't even think about it!

BRINGING USERS (B2C)

At the end of the day, when we speak about marketing and growth, this is what we have in mind: bringing users. The good news is that, if you figure out this part, you win. The bad news is that it is hard to bring users.

With a high frequency of use, your strategy is simple—invest in user acquisition until your WOM works.

Waze spent little on marketing, but just enough to remain on the first page of the App Store in the navigation category. We did invest in PR to create awareness and bring users.

Moovit spent more on user acquisition until it figured out WOM and SEO (search engine optimization).

There are fifty, maybe even one hundred ways to bring users and it is going to be a journey of failures, trying and trying and trying different things until you find the one that works.

You have to start by answering a simple question: Who are your users and where are they? Because trying to get new users for Waze in a country where there are no drivers with a smartphone is a waste of time (for instance, India in 2010).

If you don't know how to answer that question, then your journey of experiments starts by using promotions for different types of users in various places and watching the results. Once you know who your users are and where they are, then you can start thinking about other tools for running more targeted promotions.

ONLINE

Facebook, Google, Instagram, TikTok, LinkedIn, and Twitter are all platforms that allow you to place an ad or promotion online. Some of the platforms allow you to target your audience. For example, "only parents between the ages of thirty and forty with kids" will get to see your ad.

The most important thing about online promotion is that you can measure results in real time and make necessary changes immediately. So, if I need to figure out whether my target audience is twenty to thirty years old, thirty to forty years old, or forty to fifty years of age, I will know by the end of the day.

For that reason, most start-ups will gravitate toward online promotion, but that doesn't prove this is the best there is in terms of effectiveness, of bringing relevant users, etc.

The good news is that the online channels allow you to fail fast.

The bad news is that they prevent you from thinking outside the box.

Online marketing and the ability to measure results instantly is very addictive; it's easy to forget to check other promotional models.

Social Media

Social media is a special case of bringing users—reaching out to influencers who have a great number of followers. You assume that if they promote your product, their followers will follow, and in reality, some will. How many? I don't know, you don't know, and, therefore, it is worth a try.

OFFLINE

These days, we've nearly forgotten about the offline world, but once you know who and where your users are, offline outreach might end up being more efficient than any other form of promotion. Just think of an offer for "free coffee when you fill your tank" at a gas station. Would a sign half a mile before the gas station work better than a Facebook ad?

PUBLIC RELATIONS

Many people think, "What's the big deal with PR?" You organize a double-page spread article in the *New York Times*, and that's it.

Well, getting there is not easy.

You hire a PR firm, and it will take them three months of effort to try to get you this double-spread exposure. Sometimes even more. But it is not promised that you will get it. In some cases, it doesn't work. You might end up getting into a small column at a much less distributed publication. Or even no exposure at all. Remember: Even if you do get to the *Times*, it is a one-time event.

Having a successful PR machine means that you set your objectives correctly, maintain your course, and realize that it takes time. Ultimately, a good PR campaign may have a lot of impact or influence beyond just downloads.

Our experience shows that PR works in some places and, in others, it is very expensive and less efficient. One of the most important goals of PR is establishing credibility. When people hear about something new, some of them will look it up. If they find only your website and social media, it is one thing. If they find multiple media publications, it is very different.

It all eventually boils down to understanding who the audience is. In general, candidates, partners, governments, and investors rely more on references and, therefore, PR is more important, whereas getting new users may be based on WOM or user acquisition rather than PR.

PR is, at its core, local. In some cases, it may even be hyperlocal. PR may also determine your GTM strategy.

By and large, PR would work better in places where the media is nationwide and less when media is local (like in the US).

Think you can do it on your own? Don't. You will need a PR firm. They are the experts and you're not. Even if you have a very good friend who is an editor in a media group, results rely on *many* of those contacts and not just one person. The PR firm is the one with many relationships with media groups.

ATL—ABOVE THE LINE

An alternative to PR is ATL, which basically means buying traditional media ads (TV, newspaper, etc.). So, if the *New York Times* is not interested in writing a double spread article about your start-up, they are much more likely to agree to run your content in the same size but as an ad—that is, if you can afford to pay for it!

How do you know if spending $X on a TV ad during the Super Bowl is going to yield better results than a double-spread ad run five times or reaching a million users via an ad on Facebook?

Well, you don't . . . unless you try.

However, Super Bowl ads are very expensive and provide just one-time exposure. In order to utilize the ad's effectiveness, you need to build the campaign around it. A double-spread ad is also expensive, and there is no way to do a small-scale experiment. Therefore, most likely, you will try online ads, as you can start by going small scale and adjust accordingly.

This approach still doesn't guarantee that you will get better results, but at least you can try it immediately and at a low cost.

CAC—CUSTOMER ACQUISITION COST

How much does it cost to acquire a user? Over time, you will fine-tune the metric and improve on the results.

In general, CAC refers to direct spending on user acquisition, so the cost of the marketing department or the retainer of your PR agency is not included.

Over time, you will improve your CAC dramatically through trial-and-error experiments.

At the end of the day, you are measuring different marketing methods here, so you can optimize the return, spend less, and bring more relevant users.

The bottom line is equal to the total marketing spent divided by the number of users acquired in a period, including organic growth. Once organic growth becomes exponential (i.e., you gain more users than you churn), you can start lowering the marketing spend.

FTV—FIRST-TIME VALUE

How much value do you generate from a user's first time with your app or service?

- If you're Waze, then this number is close to zero.
- If it is a paid app (say, one that helps users prepare for the GMAT), then this number is the app's net price.
- If this is a pay-per-use app, then the value is from the first time a user makes a payment.

This number is super important, as it will tell you how much you're willing to spend on marketing.

In general, in high-frequency-use services or apps, or a subscription model, this number is less critical because you can calculate the lifetime value (LTV) relatively easily.

But with low-frequency-of-use services and apps, you don't know the LTV; you don't even know if there will *be* a second use. Within a few years, you will know, but you have no idea when you start what the LTV is, and therefore your reference should be first-time value (FTV).

The best example of FTV is in the travel market.

People don't travel that often and, if you get a new user for your new travel guide, you have no idea when this customer is going to show up again, if at all.

Once you figure out this number, if FTV > CAC, keep on spending more on marketing, as you're making money.

The magic number here is three—if you spend $X per active user, and if an active user generates on his or her first use more than $3X, you are on the right track. Essentially, you have found a cash-generating machine. You now need to raise capital to spend more and then figure out if the 3:1 ratio improves or not when it comes to larger numbers.

LTV—LIFETIME VALUE

What's a customer worth over his or her lifetime as a user? In reality, you don't know how long a "lifetime" is with your app or service, but you can estimate it after a year, based on churn.

Essentially, if the annual churn is 33 percent, you can assume that a lifetime for a user of your app is three years. Over time, you will learn the annual spend and the lifetime duration and then you can calculate it more accurately.

Initially, assume it is two to three years for your model, and that once you run with the model for two to three years, you can readjust. These estimates depend on if your user is paying or not, and if you're selling ads or data.

If, however, you've proven FTV/CAC > 3, then go spend. If you don't know, then keep on fine-tuning the business models until the formula fits. The fine-tuning of the models is a journey of multiple experiments.

ORGANIC GROWTH

Organic growth is simple. You do nothing and users come. It is, obviously, the Holy Grail of marketing and is usually attributed to word of mouth. Essentially, organic growth is everything whenever you have no idea of where your users are coming from.

At the end of the day, you measure net adds (new users minus churned users) divided by your total spending on marketing—that's your CAC. If you have a greater number of organic users, then this ratio improves significantly.

MEDIA AGGREGATORS

In many cases, you will find out that, when you need to make multiple experiments, working with a media aggregator is easier.

A media aggregator is a company that deploys a user-acquisition budget across multiple media types. Such a company can deploy budgets on multiple ad platforms concurrently and get you faster initial results.

Eventually, you will need to bring this process in-house, to build the expertise, the know-how, and the ability to scale. A media aggregator will be an awesome starting point, but to scale up, you will need to stop outsourcing this function. (To an extent, it may be the same with other aspects of the business such as legal, finance, etc.)

REFERRAL PROGRAMS

Many apps and services believe in WOM; they try to encourage it by rewarding user referrals. So, if you refer a friend and that person signs up, you may get a reward.

Uber used that method to fund its growth, and it turned out to be pretty successful for them. In some other cases, it turned out to be much less effective.

In general, I don't like referrals—it feels like I'm selling my friends or taking advantage of them. But that's *my* personal perspective.

If WOM is not working well enough, trying to accelerate it with a referral program may work.

SEO—SEARCH ENGINE OPTIMIZATION

SEO is how you get Google and other search engines to place you higher in their search results. In that way, when people search relevant terms on Google, you will be one of the top results.

Moovit used SEO as a powerful tool to bring users. We essentially created a landing page for every possible search of "How to get to . . .".

So, we had "How to get from Times Square to Washington Square," "How to get from X to Y by bus," and "How to get to where I need to go by subway tomorrow at 7 PM."

We created landing pages for every possible combination—anywhere to anywhere at any time.

"Wait a minute," you're probably thinking right about now. "This is millions, if not billions, of landing pages!"

Exactly.

Each one of them leads to a direct specific answer and, in many millions of cases, this is converted into a user downloading the app.

We did the same with several others of my start-ups to generate the best search results.

TNBT OR AGI—THE NEXT BIG THING OR ANOTHER GREAT IDEA

Your user acquisition plan should include the Next Big Thing or Another Great Idea (actually, many of them). Then you will be ready to go into this journey realizing that you will keep on trying

FIFTY WAYS TO BRING YOUR USERS

Once you start to think about your GTM plan and your "bringing users" plan, go into a meeting room with a whiteboard and write on it all the ways you think you are going to acquire those users.

Then, bring in the rest of the management to add their ideas to the list. Keep adding until you have fifty line items on the whiteboard—that is, fifty different ways to bring users. Then start your journey of experiments toward user acquisition.

If you don't have fifty, you're not ready to start.

The idea of fifty is simple: You don't fall in love with one method. You fall in love with the journey until you find the one method that works.

Think of finding a new source of oil.

You may need to drill fifty times, but when you detect any signs of oil, you start to go deeper and deeper. That's the idea here, as well.

At first, the fifty ways are very different, but once you get some initial traction, start to go deeper and deeper.

If it had turned out that for Refundit the best marketing was at the destination airport (to physically hand over to arriving passengers marketing material about the app), then we would have optimized in that direction, approaching potential customers at the baggage claim or after customs or at the taxi stand.

B2B MARKETING

Some years back, I spoke with a VP of marketing and sales of a B2B company, and I asked him what the role of marketing is and what the role of sales is.

"Those who can, sell. Those who can't, that's marketing," he said.

He explained further. "We have built a well-oiled sales machine that generates leads and does sales calls, then qualifies them so the sales executives can try to close deals. Then, we follow up on those leads."

"OK, that's great," I said. "But what's the role of marketing?"

"It 'prettifies the sales material,'" he replied.

I showed him a few ways that marketing can change the whole thing around and bring customers to him. He subsequently implemented many of those.

When we met a year later, this VP shared with me that the company's sales cycles were now way shorter and that he didn't need to call up leads anymore—they were coming to him!

That's the idea—even if you close deals one by one face-to-face, marketing can still do magic. Creating awareness in the market, establishing credibility, creating a way better sales toolkit and customer engagement materials—these and a dozen other ways all lead to at least one of the following:

- shortening the sales cycle
- increasing the addressable market
- qualifying leads
- increasing the likelihood of renewals
- establishing a brand name and claim ownership of a market

IS THERE WOM IN B2B?

Your initial response might be "no," but that's not true.

Imagine that you are a salesperson and your company is using the software application Salesforce. A couple of years later, you move to a different company that is still using Microsoft Excel. You immediately become a promoter of Salesforce. That's an example of WOM.

WOM takes longer and, in many cases, you've already worked on your GTM plan and your customer acquisition plan. But then you realize that you're starting to get calls from prospective customers that you didn't even reach out to yet, all from WOM.

In developer communities, this happens faster for multiple reasons, including that they are more connected and sharing as they move around more. For other apps and products, it can take a while, but once you get there, it is a flywheel that makes you the market leader.

MARKETING ORGANIZATION

Is there a recipe for building the right marketing organization? It depends on your objectives.

If you bring in a CMO early on to figure out market-product-price, then it is essentially a one-person show. This person may be your product marketing lead, but he or she still has to be a marketer, understanding users and having experience in similar and better markets.

Your CMO is *not* an outbound marketing person, a PR executive, a marcom (marketing communication) expert, or an online media buyer.

If you are looking for someone to bring users, start with someone who can orchestrate all those functions (outbound marketing, PR, marcom, online), and in the interview ask the candidate to generate fifty ways to bring users. If the candidate succeeds, tell them to start.

If your focus is on online user acquisition, bring on someone who has done that before.

Bottom line: Your first person *must* be hands-on—someone who can do the work without hiring more people.

STARTIPS

- There are at least fifty ways to bring your users—don't start the journey before you line up a list of experiments.

- Measure—If you don't measure marketing effectiveness, how will you know what's working and what isn't?

- Simply start—This journey, while it is hard, has short time intervals between experiments. So, simply start your marketing experiments ASAP.

- Know when to bring a CMO—When you start your company, you need someone to lead product-market-price strategy. At a later phase, when it is time to grow, that same person may not be the right one. Hire the person who can generate the "fifty ways to bring users" strategy.

- A sales-focused organization needs marketing to reduce sales cycles and to increase TAM (total addressable market).

Chapter 11

GO GLOBAL

There are more smartphones in India than in the US. In fact, there are more than double.

While editing this book, we removed this chapter multiple times and brought it back again an equal number of times. The final verdict was to keep it, and there is a simple reason for it. The perspective this chapter offers for when you need to figure out your going-global strategy could be valuable for you and perhaps nontrivial. I hope you will agree with me.

"Going global" as a strategy is dependent on where you start. If your company is based in the US, you may become a market leader long before you even think about the global market. If you start in a small place (like Israel, Estonia, or Sweden), your backyard market is too small and therefore you have to think about going global very, very early in your journey.

The third option is that you start in a large market like Russia, Japan, Germany, India, or Brazil and you spend too long in this market establishing your local leadership. Then, after many years, you decide you want to become global. In this case, the default won't work; you will need to define a different strategy.

In this chapter, we will discuss the ways you can become a global market leader. For that, you will need to capture multiple key markets.

This chapter will also help you figure out *where* to go, *when* to go, and *how* to go there. If your home base is a small country, then you should be thinking global before you even start. Qualify the problem in other markets, as well; think about the PMF you would need to achieve in your small country, then fine-tune that for a larger market.

Israel is a very small place, about the size and population of Massachusetts (with more start-ups). One of the critical learnings in Israel is that no VC will invest if your market is only Israel. Your ability to build a successful and large company, if you only serve the Israeli market, is slim. And it will be the same for Sweden, Estonia, the Netherlands, etc. If your market is small, you have to think global from the first day.

The question, then, is: *Where is your market?*

TOP MARKETS

We tend to think about the top markets as being the US, China, Japan, Germany, and the UK, but there are actually more (and easier) markets to win.

Think of the top internet apps or services and ask yourself, "Who are the top markets in terms of usage?" If you answered the US, you would be, in general, correct, but what about numbers two, three, and four?

The following might change over the years, but the top five markets are nearly always the same.

- Google: the US and then Brazil, India, and the UK
- YouTube: US and then Russia, Brazil, and Japan
- Facebook: US and then Vietnam, Brazil, and UK
- WhatsApp: Brazil and then India, Mexico, and Indonesia
- Instagram: US, Brazil, Russia, and Italy
- Waze: US, France, and Brazil

- Moovit: Brazil, Turkey, Italy, and US
- Uber: US, Brazil, Mexico, and UK

Got the picture?

There are some countries here that probably didn't even cross your mind as a target for expansion. But if you think about it, there are 210 million people in Brazil, 1.3 billion in India, 275 million in Indonesia, and 115 million in Mexico—these are not small countries! There are more vehicles in Brazil than there are in the UK, France, Italy, and even Germany.

SMALL PLACES VERSUS LARGE ONES

There is a big difference between the cultures of small countries and large ones. If I needed to define that difference in one word, it would be "adaptability."

In order to do business, small countries need to adapt to large places.

Large places, by contrast, can be nearly self-sufficient in terms of business and therefore don't need to adapt to the rest of the world; the rest of the world is more likely to adapt to them.

The result is nearly always the same: Start-ups that were born in a small place figure out their globalization early . . . and for good reason.

If you live in a country with a small market, as soon as you figure out PMF, or even before you've completed it, you need to go to a new and larger market.

If you are in a large market, say the US, you start in your hometown, then you go to San Francisco, and then build one metro area at a time.

Alternatively, if you're nationwide, then the entire nation is your "hometown."

In the next five years, every time you ask yourself, "Where should I invest now?" the answer should be domestic. Only then can you start to think about other places.

However, if you're in Brazil and you launch in São Paulo, and then think about Rio de Janeiro, Belo Horizonte, Brasília, Salvador, Fortaleza, and Curitiba as your next markets, the time that it would take you to create a market leadership position in Brazil is going to be about five years. Trying to figure out global market leadership then is going to be very challenging. Reaching regional leadership in Latin America is probably doable, but after five years, going from Brazil to the US or Europe is going to be next to impossible.

WHEN TO GO?

If you are coming from a small place and you aim to become a global market leader, then after two to three product iterations, even when it is not good enough yet (but it's starting to look like it is going to get good enough), your learning and improvement will become much more significant in the *large* target market and not with more iterations in your small home market.

Your objective is now to get to PMF in that target market.

If you are in the US or China, however, you only need to think about going global once you've figured out PMF at home. It's more likely you will start your "going global" journey only after you figure out growth or your business model.

The challenge is when you are coming from another large country, say Germany, Brazil, Mexico, Russia, India, Indonesia, Japan, the UK, France, etc. In this case, very often when you are ready to go global, it may be too late to become a global leader. Your journey of figuring out PMF in your home market, and then giving yourself time to grow at home and become a market leader in your home country, is on average a five-year journey.

Going global at this point becomes an issue, as you may face fierce competition already established in the target markets, and you will be competing uphill against either local or global players. It is hard to find global market leaders in the tech space that started in those large countries. In most cases, when they decided to grow globally, it was already too late to become a global market leader.

WHAT IF YOU DON'T?

If you don't go global early enough, you may miss the opportunity to become a global market leader.

There are a few reasons why you may miss that opportunity.

- **DNA**—The DNA of your company is local, the key leaders are local, you think like a local, and, therefore, becoming global requires a leap in your thought process. And in particular, you may need to replace some of the management, which is always hard. It requires you to place the expansion to other countries as a top priority. If you don't take this seriously and the entire management team is local, it will be very hard to create significant traction.

- **The next country**—If you are already five to six years old as an organization focused on the local market—say, Germany—and you now decide to go to other countries, what target country should you choose to go to? The easiest markets to win will be Austria, Switzerland, and the Czech Republic. If you started in Vietnam, then Thailand, Cambodia, and the Philippines would be the easy choices. All those will increase the market and will grow the company. They will *not* bring you any closer to becoming a market leader, unfortunately.

- **M&A strategy**—If you started in a major country, you may have spent a long journey becoming a market leader in your place of origin, and your strategy for going global is through mergers and acquisitions (M&A). If you're Groupon, for example, it would be very easy to acquire similar activities locally and then to expand globally through them, where each one of them already demonstrates its ability to become a local market leader.

WHERE TO GO

I'm going to let you in on my secret strategy: **Choose a significant market that is easy to win**. Essentially, think of all the things that make it easier to win in the top twenty countries in terms of GDP—things like the effectiveness of PR, how big the pain is, how social/connected the market is, etc.

On the flip side, think about factors that make it harder to win a market, such as competitiveness (are there any competitors and what's their position in the market?), and how expensive the CAC (customer acquisition cost) is.

The results are likely to suggest the US and China as tier one in terms of the size of the opportunity. But these countries are, at the same time, the hardest to win. PR doesn't work (or it costs a lot if you want to win), and user acquisition is very expensive since the market is highly competitive.

The UK and Japan will be the second hardest to win. If you can succeed there, though, they will both be awesome references for investors.

Brazil, Mexico, Italy, Spain, Turkey, and Indonesia may be easier to win. Plus, they are large markets by themselves. PR works in these countries, the markets are socially connected and, usually, there is little to no competition. In addition, the CAC is likely to be much lower.

Now, that's a winning formula!

One of my start-ups had figured out PMF relatively fast. The pain they were addressing was pretty significant and the value was clear.

When we decided to go to other markets, we had a lot of debate about where we should turn to next. I was a strong supporter of Mexico, Brazil, Italy, and Spain, but the team insisted on the UK, saying that we didn't have enough funding to go after the US (which is nearly always the most significant market), but the UK would be cheaper and doable.

I suggested the CEO speak with other CEOs.

"Where should I go globally?" the CEO of the company asked Nir, CEO of Moovit. In other words, "How did you decide where to go?"

"I went to Brazil, Mexico, Italy, Spain, and the UK at the same time and it was the right decision," Nir told him. "We ended up with four of those being successful. We were unsuccessful in the UK because there were some particularly strong competitors, but we won the others big-time because there was no competition, PR was successful, and our user acquisition campaigns worked well."

As of the time of writing this book, Brazil and Italy are still number one and number three, respectively, in terms of usage for Moovit.

Despite the advice he received, the CEO went back to his team and they decided on the UK. Partly, this was because of the language (it's easier for Israelis to work in English-speaking territories), and partly because this is what the investors wanted to hear.

They were, sadly, unsuccessful in the UK. As a result, they had a hard time raising capital (since they had no traction outside of Israel). When the company eventually raised some capital, it went back to Brazil and Mexico, and had much more success.

Another perspective to keep in mind is funding. If you're already successful in the US and have raised tons of money, then going to the UK is not a bad idea. London is one flight away from multiple cities in the US, and they do speak the same language.

The UK is probably five to ten times more expensive to get to the same number of users than Brazil, Mexico, Turkey, Indonesia, etc., but you will be winning a market that is hard to win—not just for you, for everyone.

Your go-to-market strategy is also based on your funding:

- The poor start-up formula: Go to a significant country where it is easy to win.
- The rich start-up formula: Go to a country that will make the biggest impact and serve as a stellar reference.

Regardless of where your start-up fits, don't forget that you must make mistakes fast. That means go in parallel to several countries with the underlying assumption that there are no market specifics (like regulation or infrastructure) to trip you up.

HOW TO GO?

The answer here is rather simple—boots on the ground and a founder to support them.

The boots on the ground can be a local partner, one that can commit a considerable effort into this activity. You can also hire a country manager whose task is to make the company successful in that country's market.

A joint venture (JV), on the other hand, is a *bad* idea. If you want to work with a local company, there should be two critical elements:

- You are important to the local partner, so they really want you to succeed; it's not just another experiment for them.
- Make sure that you can walk away if the partnership doesn't work and that you have the ability to try again in the same market with a different partner or strategy.

While the idea of sharing success and effort is good, the structure of a JV can be very problematic.

First of all, there is no way out of the structure. It is a company owned by two shareholders and, in the case of disagreements, you will end up with a deadlock. No one can do without the other and yet neither party wants the relationship to last.

The second reason is even more problematic. JVs, by definition, are inefficient—sometimes as bad as nonprofit organizations. The JV management has less incentive to create shareholder value as they are not shareholders, and the local CEO of the JV is much closer to the local shareholders than he or she is to you.

This creates a situation where the JV tends to spend more money than needed. That's what happens in organizations where their highest-priority objective is to stay alive.

The advantages of a JV can be easily created in an agreement that regulates a few critical elements:

- Who's doing what? For example, the local partner provides local support and marketing efforts, while your start-up provides the system and localization.
- What's the value created by being together and how is it split? For example, will it be 50/50 on the revenues? Something different? Why?

- Termination. What if you don't want to do business together any-more? How do you terminate? Sometimes it is with a long (very long) notice period, and in other cases with termination fees. Termination may be associated with objectives, so if objectives are not met, the termination is considered "at will."
- Budget. Who is going to spend how much, and on what?

In the example above, we ended up with two options—either use my employee as a country manager and build the local activity from scratch, or establish a local partnership agreement.

But which one?

Like many other experiments in your journey, you will have to try and see. You should start the search for a local partner and a country manager at the same time, and go with the first one you find.

In many cases, you may end up with both!

CHALLENGING MARKETS

Some years back, one of my CEOs said that we should be going to China. I asked him why.

"The market is huge!" he said.

"You're right, the market is huge," I replied. "But it also requires focus and a lot of attention."

We agreed that this was the case, but the question was: What does that really mean? To which I answered, "Are you or your cofounder going to be one hundred percent in China for the next twelve to eighteen months?"

The other cofounder was technical and not business oriented, so obvi-ously it would be impossible for the company and for him to relocate, as he is needed close to the development team. Also, going global requires business capabilities rather than technical ones.

The CEO's answer was simple.

"I cannot dedicate one hundred percent of my time and attention to China at this phase," he told me. "We still have a lot to do here."

My reply was simple, too.

"Then you are not ready for China."

If your start-up begins in Israel, most likely your major market and the most lucrative one will be the US. If this is the case, and you are already at PMF in Israel, then the CEO or one of the founders should relocate to the US to make the company a success there.

Assume a lot of funding will be required.

As a rule of thumb, you would need $10 million or so to create enough traction that will allow you to raise additional capital in the US.

If, however, you are a US-based start-up, the first market is obvious: the US. The global question will only become relevant for you many years down the road.

These four markets (the US, China, Japan, and the UK) are the most challenging for a few reasons.

- They are large and influential and, as such, they are the most attractive markets for many companies.
- Their attractiveness results in a lot of competition with a high customer acquisition cost.
- All of the marketing tools are expensive. On top of that, some markets will require a very different cultural approach.

The UK is in a very unique position. Most American-based start-ups, when it is time for them to go global, automatically choose the UK and, in most cases, this is after establishing a major position in the US market and therefore raising significant funds. As a result, their willingness to spend on capturing this market will be high.

The bottom line is, if you're a small start-up looking for your first key market, going to the UK will see you face off against the local competition and, much more fiercely, with US-based competition that is more mature and well-funded enough to spend a lot on marketing.

THE WORLD

Here's a very simplistic way to abstract the world: Look at GDP per capita and assume similar business/consumer behavior in like-minded countries. Then go and look for other similarities, such as social and cultural behavior. Finally, find your specific total addressable market (TAM).

You can get all those figures from the US government's *World Factbook*, readily findable online via a Google search.

Now, create a list of the top thirty countries by GDP. This is likely to start with the US, China, India, Japan, and Germany and, following that, Russia, Indonesia, Brazil, the UK, and France.

The next ten on the list will include countries like Italy, Spain, Mexico, Turkey, South Korea, Canada, and Poland.

While some of the countries may be surprising, you can eliminate names from the list for any reason (for example, countries that are very hard to become successful in or countries where you don't want to go).

Keep your research on the already-narrowed list in terms of TAM (size in customers, not in money), competition, the existence of the problem you're trying to solve there, etc.

When you've done all that, pick three to five countries to start.

In some cases, you may try online user acquisition to see if a particular country is relevant. Pick those where user acquisition is inexpensive. Maybe see if your network can find a local partner who can investigate further for you and who can do enough research to satisfy your gut feeling—the same as you did when you started the journey. It should be just enough so that you have conviction about which places would work.

Then start focusing on those three to five countries in parallel.

THE DIFFERENCE BETWEEN UBER AND LYFT

As I write this, Uber's market cap is about $90 billion and Lyft's is about $19 billion. If you live in New York City, you are probably using both apps. If you see the price and wait time on one is high, you try the other.

Yet, if you try to hail a Lyft in São Paulo, there isn't one. Nor is Lyft in Paris or Mexico City. Uber is global; Lyft is domestic.

If you want to be the market leader, you must think global.

STARTIPS

- The formula—Think of all relevant, significant markets and pick those that are easy to win and that suffer severely from the problem you're trying to address. You want a market where the competition is nearly nonexistent and the customer acquisition costs are low.

- Pick a big market—In the US, if you can be successful in either San Francisco or New York City, you are on the right path to win the market. You may decide to start in a smaller place, but rather quickly you will need to go nationwide or to a major market.

- Work concurrently—Think of the top markets you're trying to win and launch a few at the same time. Consider India, Brazil, Indonesia, Mexico, Italy, Spain, Turkey, and France.

- Similar countries—Outline comparisons between countries using *very* few criteria.

Chapter 12

CRISIS MANAGEMENT— SURVIVAL MODE

In any moment of decision, the best thing you can do is the right thing, the next best thing is the wrong thing, and the worst thing you can do is nothing.

—Theodore Roosevelt, twenty-sixth US president

Ⅰn the years to come, we will ask ourselves: How did we so easily give up our freedom? In 2020, when the COVID-19 pandemic started, we were forced to give up our freedom. In many countries, governments were overreacting, and people around the world paid with their freedom. Looking back at the height of the COVID crisis, for many it was a clear disaster, with both people and businesses dying.

That was not all, either.

After the COVID-19 crisis ended, we had inflation and a shortage in supplies, which were partially derivatives of the pandemic. That was quickly followed by the war in Ukraine, which provided even more fuel for inflation, an increased interest rate, and, as a result, a bearish market. Then, on October 7, 2023, the biggest terror attack ever on Israel sparked a new and intense war.

Some of my start-ups suffered significantly from broad COVID-19 crisis implications. One of them died and closed, two nearly died but recovered, and one died a few years later of what I'll call "COVID complications."

We live in times that seem to be the busiest ever in terms of external events creating a series of crises for businesses and, in particular, start-ups. This additional chapter is all about managing start-ups in crisis.

When I started to write *Fall in Love with the Problem, Not the Solution*, we were at the beginning of the COVID-19 crisis. For parts of 2020 and 2021, my family and I were closed in at home, sometimes under strict lockdown. I couldn't go anywhere, but there was a silver lining: this allowed me the time to work on the book.

The series of events since 2020 and the high frequency of them, with many businesses and start-ups paying a heavy price—among them, some of my start-ups—brought me to the understanding that, although throughout the book I state that building a start-up is a journey of failure, we didn't discuss major and global crises; they deserve a separate discussion. That is the aim of this chapter.

DECLARING TIME OF DEATH

A crisis is a threat and, in some cases, a fatal one, especially for start-ups. A human being will be declared dead if the heart stops beating or if there is no oxygen to the brain. For a company, it is simpler: a company will die when it runs out of money and is unable to pay its bills.

A company will run out of cash if it is not profitable and is unable to raise additional funds. A crisis may be a reason for either one of those, but in your journey of building a start-up, you will run into multiple times of being "nearly dead."

In that sense, if you're unable to raise capital or bring your company to profitability, then you will die, regardless of whether there is a crisis out there or not. The fact that everyone suffers from the same situation or constraints has no relevance to you as a start-up. You need to address your specific problems in the best possible way.

In a crisis that impacts you, even if it is just about fundraising, your mindset should change from "optimization mode" into "survival mode." You should, for example, take a very unfavorable investment deal if there is one, regardless of how bad it is.

In this chapter, I will bring stories from my start-ups. Some of them were able to overcome a major crisis and got stronger. Others, unfortunately, did not survive.

ORDERCHAT: A MARKET DISAPPEARING OVERNIGHT CRISIS

OrderChat, founded in 2017, solved the frustration of making restaurant reservations through a simple chat interface. The company's magic was that they had a first-generation AI (artificial intelligence) chatbot. On one side was the customer who wants to complete the reservation simply and quickly. On the other side was the restaurant. No integration with any restaurant was required, resulting in an unlimited addressable market. That allowed OrderChat, in a relatively short amount of time, to grow fast and have higher coverage than anyone else in the market.

The company's motto was "60-second chat to find and book a table at any restaurant in the world." For perspective, it took OpenTable (the global market leader in the reservations space) around seven years to reach three thousand served restaurants, whereas it took OrderChat just two years to reach this goal, based on their zero-integration approach and innovative technology.

By 2020, OrderChat had reached a good PMF, with a high user retention rate and an LTV/CAC ratio greater than three.

However, when COVID started, restaurants were either shut down or unable to host customers in person. As a result, what looked like a very promising value proposition disappeared in no time. On top of that, we were close to the end of our cash. Even ongoing discussions we had with investors ended up with "let's wait and see." Sadly, we took the decision to shut down, as we were running out of cash, restaurants were not coming back, and neither were investors.

It was a sad ending to a service that had very high retention and satisfaction with a rather straightforward and quick solution. We simply did not have enough run rate to pivot. We had a user base that liked us, but our service was no longer relevant as the restaurant industry was paralyzed for a long time. Indeed, it took another two years for people to go back to socializing while dining outside of their homes.

Looking back, we entered the crisis with not enough cash, and with traction in just one geography and with a single market (restaurants). This was a case of a "market disappearing overnight" crisis.

I still run into people who say, "We truly loved it. Any chance to bring it back?"

Thank you, Alon Schwartzman, cofounder and CEO of OrderChat, for running the company, for the journey, the opportunity, and the friendship.

WESKI: FROM NEARLY DYING TO PROFITABILITY THROUGH MOST EXTREME ROLLER COASTER

WeSki has a more complex story. The good news first: The company is doing amazingly well nowadays. WeSki has become "the Booking.com for ski vacations," allowing people to build their trip quickly and effortlessly and to find the deal that best suits them.

Building a ski vacation is complex. It is no way similar to ordering flights and accommodations. In an urban vacation, getting from the airport to the city center is easy. In a ski vacation, it might entail a three-hour drive and with very limited transportation.

In an urban area, if I had told you the hotel is great and that it is five hundred feet away from the main attraction, it would sound like an excellent location. In a ski village, what's most important is not the distance, but the difference in elevation, as well as other elements such as a ski pass, ski rental options, etc.

I'm an avid skier, and I've built nearly one hundred ski vacations. Nevertheless, even with all the experience I have, it will still take me hours to reserve the next trip.

In March 2020, all ski resorts in Europe shut down for foreign visitors. For WeSki, the crisis started when the company's team had to handle one hundred times more cancellations in one day than usual. That's when we realized that the season for us had ended in an instant and, while we had been well on our way to reaching a profitable season, we ended by losing money—and a fairly large amount, too.

We descended into a "We are going to die" attitude. We had very little cash in the bank and this season was supposed to be profitable. There was no dialogue with investors and the shutting down of ski resorts in mid-season sounded like a death sentence to us.

We tried to reach out to our existing investors, many of whom were strategic investors, coming from the travel business, but unsurprisingly, they had bigger issues to deal with, as this event was dramatic to the entire industry.

Just think about it: you are a hotel chain, COVID-19 has just started, and one of your start-ups is asking for more money. Our crisis looked like peanuts by comparison. We reached out to a fund set up by the Israeli government, but they were also unable to help. Their number one criterion was to show a major decrease in revenues compared to the previous year. Being a start-up at a growth stage, growing at 3x year-over-year, comparing our revenue to the previous year didn't reflect the blow we received in March 2020. It was unclear how long the situation would last, but for WeSki, it became clear that we had lost the entire season.

At that point, it was time to decide. No one from the outside was going to get us out of the near-death situation. It was only up to us!

The decision was taken on several levels, with the following underlying assumptions:

- This season is dead.
- Next season—we don't know, so we assumed it was dead as well.
- We therefore needed enough cash to survive until November 2022, when we would start generating revenues for the 2022–2023 ski season.

Based on these assumptions, we reduced our workforce dramatically. The founders gave up 100 percent of their pay (for the time being), and we had to raise money to last for two-and-a-half years, until November 2022. Only then did the company succeed in getting back on track and renewing its sales activity.

We narrowed down the problems.

1. There was COVID out there.
2. We didn't even know if there would be a 2021 season.
3. We had another major weight of a "SAFE agreement."

SAFE stands for "Simple Agreement Future Equity." It's similar to a convertible note or a convertible loan agreement, without the loan part—investors' money will be converted, at the next funding round, into the same type of shares as new investors in the round; often, there will be a discount on the price per share. In a way, SAFE serves as a kind of bridge loan, providing a solution for an interim investment between rounds when you need additional cash to get there.

The advantage of a SAFE or a convertible note is its simplicity and the lever it provides—you get more cash to reach a major milestone. The disadvantage is when you don't get to the major milestone or if there's a crisis that makes the SAFE a weight rather than a lever.

WeSki raised money through a SAFE mechanism, with the vision that the 2020 season was going to be profitable and afterward we would be able to raise a large funding round.

The challenge is that SAFE is very simple and allows you to get more and more investors to join with the same terms, so you may end up with a fairly large SAFE that needs to be converted in the next round. In our case, the SAFE was pretty big when compared to the amount of money that we needed to raise to survive.

Just think of the following example: You've raised a seed round and are making good progress but not enough yet for an A round. Now, you're raising $2 million in SAFE with a discount from the next round, and you get a term sheet for a $20 million A round.

In this case, the SAFE is a wash. It is about 10 percent of the round. But if you keep on bringing more and more SAFE investments, say for a total of $10 million, and you still don't have enough progress to raise a hefty round, now you have to find an investor that is willing to invest in a "Seed+" round of $5 million.

The problem is that, with the conversion of the SAFE funding, the new investor is not even the majority of the round. This is the simpler problem; a more significant issue is that the new investors may suggest investing $5 million at a $20 million pre-money valuation, with the perception that they are going to hold about 20 percent of the company after the round.

The reality is there is $10 million in SAFE being converted with a discount. So, the post-money valuation is not $25 million, but close to $40 million. Therefore, the new investor, rather than having a 20 percent stake, will end up with way less. In other words, there is a weight of more than $10 million for this round. Once the new investors realize it, they might cool off and ask you to convert the SAFE before they invest, which is going to be an issue in itself.

The state of things at WeSki went like this: We realized that this was going to be a major down round, because otherwise no one would invest, and it was going to be next to impossible to raise money from external investors.

We figured out that we needed to do a "pay-to-play"—that's a way to brutally encourage existing investors to further invest in the company; otherwise, they would lose all or most of their value. "If you want to play, then you have to pay."

Given the status of the travel market at this phase in the pandemic, I told Yotam Idan, the CEO, that while I was fully supportive and would invest personally, at the same time, I believed there was less than a 50 percent chance that we would be able to pull it off.

And then . . . Yotam pulled it off.

It was like extracting multiple rabbits out of a hat. First, he told the SAFE holders that, even though we had promised them something, we were going to change the terms of the SAFE. Then, he approached the existing investors, telling them they could either invest or get diluted to a very small holding position (or else the entire company would die).

Yotam was able to raise money, mainly from the existing investors, and was able to keep WeSki alive until the company hit profitability in the 2023–2024 skiing season. It was not easy. There were many sleepless nights for the team and they started to grow grey hair.

During this period, until Yotam got it, we held multiple meetings (mostly in my kitchen) with the leadership team (Yotam Idan, the CEO; David Benzimra, the COO; and Pavel Elkind, the CTO). When we spoke about product development, Pavel would remind us that "the entire R&D team is right here." He was right in an ironic sense: Pavel was the entire R&D team for the "COVID-19 season," David was the entire operations team, and the entire company was down to just a handful of people.

Thank you, Yotam, and your amazing team, for guiding us out of the woods. While the verdict is still out, WeSki appears to be on the slopes toward a final, successful run.

"PAY-TO-PLAY"

What is a severe down round? What is the impact of a "pay-to-play" approach? Think of the cap table of a company. For the sake of the discussion, let's say that 30 percent of the company's shares are owned by the founders, 10 percent by the employees through different types of employee equity incentive plans, and 60 percent by the investors. Let's also assume there are six investors with 10 percent each.

The new down round I am envisioning here looks to raise $2 million at a $500,000 pre-money valuation. The post-money valuation is now $2.5 million. So, the new investors will have 80 percent of the company, while the rest of the shareholders (those who had previously invested) have 20 percent altogether. That means that the employees' portion is reduced to just 2 percent instead of the 10 percent that was there before. That's certainly not enough to keep them committed to the journey, especially with the new (low) salaries and a high level of uncertainty.

This turns out to be even more significant when you think of the founders: Their 30 percent is now down to about 6 percent, and this is only the beginning of their journey. We have to allocate a lot more for the founders and employees.

We came up with a new plan that allocated 30 percent for founders and employees, 68 percent for new shares (those who "pay-to-play"), and 2 percent for previous shareholders who choose not to participate in the new round—that is, they don't pay and therefore don't play. The idea was to encourage them to participate and save the company from death.

If you are an investor and participate, you'll get diluted by about 30 percent (the allocation for new equity for founders and employees). If you don't participate, you'll get diluted by about 98 percent, so that your 10 percent turns into 0.2 percent.

That "pay-to-play" magic (forcing nearly everyone to participate) is a one-trick pony. It will usually work a single time; you will not get investors' collaboration again in the future. They will simply lose faith in you and in your ability to recover their losses.

FROM "ALMOST DEAD" TO BACK IN THE AIR

This story is about another start-up in which I am involved, operating in the travel industry, that was severely impacted by the pandemic.

Up until March 2020, the start-up was doing well and was funded. However, when people were in quarantine, no one was flying. I recall that when I did travel, I was nearly the only one at the airport and my taxi driver for the last fifteen years told me that I was his only client for that month.

At the time, no one had any idea how long the COVID-19 crisis would last, but soon everyone realized that this was going to be much longer than anyone had imagined. We would have to adjust to the new reality. The company had to place most of its staff on "unpaid vacation" status, which was partially funded by the government, but we needed more money to continue.

We ended up with an even more severe down round (compared to the previous example): a 100:1 dilution factor. So, if you had 5 percent of the company beforehand, you would end up with five basis points. That round was led by an external investor, while the existing investors that did not participate were diluted to close to zero.

Trust me, I can share dozens of pages of roller-coaster stories—around my companies, COVID, and fundraising during this period—but I think you get the picture.

All that being said, this company continued to add clients and develop its product in a way that, when life went back to normal, it enjoyed an even bigger client base.

Thank you to the never-give-up CEO and the team for taking us through multiple "almost died" scenarios and putting us on the track to being successful despite the severe crisis.

At the end of the day, founding CEOs get used to this "almost die" status and, throughout the journey, they all face it multiple times. That's why "never giving up" is probably the most significant behavior a successful start-up CEO should own.

REFUNDIT: DIED DUE TO "COVID COMPLICATIONS"

Refundit dealt with the frustration of tax-free shopping. The company was operational in a couple of smaller countries in Europe before COVID. When COVID came calling, there were no travelers into Europe, nothing at all, nada. The company was well funded, so we decided we were going into hibernation mode, reducing the team to very few people, with the intention to reignite when we could, and cutting the burn rate to a level that would give us a very long run rate.

We were stuck in hibernation for a couple of years and then, when we were ready to try to reignite, we discovered that all of the ongoing dialogues we had with different tax authorities in Europe needed to restart, as well.

After a couple more years of trying to reengage different countries in Europe into our hassle-free tax refund model, we were approaching the end of cash on one hand and increased frustration amongst the team derived from the no-progress status on the other hand.

We eventually decided to shut down the company.

The problem we were addressing was still there, but I didn't want another journey that relied on government regulations or decision-making. They are not good at it, and in too many cases throughout my entrepreneurial journey, they obstruct innovation.

I call this "Died due to COVID complications." Thank you, Ziv Tirosh, for the amazing journey, excitement, and passion to make an impact.

THE IMPACT OF BEARISH MARKETS ON EARLY-STAGE START-UPS

Let's move beyond the physical impact of COVID.

- What about inflation and interest rates?
- What about the escalation of the war in Ukraine in 2022? (At the time of writing this chapter, this had been ongoing for more than two years already.)
- What about supply chain limitations and a bearish market?

At the end of the day, a company dies if it runs out of cash, which, as I noted above, can happen if it is either not profitable or cannot raise capital to continue operating. Add to that the 2008 subprime mortgage crisis and the dot-com crisis of 2000 and you end up with a very simple realization: Crises make fundraising harder—and for a very good reason. Uncertainty drives investors away. Their appetite for risk decreases and the result is that their willingness to invest is much lower. Therefore, the number of deals decreases. Getting funded becomes harder and companies have to be more attractive than usual to investors.

Let me demonstrate this concept with the 2022 bearish market. It started in 2021 and ended with an all-time high in the S&P 500 index. Within a year, the market went up by about 30 percent, people got richer, and their risk appetite became higher.

At the same time, the interest rate was close to zero, which meant there were no real alternatives in which to invest money. Then, 2022 started with a combination of events: the war in Ukraine, the supply chain crisis, and inflation, all of which led to increasing interest rates and a bearish market.

As a side note, 2021 was also a year of "money for nothing," which drove inflation. There were two main sources of this money for nothing: the government poured money into the public during the height of the COVID-19 pandemic, and the S&P's dramatic rise drove spending up. Demand increased, prices went up, and we all got the result: inflation.

The mindset of an individual investor can shift very quickly, from an appetite for risk to being more conservative. The bearish market of those years eliminated a good chunk of the profit that many investors planned to invest in start-ups. The interest rate got to a level that they could get 6 percent risk-free. All those reasons changed the thinking of most investors and, rather than looking for high-risk, high-return investments, they sought out more solid, safe alternatives.

The impact on the market was even more dramatic.

Having the S&P down meant no IPOs were on the horizon, so companies that planned on going public had to wait, perhaps two to three years. In this situation, the only remaining alternative for those "almost ready to go public companies" was getting further investments from existing investors.

The implication of these changes was fewer resources for investment allocation in earlier-stage start-ups and less money for new investments. This ripple effect made the earlier-stage companies even less attractive than companies that had already demonstrated some traction or that had figured out their product-market fit (PMF). But no matter the reason, all valuations ended up way lower.

The challenge here is that it can take two to three years to recover and such cycles can last for about ten years on average. The start-up side needs time to adjust. Their belief that they can get high (hyperinflated) valuations needs to be readjusted, and this takes time. This cycle has occurred similarly in all bearish market cycles—in 2022, in 2008, in 2000, and in 1984.

The significance for a start-up will always be the same—it becomes harder to raise capital. In chapter 5a—"Ride the Fundraising Roller Coaster"— I described raising money as a roller coaster in the dark. In a bearish market, it is even darker. Raising funds will be at less favorable terms, will take longer, and you will hear more noes. The general state of mind of investors will be, "Let's wait and see," which can be extremely frustrating for entrepreneurs rushing to realize their visions.

For VCs, it is even more frustrating. Just imagine the following.

First, some of their perceived amazing investments at 2021 valuations just raised a down round and the investors have lost money (book value). Then, it is harder for their existing portfolio companies to raise capital. As some VCs are committed to helping their portfolio firms, they therefore refrain from making new investments.

In that situation, if you are an entrepreneur looking for your first round of investment, the odds are not in your favor, but it was hard anyhow. Statistically, even without a global or local crisis, only about 15 percent of start-ups will get funded. Go back to chapter 5a to increase your likelihood of becoming one of those 15 percent.

FIBO: A CHANGE IN REGULATIONS CREATES ITS OWN CRISIS

The story of Fibo is a different one, yet still relevant.

Fibo allowed people to file their tax returns in a very simple way. When we started, we realized that tax returns are always complex and often very expensive to file. We decided that we would make it easy and defined that as "filing in less than five minutes." We ended up with "filing in three minutes," which was even more amazing.

People loved the service. We launched it in Israel where filing taxes is not mandatory and therefore most people don't file as they find it too complex. That results in them losing out on significant sums of money they are entitled to as part of their tax returns.

Once we had simplified the process, the number of people who filed their tax returns in Israel increased by 25 percent from August 2021 to the same time period in 2022. Ninety percent of the increase originated from Fibo users—this created more work for the tax authorities, which now had to review more filing. The additional work drove them to shut us down.

For me, this was my biggest frustration. We had identified a problem worth solving, had assembled an amazing team led by CEO Roi Kimche (with whom I would love to build another start-up), had figured out our PMF (returning users), had developed a solid business model (you pay only once you get a return), had figured out growth, and had a 15:1 ratio of value to the company vs. users' acquisition cost. We had nabbed a 20 percent share of the market in just a year . . . and then got shut down by the authorities!

The company was on the verge of being profitable with nearly no cash reserve, but we hadn't demonstrated any traction outside of Israel yet. Therefore, we had to start from scratch should we want to go elsewhere. While that was something we wanted very much, at this stage in the company, none of us wanted to deal with tax authorities abroad.

This example has nothing to do with COVID, the Ukraine war, not even with the bearish market, and certainly not with inflation or interest rates. Still, it's an example of death due to an external reason.

OTHERS IMPACTED BY A CRISIS AT THE SAME TIME IS OF NO SIGNIFICANCE TO YOU

Pick your crisis: COVID-19, a war, a bearish market, not figuring out PMF, the inability to reach profitability on time, or simply the hardships of the journey. Does the reason for the crisis make a difference?

I would claim the fact that the market is unfavorable, or that it is hard to raise money for everyone, not just your company, doesn't matter at all. The fact that other people also suffer from the same problems is of no importance. It is *your* responsibility to solve *your* problems, whether it is harder due to external reasons or not. Remember, it is going to be hard anyhow, even without an external crisis or impact.

A Crisis Perspective

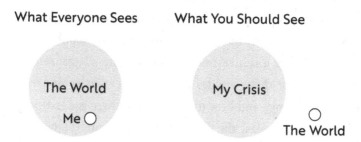

What Everyone Sees   What You Should See

The World   My Crisis

Me ○   ○ The World

The Only Thing That Matters Is YOUR Company

A crisis will end up being a good excuse for failure, but if you want to be successful, simply don't give up. It is resilience that makes entrepreneurs successful.

A JOURNEY FROM ONE CRISIS TO THE NEXT

We've defined the start-up journey as a three-dimensional journey—a *long, roller-coaster* journey of *failures*. I would like to add another dimension: *Building a start-up is **a journey from one crisis** to the next.*

While the *reasons* for a crisis are of less importance, the *type* of crisis still matters because your execution plan will change accordingly. A wide-impact crisis, for example, is likely to enjoy a wide-impact solution provided by the government or a change in regulations. Wide-impact crises also provide plenty of references to learn from.

Think of airlines during COVID-19.

An airline is a very operational-intensive company; when passengers drop by 95 percent or so, as they did during the COVID crisis, the airline simply cannot survive, certainly not if they don't have more than a month of run rate. And yet, most of the airlines are still here.

The answer to how it happened is government aid. Governments helped the airlines, as well as many other players across a number of industries perceived as mission-critical. Once a crisis is not just yours, there will be other solutions for the market to survive.

In some cases, the industry adapts fast. For example, restaurants were preparing significantly more food deliveries, which could be even more profitable and require less investment than running a restaurant.

Let's look at the examples I presented earlier to understand what it is you need to change and how to adapt when there is a lasting crisis.

Fundraising, sales, the organization, run rate (budget), and aspects of managing your people, investors, and the board of directors are all likely to change.

A Major Crisis = Something Major Disappears

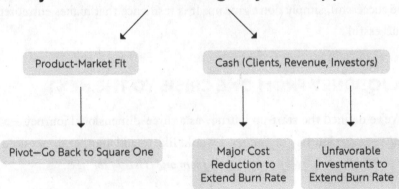

INTERNAL CRISES

When you face a company crisis—for example, your biggest customer leaves or a system that serves millions of people crashes—it is an event that needs urgent care. Fortunately, the duration of the situation usually lasts only a short time and doesn't always require a change in strategy or a company's plans for the future.

Sometimes, though, it does—for instance, if there is a realization that a customer churned because your company's product or the customer service perspective was not ready. In cases like these, you'll need to adjust your plans accordingly.

Occasionally, you will realize that you have not reached PMF yet, and you therefore should slow down sales (or hold off sales completely) until you fix the product. The general approach here is to fix what needs to be fixed and then continue with your plan.

INVESTOR CRISES

When the crisis is of an investor who withdrew from a term sheet resulting in your funding plan going down the drain, you might face a bigger problem. Adjustments will have a bigger impact. Just imagine that you have two more months of run rate, and your term sheet was withdrawn. If you do nothing, you will die in two months. You will have to adapt fast. There are three ways to extend your run rate dramatically: reducing costs, raising capital, and delaying payments.

EXTERNAL CRISES

Let's look at an external crisis like COVID-19 was for travel companies, and then look at a bearish market situation for *all* companies.

In the first type of crisis, you will need to recalculate your entire route, perhaps even redefine yourself. The second type of crisis deals with the funding challenge only.

The reality is that you act the same whether it's a global crisis or just your company's. When COVID started, WeSki had no market, and neither did Refundit or OrderChat. While companies will die if they run out of cash, they will get there even quicker if there is no market!

THE IMPACT OF THE CRISIS ON YOUR START-UP

You spend a good deal of time trying to understand the consequences of a crisis, making assumptions, and understanding the situation. These are the parameters you need to evaluate before making your decisions:

- How long?
- What's being impacted?
- Is our company still relevant?
- How much run rate do we have?
- Is there something else we should be doing?

With Refundit, it was rather simple. We had just completed a funding round a short while before COVID, so we had plenty of cash and more than two years of run rate in normal operation.

For how long would the crisis last? No one knew. We decided to wait for a month and then looked into the increase of panic on the one hand and of governmental actions on the other. We reviewed the history of the previous most wide-ranging pandemic (the Spanish flu one hundred years ago) and assumed the impact of COVID would be long, lasting for at least a year.

From the perspective of what's being impacted? Everything! There were no tourists in Europe, and nearly no one traveled anyhow. We could not keep on evolving the product as there was no feedback from users.

We could have continued to develop our governmental relationships with different countries in Europe, but due to the lack of tourists, the perception of our business opportunity had moved way lower on their agenda—for the time being, at least.

We made two decisions regarding people and the direction of the company.

- With our people, meaning employees, it was rather easy. The Israeli government (as well as many other governments, globally) offered support in the form of paying social security for "unpaid forced vacations." We decided to send 100 percent of our employees to this governmental scheme for as long as the money kept coming.
- The strategic decision was hibernation. We decided to keep on running with a very small team that would allow us to reignite the company after the crisis. The expected burn would allow us two years of run rate under hibernation and then another year and a half or more for reignition.

The reality, however, was very different.

While our budgetary plans were rock solid when it was time to spring out of hibernation, it turned out that European governments and their respective tax authorities were way slower to react post-COVID. We spent almost two years of "almost there" with Greek and some other European tax authorities until we eventually died at the end of 2023.

WeSki was more challenging.

At the beginning of COVID, we had a run rate of about two months, so the real crisis was that we were about to die. Almost all employees were immediately sent on the government-paid vacation I described for Refundit. We accepted a down round that gave us two-and-a-half years at a very low run rate (with the underlying assumption that the pandemic would last two skiing seasons).

With a very small team and no customers, the company took three major measures in those two lost seasons:

1. We improved the product for our major market—UK-based skiers traveling to the Alps.
2. We integrated more and more inventory providers into the platform. (These first two actions allowed us to quickly recover after

COVID-19 and demonstrate significant growth in the 2022–2023 and 2023–2024 ski seasons.)

3. In addition, we complained and swore about COVID every day; that was decidedly **not** helpful.

With SeeTree, it was a completely different story.

SeeTree helps tree growers increase their yield, as you may recall. At the beginning of the COVID-19 pandemic, SeeTree was actually in pretty good shape, both in terms of engaging customers as well as in terms of dialogue with investors. But these two activities were led by the CEO, who is based in Israel, and who was unable to travel for the time being.

While that was the case everywhere, when dealing with farmers who buy when they trust you and trust you when you show up on their plantation with your shoes covered with mud, Zoom simply didn't cut it.

New sales slowed down and the company was unable to meet its business objectives. Trying to raise capital under these conditions thrust us into a vicious cycle of chasing our own tail. Over that period, the company transformed itself by modifying its product and pricing model, by focusing on R&D projects, and significantly cutting manpower and burn rate. The company succeeded in executing these major changes, without losing important customers.

Only then—and it took a long while—was the company able to raise the funding it needed to get back to a growing and successful business execution.

MAKING MISTAKES FAST

From this, we can draw the following conclusion: You have to be *quick and decisive* with cost reduction and chasing the tail cycle of fundraising. In chapter 2, "A Start-Up is a Journey of Failures," we spoke about the importance of making mistakes fast.

Here's an example that demonstrates that urgency.

Let's say that you have $2 million in the bank and your monthly burn is $400,000, so essentially you have about five months of run rate (excluding any shutdown costs). Now, a crisis arrives. It could be any crisis—external, market, internal, or maybe not even a crisis, just a realization that the product needs more time.

You realize you need a longer duration to survive—say, twelve months and not five. This means $2 million divided by 12, providing a $167,000-per-month burn.

If you wait three months until you act, you will already have burned $1.2 million, leaving only $800,000 for the additional nine months of the year. That comes to $89,000 per month.

If you wait five months, you will have zero dollars left for the additional seven months.

The hard decision you must make today is either to reduce costs immediately or keep on running until the last minute, with the belief you'll be able to raise additional capital during this period.

Here's another example. Let's say that you have $500,000 per month in revenues and $1 million in expenses, and you have $3 million in the bank. Your net burn, therefore, is $500,000. You would be running out of cash in six months while, at the same time, you'll be trying to raise capital.

If you had asked for my point of view, my next question would be: "Can you reduce your expenses by half and still maintain the $500,000 revenues?" If the answer was yes, then perhaps the best approach would be to wait until the last minute, and then, if you're unable to change the revenue stream or raise capital, reduce expenses to $490,000 overnight and become profitable.

THE DRY WHEEL OF NO TRACTION

It can be tough to realize you're in the midst of a "chasing-the-tail" vicious cycle syndrome because often you're chasing your own tail and you don't even know it! The nature of the beast is that you get too engaged in the fundraising and it takes longer than you expect. Sometimes, it is the other way around.

The result is that the company is not executing its plan mainly because its focus is on fundraising. That feeds itself and instead of having a flywheel of traction, you end up with a "dry wheel" of no traction.

Investors who were engaged at the beginning of the dialogue started getting cold feet due to this "no traction" or a lack of traction from other investors. You find yourself starting new conversations with new investors. You keep on updating the business plan for the investors' presentations because you realize that the previous one is outdated.

What you should do is make a leap forward rather than chase your tail; acknowledge the situation that you are a beggar, not a chooser; and lower your fundraising expectations. The faster you adapt, for example, to accepting a lower valuation or to a less ambitious plan (and therefore aspire for smaller fundraising), the more likely you are to be successful. This is the best way out of the "dry wheel" cycle.

Ask your current investors what would be an attractive deal for them if they saw you now for the first time. This is the kind of deal that you should be looking for—one that is attractive for investors even if it's not necessarily the best deal for you.

WHEN YOUR INVESTOR CATCHES COLD FEET

It is easy to understand that investors typically tend to stay "on the fence," waiting to see how much progress you're making and then, even though they liked you, eventually deciding not to invest.

But what if they have already signed a term sheet? I've seen enough investors who got cold feet after signing a term sheet. It doesn't happen often, but it can happen, especially amidst a crisis.

That is one of the most challenging crises you will encounter because you may have already ceased conversations and negotiation with other investors, or maybe you harnessed other investors to join the round based on the term sheet you've got in hand, and now you need to tell them that the lead investor got cold feet.

Here's how it probably sounds to the other investors: "If the lead investors have decided not to invest based on their due diligence process, we should stay away from this deal, too!"

How cold can cold feet get? Very cold, like shying away from a signed term sheet or from a signed definitive agreement, and not transferring the money. How about telling you the check was in the mail, literally for months (that's perhaps the most accurate description I've heard for "snail mail")?

A CRISIS SHOULDN'T STOP YOU FROM STARTING YOUR START-UP

When is the right time to start your start-up? Or the right time to raise capital? **Today!**

You cannot wait for the timing to be ready because it's never the case. If you think that waiting plays to your advantage, it doesn't. I know some people who have been waiting for a couple of decades for the right timing. Guess what? They are still waiting.

That said, timing indeed matters—and luck even more. Many start-ups have failed because of timing. Waze nearly died because of the timing of Google Maps' launch, which made it nearly impossible for us to raise capital for our second funding round.

But when you consider the reasons start-ups failed, not figuring out PMF is the number one reason. Professor Paul Nutt from Ohio State University researched hundreds of business decisions taken over some twenty years. About half of the businesses analyzed in his research failed because they tried to solve the wrong problem. What's number two? The inability to make hard decisions, in particular about the team.

Timing is actually *less* of an issue for the failure or success of a start-up. Is it harder to raise capital amid crises? Yes, it is, but it is hard anyhow.

Should you start a new fintech start-up when there are so many macroeconomic uncertainties? If your value proposition is clear, then absolutely yes. If it is not, your inability to be successful is because of that and not due to the crisis.

Timing and crises always sound like good excuses, but at the end of the day, this journey is about never giving up, figuring out the value proposition (i.e., your PMF), and ultimately building value. Guess what? Creating value takes time, way more than the duration of a crisis. In fact, the journey is so long that, even if you don't know it yet, you will most likely run into a crisis period at least once.

CRISIS MANAGEMENT REQUIRES HARD DECISIONS

At the end of the day, the hard decisions that need to be made are very few:

1. Direction of the company
2. The team
3. Shareholders (investors)

For each of them, it is about what to do and when. The most important element is to keep everyone aligned and ensure transparency amongst all stakeholders.

People are not stupid. Your team knows when there is a crisis. While it's you who must decide what to do, you also have to communicate those decisions—the sooner, the better.

Once you have decided what you are going to do (i.e., the direction of the company), you gather the Board of Directors (BoD) to get their approval of the plan and, around the same time, you get all your teams together and tell them, "This is what we are going to do and why, and this is what it means."

For example, you need to extend your run rate until the crisis is over. You will need to cut costs by 50 percent, which means that management is going to go through a major salary cut and about a third of the team will have to go. You tell the team, "This will extend our run rate by X and allow us to recover once the crisis is over." If you do that with empathy and decisiveness, everyone will follow.

With your investors and BoD, it may be somewhat more complex.

First, you have to find out which of the investors is going to support you, regardless of the other investors. A response like, "If everyone invests, I will, too," doesn't help you; you need someone to stand by you, regardless of the others.

If you need more money, go to the BoD and tell them that you need funding and you are ready to take any deal that is on the table, including major down rounds and "pay-to-play," if these are the only options. Then, you have one-by-one discussions to see how supportive the investors are. You're optimizing the run rate and not the investment deal. It is about your survival and nothing else.

THE ISRAELI SPIRIT AND CRISIS RESILIENCE

When it comes to survival, I would bet on Israeli start-ups to have a higher likelihood of enduring.

Four elements make up an effective start-up ecosystem. Israel has five, which makes the country one of the best places in the world to build tech companies. As a result, Israel has the highest number of start-ups per capita in the world and is a leader in "most attractive ecosystems for start-ups" and in the number of acquisitions by global tech leaders and multinationals.

The four elements are:

1. Entrepreneurs
2. Investors
3. Engineers
4. Experience

The fifth element is an Israeli-specific foundation: a derivative of mandatory military service.

Let's look at each of these elements in turn.

1. ENTREPRENEURS

Israel has a proportionally greater number of entrepreneurs than any other country in the world. One major reason for this is a low fear of failure.

At the end of the day, people will choose the path of entrepreneurship when their passion exceeds the sum of fear of failure plus the alternative cost. Therefore, lowering the fear of failure is the key to creating more start-ups.

How is it done? Regulation—for example, no penalties for failures, lower taxation on success, etc.—and media coverage portraying entrepreneurs as heroes will assist in achieving this goal.

2. INVESTORS

Putting money into the overall tech ecosystem should be considered extra-lucrative for investors, thanks to increasing return and decreasing risk.

Increasing the returns of the ecosystem can be achieved through the involvement of governmental funds. For example, matching programs for foreign investments, reducing risk by having system stability, a tax transparent system (i.e., no taxation of the investors in the ecosystem), and a stable democracy.

3. ENGINEERS

We simply need to have more engineers. Governments can easily increase the number of engineers by providing work visas to non-locals who want to be part of an exciting and growing ecosystem.

The US is a pretty effective example of this; Canada is even better.

It is a matter of decision. The alternative is encouragement via taxation—say, offering a ten-year discount for engineers once they've completed their studies. In the end, those engineers will be paying more cumulative taxes than others, so the investment will return itself.

4. EXPERIENCE

Entrepreneurial experience is critical to making fewer mistakes, which increases the likelihood of success.

This is also the reason many entrepreneurs and businesspeople opt to write books about their careers and the business world in general. This was, in fact, the motivation for me to write this book—to share my experience with readers and increase their chances of being successful.

The new generations benefit from the previous ones' experiences. Waze was, at the time, the biggest exit in Israel (and in the world) for a consumer app. Since then, many other Israeli companies have been sold for more than a billion dollars and, before the current crisis (in 2021), there were about seventy unicorns in Israel. Their founders pay it forward to the ecosystem, helping their peers and the less experienced entrepreneurs.

5. MANDATORY MILITARY SERVICE

The X factor, what is most unique about the Israeli ecosystem, is the country's mandatory military service.

At age eighteen, all Israelis (both men and women) are recruited for two to three years of duty. Consequently, they develop a set of behaviors, values, and skills that will serve them later as entrepreneurs. That includes a "never-give-up" attitude and the ability to work well in teams, trusting your teammates, leadership, and responsibility.

These skills simply make people better entrepreneurs—and probably better professionals throughout their lives.

The most significant part of military service is that you join at a very young age and when you complete it, you are still very young. This enables people to take all the experience they have gained and use it in their personal and professional lives.

For the last three decades or so, Israel has cultivated generations of entrepreneurs based on these foundations—educating them to never give up and not to be afraid of failure, providing tax benefits and other incentives, building special funds to support tech start-ups, and more. This is what's made Israel the most phenomenal place to build a start-up.

While there is a state of war in Israel at the time I'm writing this chapter, and many investors will shy away from investing in Israeli start-ups these days, in my mind, it should be the other way around.

Israel, even in the middle of a war, is in my opinion a great bet, the best place to invest in, for two main reasons:

- A generic one. Tough times create strong people → strong people bring good times → good times create weak people → and weak people bring tough times again.
- Coming out of the tough times, Israel will not only prevail but will become much stronger and its start-up ecosystem will be even more successful. If you ask yourself how we got to the place we're in now, well, weak people bring tough times.

Golda Meir, the first—and to date the only—female prime minister of Israel, famously told US secretary of state Henry Kissinger during the 1973 Yom Kippur War, "We will always win because of our secret—we have no other place to go." This never-give-up attitude is one of the cornerstones of Israel and its start-up ecosystem. Let me stress this point one last time: The never-give-up approach is the most important behavior of a start-up CEO.

Let me share with you how the current war impacts fundraising.

I'm in the middle of creating a new investment vehicle to finance my start-ups. I call it the "Double Down Fund," because it aims to invest in the most promising start-ups I've built, those that have figured out PMF and are likely to reach profitability in the near future and still enjoy lower valuations. Among them are those who were forced to accept a major down round during COVID.

We were in the middle of a discussion with a Brazilian money manager who wanted to offer customers to join the fund. There was a lot of excitement among the customers to invest and a high desire to become part of my new fund. Then the war in Israel started and the group said they preferred to "wait and hold."

What seemed to be a rational decision that made perfect sense to the investors was frustrating for me and my start-ups. But this is pretty standard behavior of investors during a crisis. You should be holding your position during a bearish market. While this is the recommendation of most financial advisors, it turns out that many will be selling their position rather than holding it. Looking over the horizon, the current war in Israel is a crisis opportunity; in the long run, it will be an awesome one.

SUMMARY: WILL YOUR START-UP SURVIVE?

At the end of the day, you shouldn't care if the crisis is just for you or if someone else has a similar problem. Your crisis is yours, regardless of whether it is global or local, market- or industry-wide.

But when there is a crisis that impacts you, you certainly should prepare for it. Your preparation should be in three major areas: people, funding, and customers. These are all derivatives of the (updated) direction of the company.

You shouldn't prepare for a crisis if there is no crisis. But once there is one, get ready to deal with it and make your decisions fast and with transparency.

Having said that, well-funded companies—and Israeli start-ups in particular—have a higher likelihood of surviving any crisis.

The journey you embark on with your start-up will be long and you will most likely face at least one crisis. There is nothing to be afraid of, but nothing to be ignored, either.

STARTIPS

- **What kind of crisis is it?** It doesn't matter. It can be local, global, or just your company's. It should only concern you if this is YOUR cash-based crisis in which you need to preserve cash, or if it is a PMF crisis in which you need to pivot.

- **It is only you.** Regardless of the type of crisis or who else faces the same or similar issues—it is only you who has to solve it for your company. Do not rely on anyone else to do that for you.

- **Never give up.** In a crisis and throughout your journey, this is by far the most important behavior of a start-up CEO.

- **Your team members are your most important stakeholders.** They will be the people who take you out of the crisis and those who will benefit afterward. They are also aware of the crisis, so there's no point in trying to "hide" it.

- **Transparency and empathy.** Your team knows there is a crisis, and your leadership is at stake. Once everyone knows, you have to act. Tell everyone, "I know there is a crisis, this is what we are going to do to survive, this is how we are going to overcome it, and here are the possible consequences."

- **Act fast.** If everyone knows, then the time to act is critical. The longer you wait, two things can happen: you will lose your leadership (because everyone knows) and you will quickly run out of options that you might have had earlier.

- **How many times did you "almost die" and you are still here?** Forgive the metaphor, but entrepreneurs are like cockroaches. They will never become extinct. It is believed that they can even survive an atomic bomb blast.

- **A crisis can be an opportunity.** Perhaps that's the time to refocus, become leaner, or acquire other struggling companies or market share.

- **Cash crisis.** Change your mindset to "survival mode" and be flexible. Take the necessary actions to preserve your start-up, even if it means accepting unfavorable deals or firing people.

- **Turn to your investors** to support the company, even at the price of a down round.

THE FRONT-ROW VIEW

I've mentioned some start-ups of mine that severely struggled during some of the recent crises. I've asked the CEOs of several of these companies to share their stories of what it looks like from the front row of the roller coaster.

WESKI: FROM NEARLY DYING TO PROFITABILITY THROUGH THE MOST EXTREME ROLLER COASTER

By Yotam Idan, Cofounder and CEO of WeSki

Reflecting on the burst and impact of COVID-19, it's unbelievable for me to see how WeSki navigated through that storm and got to where it is today.

In February 2020, our office in Tel Aviv was buzzing with anticipation. We were on the cusp of closing our third official ski season, boasting robust 2X year-over-year growth, and were already strategizing on how to make our self-service model a success. At that time, our customers still relied heavily on our travel agents, who we called "Ski Experts."

Our product was still in its infancy, experiencing occasional hiccups, making it challenging to build trust. To overcome this situation, we had a team of twelve ski experts diligently sitting at a long table with phones and headphones, reaching out to sales leads and selling them ski trips over the phone.

We had twenty-seven employees in total, and I had fundraising for two months already, discussing a possible term sheet for our seed round with a few investors, as we were running out of cash quickly, and the "ski sales season" was about to end.

Around that time, we followed the news about the new virus in China but didn't pay much attention to it. A few weeks later, the news started talking more and more about it, and we followed the development a lot more closely. However, we knew there wasn't much we could do about it, so we decided to stay focused on running our current ski season, which was in its peak season. Things escalated quickly every day, although most of our trips were going well with no interruptions.

Crisis Hits: March 2020

It was the morning of March 15, 2020, when all the European resorts closed and everyone already there was evacuated. At the same time, governments around the world, including Israel, decided to "close the skies" and, within forty-eight hours, no planes were allowed to enter the country.

While everyone was in a panic worldwide, our office in Tel Aviv was in complete chaos! We still had over one thousand customers waiting to go on their ski trips, and over a hundred were being evacuated from ski resorts with nowhere to go and no flights to go back home.

Our phones didn't stop ringing. We had around twenty of them in the office, and all our customers were calling customer service, panicking about what would happen with their upcoming trips, screaming at us, frustrated by the situation, and asking for immediate refunds.

A few even physically came to our office, yelling at me as if I was the one spreading the virus around the world. Of course, we understood their situation and probably would have acted the same way, but there wasn't much we could do that day—all of us at WeSki, together with the entire travel industry, were still trying to figure out what was going on.

We split everyone into teams. Some were customer-facing, some focused on repatriating customers who were stuck abroad, and others called our suppliers—hotels, airlines, transportation companies, etc.—trying to get information on how to sort out our upcoming bookings and when we should get our customers' money back.

Adapting to Chaos: Moving to Survival Mode

The situation was evolving rapidly. David, Pavel (my cofounders), and I had numerous rapid-fire discussions that day, devising a strategy to navigate the chaos. Fortunately, we were quick to grasp the situation. With almost no cash in the bank, refunds were only viable once we received money back from our suppliers, a process that could take time.

So, we devised a plan to sign customers on refund deals, offering them a portion of the money in cash and the rest in WeSki credits until we could recover the funds from our suppliers. By the end of that day, we had a clear understanding of our next steps and swiftly transitioned into survival mode. I scheduled an all-hands meeting for the following day, informing everyone that we had to place them on unpaid leave until further notice and assisting them in accessing the government's unemployment emergency aid.

With salaries halted, we suddenly had more time to think strategically about our next moves. The office remained in a state of chaos for a few more days, but most of our team members continued to show up each day, volunteering their time to help us navigate the crisis. We would leave the office each night around midnight, and the phones would still be ringing incessantly. In a matter of days, we transformed from a company specializing in selling ski trips to becoming reluctant experts in managing cancellations and refunds at scale.

Then there was silence.

The first lockdown was on, and we were all at home with our families, trying to understand what to do with the apocalyptic news we were receiving. By then, we had managed to take care of a big chunk of our customers, although it took a few months for many of them to close the cases.

By the time we finished that part, David, Pavel, and I were sitting together for days with no real sense of what was going to happen, moving from complaining about the situation and the governments implementing various levels of lockdowns to thinking of our next steps and strategy together with Uri and Ariel from The Founders Kitchen fund, and a few other investors and advisors.

It was unclear at that point how long the lockdowns and the virus would be with us and when travel would reopen. What *was* clear to us—and what we've always communicated to our shareholders—was that we were not ready to quit. After four challenging years as young entrepreneurs (building a start-up is challenging even without a global crisis), we had just started to see product-market fit with WeSki. We simply could not let go of that glimpse of our dream come true.

By the summer of 2020, the most severe of the initial lockdowns had stopped and international travel was back. As a bunch of optimistic entrepreneurs, we were convinced that COVID-19 would be over in just a few months.

However, just a few months later, a second wave would come and bring us all back to square one. While we were getting more experience in these circumstances, our cash balance was running low, and going into another winter season with no ski holidays on the horizon didn't help.

That's when things became really challenging.

Not only was it almost impossible to find investors interested in meeting with us, but once we did, most of them were trying to convince us to close shop and open a new company in another field. Finding our motivation every day was not easy and we started questioning our future and the chances that WeSki will ever succeed. Luckily for me, I have the two most driven and passionate cofounders. Each time, one of us was more motivated than the others and kept the team spirit up when one of us was down.

So, we kept ourselves busy in creation. We believed that the best use of our time would be to focus on our product, fix everything that wasn't working well in the customer journey, and prepare for the day travel would be back.

The best part was that we had lots of time to focus on it without thinking of sales and operating a ski travel business. We learned a lot from the customers and data we collected in the first four years of WeSki, and our product had many broken areas that needed to be fixed.

The biggest challenge was that we had almost no other resources but ourselves, three founders, and one employee who didn't give up on WeSki. In addition, we had to fix an online self-service product with no traffic or customers using it. It was literally guessing in the dark.

We sat together on every piece of the customer journey and focused on what would drive skiers to book their annual ski trips without talking to any of us over the phone. Thus, piece by piece, we improved each step of the funnel, waiting for COVID-19 to be over so we could test it with real users again.

Fundraising was a whole other story.

As the winter of 2020–21 approached, COVID cases were rising again, and investor sentiment around travel was just off. No VCs were open to it and rarely would we find an angel investor or a family office even willing to have a Zoom meeting with us. They were mostly nice to me but didn't show any genuine interest.

Pay-to-Play Funding

After a few weeks with zero progress, we started looking for alternative ways to raise money.

- Crowdfunding seemed like a good idea initially, but it couldn't work for us legally.
- We weren't eligible for most government loans and aid packages besides some small amounts here and there.
- We even had a few meetings and deal discussions with a leading travel agency on creating a merger with them.

Eventually, all these options couldn't work for us, and time was passing by while we had only four months of runway to go.

By that time, around January 2021, lockdowns were back worldwide and it was clear to us that investor sentiment about travel would not change anytime soon. We were left with our last option to save WeSki—creating a pay-to-play funding round from our internal investors, hoping that they would believe, like us, that when travel returned, WeSki would flourish and take advantage of the market recovery situation using the product and technology we'd built during that year.

We started planning the round with Uri and Ariel, consulting with our advisors and other investors on the round structure, and trying to figure out how to make this work for all our stakeholders.

On the one hand, the round size had to be big enough to sustain us until the pandemic was over, and our product would work as expected to bring us to a profitable state. On the other hand, we had to be aggressive with the investors who wouldn't join the round by creating an almost artificial reason for them to invest.

By that time, we had four groups of stakeholders to take into consideration:

- Pre-seed investors—a dozen investors, mostly angels, who had been backing us since our first round in 2017.
- SAFE investors—a group of a few investors, corporate funds, and angels who had an open SAFE agreement with a CAP (CAP = maximum price) and a discount on the next funding round's terms.
- New round investors—all the investors (existing and new) that would invest in that round.
- We three founders and future employees—as we would lose most of our equity from the round dilution, we had to be compensated to a level that made sense for us to run the company for another five to ten years.

After endless meetings and listening to all our stakeholders' points of view and advice, we finally came up with a plan that would benefit all the stakeholder groups that would participate in the round, along with a business plan we founders believed could be executed. I will always remember that last meeting with David, Uri, and Ariel, just before we started the process in front of all shareholders.

We presented them with the final round structure and targets and listened to their feedback. It was like we were going into a fight against all odds. They encouraged us and were willing to help wherever necessary, but they also were fully transparent by saying how low the chances were that we would nail this and get the amount we needed. At the same time, they saw our passion for making this work and gave us their blessing.

Eventually, it came to one simple equation: either we would make it happen or we would be forced to close the company. It was a clear-cut, no-more-chances, do-or-die situation. And so, we did.

The calls were challenging and a bit tough sometimes, as not all of our investors liked the plan as it was, and some even thought we were being rude and aggressive by creating this pay-to-play mechanism. I decided that no matter what, we wouldn't change the plan again and would just stick to it, even if some investors did not support or even opposed it. I knew it was the only chance we could pull this off, and eventually, it would be in favor of all our shareholders.

Against All Odds: Closing the Round

It took around three weeks of back-to-back meetings with investors, lawyers, my cofounders, and advisors to get the first significant commitments that ignited the round. With our existing investors, we got to a bit under 50 percent of our round target. It was a good start but was still far from what we needed to close the round, especially since almost no new investments were made into travel start-ups that year. The situation was based on verbal commitments only, so nothing was tying anyone up to invest, which meant that until we reached our round target, no individual investor would take the risk.

From that point on, the clock was ticking, and I knew we didn't have much time to bring in the rest of the round target before the first investors to commit would start to change their minds. Luckily, we had a great relationship with the people from Founders Factory, a UK-based accelerator program we attended in the early days of WeSki.

The team at Founders Factory conducted an online investors' webinar where their portfolio companies could present their start-ups and investment opportunities to many investors in the UK all at once, and we were allowed to join. I made the best presentation I could, perfecting it to drive opportunistic investors to see the opportunity of the low valuation we gave at such a stage of the company, despite COVID still being active. It was a long shot, but I couldn't miss any opportunity at that stage.

Against all expectations, that single presentation was a huge breakthrough!

The next day, I got over ten introductions to highly qualified investors that turned into introductory calls in a matter of hours. The following week, I was in back-to-back meetings with new investors, and in just a few days, with lockdowns still in place, new investors committed to all of the remaining amounts!

By the end of March 2021, following the infinite tension of closing and signing the investment agreements, the impossible became real and we successfully closed the round. From almost no runway, we had endless time to work without worrying about cash for a long period.

Recovery and Growth

That round completely changed our situation and gave all our focus back to our product and our self-service customer journey. The market and travel, in general, were still slow and bumpy, and there were significant doubts about whether we were going into another closed ski season. Things started to change in September 2021 and people's attitudes toward traveling became less frightening.

Finally, we got the chance to test the new version of our product. We slowly restarted our marketing campaigns and suddenly saw sales coming in. These were self-served bookings, so there was no need for any phone calls to ski experts.

Every few days, we doubled down on marketing, and following that, we directly doubled our sales. Our self-service funnel not only started working, it was booming! All of our hard work finally paid off. Each of us ran a few areas by ourselves, and after a few weeks, we worked nonstop every day and started hiring people to help us run the season. We gave it all we had for all of that winter, and by the end of the 2021–22 ski season, with seven employees in the office, we not only smashed our sales targets by nearly 50 percent, but we did three times more revenue than we did with twenty-seven employees pre-COVID—all thanks to our hard work on perfecting our product and customer journey.

Fast-forward two years to 2024: We kept growing rapidly in sales and team size. With over twenty times the revenue we did pre-COVID and a team of almost forty full-time employees, we've reached our first profitable year and made countless improvements across our company.

We are still facing enormous challenges, including a financial crisis followed by a horrible war in Israel and many of the day-to-day challenges that every start-up has. But, based on our experience, it all seems small and easy compared to COVID-19 and the disappearance of the ski holidays market for nearly two years.

What would we have felt like if we had closed the company when all odds were against us?! Well, we're lucky we don't know the answer to that question. It was a real team effort, and thanks to my truly amazing cofounders, investors, and advisors, we managed to survive the impossible and get to where we are today.

And we know it's still only the beginning of the WeSki story.

REFUNDIT: DEATH DUE TO COVID COMPLICATIONS

By Ziv Tirosh, Cofounder and former CEO of Refundit, now CEO of Pluro

As Uri has phrased, Refundit died of COVID complications. It's the perfect way to put it.

Refundit faced the onset of COVID-19 only a few months after securing a $10 million Series A funding round. We had money in the bank, and we were running multiple business development (BD) processes in several EU countries.

For Refundit, attempting to "fix" the very broken VAT refund process for tourists, business development meant heavy lobbying in our target countries. We needed to change the existing—and may I say antiquated—VAT refund regulations in each country, to allow for a full digital solution. That required amending existing regulations and/or laws.

We met with various financial, tax, and tourism authorities, small-to-medium businesses (SMEs), and many more. We worked with local consultants as well as tax lawyers in all relevant countries, but what we were attempting to do required our physical presence. It was about obtaining support among government officials, many of them highly ranked, then clarifying what we were proposing and why it would be good for each of the local economies in the countries we were in touch with.

It was about building trust and supporting them in the process. That proved more difficult than we had envisioned. Think about it: these are, in many cases, rather conservative government officials (finance and tax people) supervising the maintenance of processes, and along comes this Israeli start-up proposing disruption in an area that's not really at the center of their attention (because who cares about tax refund to travelers).

So, it required many meetings and a lot of convincing. I traveled extensively. For close to three years, I was in Europe every week for a total of hundreds of meetings. Just to name a few examples: seventeen visits to Madrid, sixteen to Athens, thirteen to Brussels, and the list continues.

Probably the most important element in the business development journey was trust building through consistent communications and visits.

COVID Brings Everything to a Halt

Then came COVID . . . and everything stopped. Everything. And with it, all the dialogues and ties we were gently but surely sowing around Europe. It all collapsed. Governments essentially shut down for weeks, then slowly began working from home in a very defensive mode until they gradually returned to work in hybrid mode.

For Refundit, that meant going back to square one after the dust settled and starting all over again. During this time, everything imaginable occurred.

- Governments collapsed.
- Officials either retired or were replaced.
- One of the most enthusiastic supporters of our solution passed away.

If it could happen, it did. So, we had to rebuild relationships from the ground up.

Since we were OK financially when COVID started, we gave it a few weeks before starting to react. Like many others out there, after the first wave had passed, we were optimistic . . . but then wave two of COVID hit, and with it came the realization that this would be long.

Then we reacted.

We moved the company into hibernation mode, understanding that the only thing we could do now was weather the storm and save our cash for later. I cut the team from fifteen to five, leaving the bare minimal essential team. With this team, we could rather quickly move out from hibernation when necessary. Needless to say, we cut our burn rate dramatically.

At the same time, we also readjusted our business development focus. With the understanding that our BD efforts were very lengthy and depended on too many parameters, including local politics, change of government, etc., we initially took a wide approach. Prior to COVID, we were running BD processes in fifteen countries. Once we went into hibernation mode and as part of us cutting our burn rate, we decided to focus on just four countries.

A Breakthrough and Another Setback

Within the countries on which we focused efforts, it was in Greece where we had the most advanced process. So much so that, in April 2023, we finally received a green light from AADE, the Greek Tax Authority, to get ready to provide our services to tourists visiting from outside the EU. We were ecstatic and confident that we'd broken through into our first significant market.

That was a pivotal moment in our post-COVID life. We had a breakthrough. Being a start-up aiming to focus efforts, we then cut our BD efforts in other countries and concentrated our resources on Greece.

We needed that one first country where we could show a live business. But three months into the process, the Greek Tax Authority submitted our proposal for another review by their legal department.

We were put on hold once again for an unknown period. It was back to COVID for us. We waited and did all we could to support the right outcome.

After four months, in November 2023, we were informed that the outcome was positive and that we could proceed. We just needed a final signature on a new decree by the head of the tax authority. He was supposed to sign within three weeks.

Again, we celebrated . . . too early.

In May 2023, there were snap elections in Greece, followed by a reshuffling of government. The result was a new Minister of Economy (Finance). As we were awaiting the final signature on the decree by the head of the Tax Authority, which would finally allow us to operate, a new requirement was presented: the Tax Authority wanted to ensure that the new minister supported the change.

So, we waited, continuing our efforts with decision makers to make it happen.

As far as we understood back then, the new minister approved—but that final signature never arrived. Then, our runway ended. Reason of death: COVID complications.

Personal Reflections on a Roller-Coaster Journey

On a personal level, the Refundit journey was my second start-up roller coaster. It was hard and demanding, fulfilling and emotional, as always. There were days of elation and days of frustration, as always.

It was super difficult to raise our A round, and I walked for months in what Uri calls "the desert of no traction," hearing tons of noes from investors and taking it personally every time because for me it was personal. This was my baby. And then we headed to the next investor's session, taking a breath and starting all over again.

Eventually, we were blessed to find our "Yes" and closed the $10M round during Q4 2022 with awesome investors, led by Amadeus Ventures, the corporate venture capital arm of Amadeus, the travel tech giant.

By March 2020, we were on a roll. The team and I were highly motivated and optimistic. We were making good progress; we had money in the bank. Then, boom, COVID. What a roller coaster. I went from a packed agenda with weekly meetings around Europe to an empty one. Nothing. Just sitting at home and waiting, and waiting. Everyone went through that, but ours lasted longer, and it was horrible.

As the world came back to life, we remained with zero or very little business activity, hibernating, waiting for governments to get back to work and to be willing to rediscuss our disruptive model, which meant that tourists from outside the EU would be able to easily receive VAT refunds on their shopping.

It was long and the roller coaster went on and on and on until, finally, came the green light from Greece! Elation! Happiness! We did it!! Our wait was worth it! And then a full stop again, and then "maybe," then a second "Yes." And then death . . . "death by COVID complications." This was sad and frustrating, feeling like a personal failure and an embarrassment

And yet, I'd do it all over again!

Because there is nothing like this journey of creating a new do-good business in the world. When you are in it, it feels great, real, and it's about being surrounded by awesome people and together fighting a good fight. Nothing comes near it. Nothing.

So, in fact, while writing this text in May 2024, I've just begun a new start-up. Starting from zero once again (and yes, Uri's involved, of course) . . . Visit me on LinkedIn for more details.

When Refundit closed, I posted this "requiem" on LinkedIn.

After 6.5 years of existence, Refundit has reached the end of the line. Sadly, we will not be fixing the "broken" VAT refund scheme for tourists in Europe. We leave the arena as it was: antiquated, inefficient, and mostly in the hands of a monopoly—Global Blue. The right of tourists for VAT refunds will remain in many cases theory only, as close to $20B/year will remain unrefunded, and European SMEs will remain out of the scheme. In other cases the refund will be possible, but only via GB, which, enjoying its position, will continue charging exorbitant fees of 20%–70% of the refund (!), in many cases undisclosed to the tourist, just because there's no supervision and they can . . .

So, while our journey ends with failure, I believe we laid the ground for a future solution. Over these 6.5 years, we held hundreds of conversations with Ministers; MPs; Heads and leaders of Tax, Customs, VAT, and Tourism authorities; and many additional government officials, literally all over Europe. We presented the market failure and its disadvantages to tax authorities, retail, and tourism sectors. We also presented them with a digital flow that would have fixed the problem and created real measurable value for all stakeholders, including the inclusion of SMEs in the scheme (80% of businesses . . .) and an increase in tax revenue.

In times in which taking responsibility for failure is not obvious . . . I'll be obvious—this is my failure . . .

I have three special thank-yous, before Refundit says goodbye:

Thank you, my friend, Uri Levine, for the idea, the partnership, and the support along the journey. It's been an honor and a privilege doing this with you. I'd do it all over again with you.

Thank you to our investors who believed in us.

And last but surely not least—a big thank-you to the Refundit team. You guys were awesome and did great and it's been a pleasure working together. Can't name you all here, but the last ones standing: Yossi Raz, Cristian Samoilovich, Oren Divon, Lior Kupersmidt, Ami Eyal, Avraam Rynkov.

Happy New Year and fingers crossed that 2024 will bring peace to Israel and its neighbors and end all bloody human conflicts.

Ziv Tirosh

WHEN ALL POSSIBLE BAD THINGS HAPPEN AT ONCE

By Aviel Siman-Tov, Cofounder and CEO of Oversee (formerly FairFly)

The Pre-COVID-Era Status

Oversee is a technology company that helps enterprises optimize their travel budgets (one of the top three expenses for enterprises) and assists global travel agencies in staying competitive through its automation tools, which improve operational efficiency, increase profitability, and better retain clients.

In early 2020, our primary product was "Price Assurance," which helped companies manage their travel expenses by finding better prices for the exact same flights already purchased by their employees.

It took us about two-and-a-half years to reach many enterprise clients, and by the end of 2019, we anticipated ten times increase in the number of customers and, accordingly, in revenue for the following year. After years of pivots—from B2C to B2B and micro-pivots in our go-to-market strategy—we felt like we had finally hit our stride.

We understood exactly what significant problem we were solving, for what size of companies, and who we were specifically targeting in the organizations.

End of 2019

We didn't have enough money in the bank to support the expected growth, but there was a lot of interest from investors to invest in the company. So, at the beginning of Q4 2019, our board unanimously decided to accelerate growth by hiring more team members. Since two funds were very interested in investing in us, we felt confident that we would be able to raise the money needed to support this rapid growth.

Some of our existing investors reassured us with a general sentiment of, "It'll be fine, keep growing, and the funding will come." This implied that, if external investors didn't come through, the existing investors would take over the entire round.

January/February 2020

I flew to New York to meet one of the two funds that were very interested in investing in us. I had already met with them a few times in the past, and we had finalized the terms of the funding round. I remember them telling me, "We think you should take more money than we agreed upon because you'll need it for growth, and we believe the market you're in is very attractive."

At the end of the meeting, I overheard them discussing the location of their next meeting, considering changing it because of "this coronavirus thing" that they didn't want to risk catching.

I didn't realize at that moment how relevant this conversation would become for our company and that "this coronavirus" was about to turn our lives and the company upside down.

At that time, we all thought it was a disease mostly confined to China. We had no sense that it would become our problem, too. In the early days of the company, a venture fund from Hong Kong had invested a small amount in us. About a month before my trip to New York, Hong Kong was completely shut down because of the coronavirus. Our investors there were locked in their homes. When I asked what they needed, they said masks and hand sanitizer, so we sent them a big box.

We didn't imagine that we would be in the same situation within a couple of months.

Back to New York

I finished the meeting with the investors and rushed to the airport. I flew to a big conference in London for three days and then returned to Israel. Two days after returning from the conference, a directive came out stating, "Anyone returning from an international conference must go into fourteen-day isolation."

A few hours later, our system alerted us of a significant drop in revenue (we have alerts for various issues to catch problems in real time). How significant? Thirty percent. The next day, the drop was already 90 percent. The day after, it reached 99 percent.

Within two days, we went from having enough money for about six months (which included an assurance from some of our existing investors that they would add more money to their investment to give us more "negotiation space" with new investors) to a situation where significant revenue (millions) that the company relied on as part of our runway had evaporated.

Due to the impact of COVID-19 and the sharp and immediate revenue decline, we suddenly had only enough money in the bank for some two months of operation. That was it. Most of our employees at that time were entitled to thirty days' notice (with pay) in case of termination or resignation, so if we wanted to downsize the team, we had to do it immediately. Even then, it wouldn't improve the company's cash burn because we still had to pay another month's notice.

I remember calling Uri and telling him, "We need to inject money from investors into the company immediately or there won't be a company!"

Uri replied, "Aviel, all your investors and their investors have lost about 50 percent of their holdings in the stock market over the last seventy-two hours. I'm not sure what to tell you. Think of creative solutions!"

A few hours later, I got on a Zoom call with the entire team. I told them:

We are in an unfolding event that is unclear when and how it will end. We will need to take tough steps to protect the company so that the company can protect us. However, before making such decisions, I ask you to take the next forty-eight hours to ensure:

1. You and your family have enough food at home.
2. You have cash on hand.
3. You have all the necessary medications.

If you lack anything, let me know, and I will arrange for a delivery to your home (or transfer money to your bank accounts).

I ended the call feeling we were doing the right thing, ensuring the basic needs of the team and giving them a sense of security (as much as possible)—for them and their families.

After the call, we went straight into a management meeting. I presented the executives with the situation as I saw it:

1. We need to significantly downsize the team; within twenty-four hours, we need to decide how and by how much. Those who delay making tough decisions end up having to make tougher ones to compensate for the lost time.
2. Our main product is irrelevant in a time when people aren't flying. I asked Oded, our VP of Product, and Ami, my cofounder and CTO, to conduct quick research and come back with a recommendation on what product we can build that can provide value today to our customers until they start flying again.
3. Our primary mission is the survival of the company. Survival is paramount.

After two days, I got on separate Zoom calls with each and every team member (approximately thirty-five people), explaining whether they were to be let go, placed on an unpaid leave, or could stay with the company, albeit with a significant pay cut (up to 70 percent). Although each of the management members or the HR lead could do that, I thought it was better that each of them hear it directly from me.

Back then, the government paid a monthly amount of up to $2,500 for each employee who was moved to unpaid leave. This way we could get some team members "paid" and hopefully be able to bring them back on full salary, without paying the month notice period. Obviously, this didn't prevent the employees from choosing to terminate their employment and get paid for the full thirty-day notice.

Amazingly, no matter who I spoke with or what news I delivered, they understood the issue, thanked us for the respectful and professional way we were handling this crazy situation, and reassured me that I was doing the right thing and that they fully understood where it was coming from.

We founders, of course, gave up our salaries entirely during that period.

Since we didn't anticipate hiring new team members for the next eighteen months, we had to let go of our HR lead, too. We asked her to help each of the employees with whom we parted ways to revise their résumés during the advanced notice period, and I personally sent these soon-to-be former staffers to friends who run companies. We ensured that each of them found their next job.

To help the departing team members, we gave them their laptops as gifts, so it would be less challenging for them to find their next job and not have to deal with buying a new computer.

For the team members who stayed with the company or went on unpaid leave, we offered a significant amount of stock options (three times what they had before), understanding that those who stayed were like a founding team of a brand-new company and were taking a lot of risks. Accordingly, it was right to give them the opportunity to earn a substantial reward someday.

For the team that stayed on, we significantly cut their salaries while also telling them we couldn't promise they would get the cut money back because no investor would invest money in the company to pay off "old debts."

We called each of our clients and asked how we could help. Where there were locked-in contracts with us for ongoing payments, we offered a significant discount to reflect the situation where clients weren't receiving value.

We realized we were rebuilding the company for the post-COVID day.

Ami Goldenberg, my cofounder and CTO, and Oded Zilinsky, our VP of Product, came back with insights on what product we could build that would provide value to our customers when they weren't flying at all.

We knew that a significant part of travel budgets (flights/hotels) in companies is booked months in advance. After conversations with many of our customers, we understood that all these companies were "stuck" with vouchers issued by airlines for flights and hotels that their employees had already booked and paid for. The customers effectively exchanged their travel budget money for airline vouchers.

Each airline defined different rules and expiration dates for the vouchers with varying usage conditions. For someone managing the travel budget in a company with thousands of employees, there was neither the time nor the tools to analyze the expiration dates of thousands of flight vouchers.

We realized that such a new product would help our customers today. However, as the world slowly returned to travel (we anticipated this happening gradually over two years with various ups and downs given the nature of the pandemic), it would become less and less relevant because the vouchers would either be used or would expire.

Within about a week, the team built a working beta version that showed travel managers in enterprises how many vouchers they had, on which airlines, and the vouchers' value and expiration dates. The new product also helped them understand immediately what in their inventory was about to "expire" so they could time their use—or at least know they existed!

We offered this product to our existing customers for free. For new customers, we offered it for free as well, but on the condition that they also purchase our main product, which finds price drops for the same seat on the same flight or the same room in the same hotel after the booking is made.

We also provided our main product for free at this stage. It was of no added value to those not traveling, anyhow. However, we added a small but significant clause stating that new customers would use our price assurance product for free from now until they returned to a "budget level of 20 percent compared to 2019."

For example, if a company had a 2019 travel budget of $100 million annually, they would use our price assurance product for free until they returned to a usage level of at least 20 percent of 2019's figure, meaning a usage rate of $20 million annually. Since we assumed COVID wouldn't end in one go but would have further "outbreaks," we also defined that once the customer reached 20 percent of their 2019 budget, they would get another six months for free, provided that, at the end of it, they committed to continue with us for another three years at full payment.

What we essentially did was provide the product for free during the "lull" period, knowing we wouldn't make much money from it anyway, combined with a free product that solved an immediate problem for customers, under the assumption that someday companies would start flying again and then we would have a lot of new customers for our main "Price Assurance" product.

We called this "The Slingshot." We stretched and stretched, building the company for the day after COVID, with the intention that, when COVID would end, we would grow very quickly based on the existing customers, and the revenue would grow at the pace of the market's recovery, which we then expected to be very rapid.

Meanwhile: Money Injection

I called Uri and told him we needed to inject money into the company and that I didn't see how this could happen from an external investor in the middle of a global pandemic.

"Whoever invests in the company now will invest in you because they believe and trust you," Uri, with his endless optimism, told me. "In general, I've always said that as a CEO, you're a world champion in wrestling with your back against the wall [what's called a 'Wartime CEO'], so it sounds like our back is against the wall. I trust you."

Uri has the ability to quickly identify the most critical issue and focus on it. In that conversation, the issue was that I needed to believe it was possible to raise external money at such a time.

I finished the call with Uri understanding that the only investors who would invest in a travel company during such times were those I had already met a few times before. After all, who invests in a company in our industry when no planes are flying?

I made a list of five investors and told each of them the same thing in a short phone call:

We will get through this. We have a strong customer pipeline and a strong team. Now is your chance to invest in the company on good terms because later you won't have this opportunity anymore.

I called five investors. Within two hours, I had two noes and three maybes.

After two months, I was left with three noes and two maybes. The two maybes eventually became two yeses, and we raised an $8 million round in July 2020, at a time when there wasn't a single plane in the sky and it was unclear when, if ever, there would be one again.

Together with our existing investors who continued to invest in the company, these new investors are a key reason why we are still here.

Uri Levine, Ariel Sacerdoti, Alon Lifshitz, Yodfat Harel Buchris, Eyal Dior, Ron Ostroff, Yidi Schwartz, Yash Sandesara, Paolo Rubatto, Alexey Reznikovich, and Vitaliy Podolskiy, thank you for your trust and support. With your help, we have done and are doing miracles.

Fast-Forward to 2024

We started 2020 with big dreams. Our team was about thirty-five to forty people. Within days of the pandemic outburst, we had to let go a third of the team and put another third on unpaid leave for as long as possible. Essentially, in 2020, the year of COVID, within a few days, our team size decreased from about thirty-five to forty team members to seven.

Despite everything, we didn't lose a single customer, and in 2020 itself, we grew our customer base by 7x. This was a huge win of our sales team, led then by Ric Woolf who managed to keep the team highly motivated in challenging times.

Today, we have thousands of customers, including some of the world's largest companies across multiple fields, using our products.

The level of customer and partner satisfaction is unheard of.

And us? We joke that our company has nine lives. How do we know it has nine lives and not four or seven? The answer is because we've used all nine lives so far.

Chapter 13

THE EXIT

The end is just the beginning of a new journey.

—Adi Barill, media consultant

I t was the first of May, 2020. Moovit was just a few days away from closing its acquisition deal with Intel for just over a billion dollars when Intel came up with a new demand.

"We want one hundred percent of the shareholders to sign off on the deal, including all those who have proxies and even those with just 0.01 percent of the shares," Intel told us.

Moovit CEO Nir Erez thought this was a no-brainer. There were about a dozen such shareholders, and they had all signed off on the deal already, but Intel insisted that we also include ex-employees who had exercised options.

Moovit's legal team tried to explain to Intel that there was no need, as they all have a proxy to the board of directors. But Intel wouldn't budge.

Moovit was eight years old at the time of the acquisition, with about two hundred employees, but over this period, there were about seventy employees who had left the company and exercised their options. Therefore, they owned "ordinary shares" of the company, shares that were held by the trustee of the stock option plan.

Nir and Moovit cofounder Roy Bick divided the work of calling all seventy ex-employees over the weekend. After the deal was closed, Nir told me that weekend was the *most rewarding* part of the entire journey. He loved calling those tens of ex-employees, telling them there was a deal and they should be expecting a very nice reward—a life-changing event for many— and that all this was going to happen the following week.

Some of those employees had just left recently; others departed years back. No matter what their situation was, all of them were speechless.

For Nir, each one of those calls was an amazing moment of distilling the entire roller-coaster journey into the essence of value creation for all employees who had been part of it.

When Google acquired Waze—an event that changed the life of all 107 employees in the company at the time, as well as a few who had already left—we told all the employees at once. We hadn't yet learned about the power of one by one.

This experience brought me to the understanding that when I do my next exit announcement, it will be one by one, as Moovit did, and allow each employee to have a moment of private celebration.

THERE IS NOTHING LIKE THE FIRST TIME

In previous chapters, we compared a first-time user experience to a first kiss; we spoke about falling in love with the problem and falling in love in order to commit yourself to the long, winding, and very demanding roller-coaster journey. But there is nothing in your life that prepares you for that first exit (except maybe your first baby).

When it hits you, you experience an emotional roller coaster. All at the same time, you feel pride and concern, lucky and rewarded. The ups and downs are now on a personal level and not just about your start-up.

You start to think about the life-changing event that just happened.

You imagine your future, then you go back to making sure the deal will happen.

You think of all the people who joined this journey, and those who helped you throughout.

You think of your family and the people you will help afterward with the resources that you will soon have.

You think about your next start-up.

At the end of the day, this is a life-changing event. Nothing is going to look the same anymore, and there is nothing that prepares you for that.

Earlier in this book, I advised you to find a mentor and surround yourself with other CEOs with whom you can share your loneliness.

Now, I would say, add to the list someone who did it before if you're going public, someone who took their company public, and if you're going for an M&A, someone who sold their company before. They might be able to provide yet another critical perspective.

THE "WOW" EFFECT

When you get an offer you like, two things happen, often concurrently.

- The first is that you think about what it means for you and start to imagine the day after.
- The second is that you must ask yourself, "What do I need to do right now?"

In general, once there is a proposal, one of the most immediate things you do is simple math, calculating: "What's in it for me? For my team and employees?"

When Waze was acquired, it felt like "WOW, BIG WOW, this is like nothing I've ever experienced before." It was ten times bigger than anything I'd made that far—enough to retire on, enough to take care of the next generation, enough for nearly everything I could imagine.

I'm rather a simple person. My idea of fun is spending an entire winter at an Airbnb apartment in a ski resort; I don't need to own the resort, nor a chalet there. But I have big dreams, of making a bigger impact and continuing to create value for many people again, and again, and again through my start-ups.

Do you immediately start to imagine what's going to happen the day after? Not always. Other questions may come to mind, such as "Who do I need to support and help?" and "What other promises have I made to myself?"

But the real WOW when we sold Waze was someplace else.

- How about the biggest amount ever paid for an app? (That record didn't last too long; it was just a few months later that Facebook acquired WhatsApp for much more.)
- How about the recognition that you've changed the world?
- How about the impact this will have on so many people?
- How about a little bit of local pride, becoming the only Israeli consumer app to make it to the unicorn club?
- How about becoming an entrepreneur celebrity?
- And, of course, there is the large amount of money that changes your life.

I was doing well before the exit. I actually had a few mini-exits beforehand.

At Comverse, I had stock options, which I used to build my first house.

At Waze, we sold secondary shares in 2012, and I was able to take home what, for me at the time, was a lot of money.

Then comes a $1.15 billion exit.

Some people imagine (and I run into these cases all the time) that if I sold my company for a billion dollars, I must have $1 billion somewhere in my pocket, right?

Well, I owned less than 3 percent of Waze on the day of the acquisition. Still, it came out to $30 million. That sounds like a lot of money, and it *was*. It was a life-changing event for me. I never saw so much money.

I was forty-eight years old at the time.

But then you pay taxes, you get divorced, and you end up with much less. It was still enough for me to retire, but that never crossed my mind. I only thought about making a bigger impact, and I have invested most of the money into new start-ups that I have been building ever since.

MY BABY

There's another side to the exit: Your company is not yours anymore.

I recently spoke with the local branch of an American company that had acquired an Israeli start-up two years prior. In the call, they said, "We used to be called XYZ, but we are not allowed to say that name anymore." (And no, it was not Voldemort.)

While what's going to happen to your baby is part of the negotiation and dialogue with the acquiring partner, there are really only two options: Your company won't be yours anymore, or it will be.

- Waze stayed Waze for at least nine years after the acquisition.
- Moovit is still Moovit and Nir stayed on as CEO.

That's not always the case, though.

Intel acquired Telmap and, two years later, decided to shut it down.

At the time when Intel/Mobileye acquired Moovit, autonomous vehicles were important to them and as a part of that, autonomous public transportation was as well.

But what if they change their strategy?

Giving up your baby means you *let it go*. The baby is no longer a baby. It is mature now, and you're setting it free rather than giving up on it.

Now, for the sake of discussion, assume that your company's identity and independence *won't* last after the acquisition. Does this change your point of view on the deal? If it does, don't sell. If you assume it will take ages before this happens, don't worry—most likely you won't be there when it does.

YOU, YOUR FAMILY, EMPLOYEES AND REPUTATION, YOUR WORLD, AND THEN OTHERS

OK, so a life-changing event has happened, and you think you know what it is you want to do next. Here is the *real* order of importance of things you should think about.

You should put yourself first, and, to be clear, this refers to a combination of many things: your well-being, ego, alter ego, your reputation, the next X years, your future.

Imagine all those, and ask, "Is this good for me?"

Now consider the alternatives and the risks associated with them.

Your family comes next. What does it mean to them?

Waze's exit was all over the media and, to an extent, a bit too detailed. A few days later, when my daughter's high school class was supposed to go on a rather expensive field trip, the teacher told the class that, now, my daughter can easily sponsor the field trip for the entire class.

Think about what there is to gain and what there is to lose. Is it good for your family?

Next come your employees—those who were instrumental in getting there. Is this going to be a life-changing event for them? Did you take care of them? Do you feel proud that you did?

If not, it is not too late to fix it in the deal structure. Make sure you do. Read the beginning of the chapter again; you really want to be proud that you took care of your employees.

Once you've addressed yourself, your family, and employees, you'll want to consider the rest—the board of directors and the shareholders. Of course, they should be happy, but when you are juggling priorities, they are the last ones you should be thinking of.

EMOTIONAL EXTREME ROLLER COASTER

You know by now that building a start-up is a roller coaster, and we already established that fundraising is like a roller coaster in the dark—you don't even know what's coming. These are all just basic training for what's coming when you contemplate a merger and acquisitions deal.

In January 2013, the Israeli press was insisting that Apple was set to acquire Waze for $400 million. The reality is that we never spoke with Apple, but many people came to congratulate me, on one hand, and to ask for financial support on the other hand. It got to the point where I had a hard time convincing my mom that I could not support a certain distant relative because I don't really have $400 million. And I needed to argue with the most amazing argument—"But the paper said . . ."

At that time, however, we were in dialogue with Google. They offered us $400 million, which we turned down. We turned it down because we thought we could do better. We had made amazing progress, so we thought we should keep on going. This sum of money meant close to $15 million for me on a personal level, way more than what I'd made until then. This is why it becomes so personal and extreme. With fundraising, you are thinking of your company's plan and vision. For M&A deals, your dreams and family become part of it, as it will change your life and theirs.

EVERYTHING IS PERSONAL NOW

Until there is a deal on the table, your equity is considered "paper money"—maybe it will materialize, but in reality you cannot buy anything with it.

When there is a deal on the table, however, this is *real* money and, most likely, you will treat it differently. At the end of the day, the decision to sell a company is about 99 percent personal. You, your cofounders, and your management team must ask the question of what it means for you. That question very often drives your gut feeling and decisions.

But there is more to it.

The reward is quantifiable. Recognition isn't. An M&A deal is both reward *and* recognition for the entire journey, in which your long journey is recognized by the industry and the start-up community—essentially, by everyone.

For some, the reward is the most important part. For others, it's the recognition or the impact. It is the combination of these two parts that makes it personal.

Now, this is critical to understand: *Personal does not necessarily mean rational.*

Occasionally, entrepreneurs come to me for perspective. They want to know if they should sell or not.

"What's your gut feeling?" I ask them. "Because I can give you five to ten reasons why you should, or five to ten reasons why not. What is it that *you* want to hear?"

THE WAZE M&A ROLLER COASTER

The media reports that Apple was to acquire Waze for $400 million, though not true, became a roller coaster in and of themselves. Employees kept on coming all day long to ask what it meant for them, and many friends called to congratulate them.

My immediate family was easy to handle. I told them, "Read my lips: There is no deal, that's it," although it was admittedly hard to explain why the newspapers and the TV stations had reported a deal if there was nothing there.

While an offer from Apple was not even on the table, the double-spread newspaper articles that were published at the time potentially triggered Google to make an offer of its own that January.

Noam Bardin, Waze's CEO, called me to say that Google had invited him and the team to Google's "secret room" in Silicon Valley. Amir and Ehud were in town so they were ready to go that same day. I really wanted to be in that secret room, too, but I was in Israel, and I wanted the meeting to happen sooner rather than later even more than I wanted to be there.

Noam, Amir, and Ehud called me right after the meeting and said Google agreed to offer an M&A in cash. A few days later, we received the term sheet from Google and were disappointed to discover that the actual proposal was $400 million. At the time, we were on the right track and we still had plenty of the cash that we had raised just six months beforehand.

I had already been thinking we should try to raise $50 million to $100 million at a higher valuation than $400 million. There were initial discussions about a fundraising round at a valuation of $700 million.

The offer of $400 million would have meant a life-changing event for me, but I thought that we could and should do better.

We celebrated the moment and the offer, and then we decided to say no. We also decided that we were not going to sell for less than $1 billion.

Putting things into perspective, there were no acquisitions like that at the time. There had never been a three-comma deal for an app before.

Then came the second offer.

In April 2013, a US company, one of the top ten companies in the world, that did not have maps and thought that maps and community would be awesome for their offering, reached out to us saying they might be interested in acquiring Waze and that we should discuss the future.

It was too early to even consider how serious they were, but after a week, when we thought we had a good understanding of the shared future, they put a term sheet on the table with a price tag of $1 billion.

The only problem: The proposed deal was mostly a stock deal. Now, they were a publicly traded company, so it was as close to cash as possible, but the amount might also go up and down due to fluctuations in the stock market.

I was in the office supporting Noam in his fundraising journey and preparing for due diligence when the offer came in.

The following is what was going through my mind.

The $30 million I would earn would be a life-changing event for me.

I thought about all the people at the office. "OK, this guy is going to enjoy a life-changing event, and that guy, too, and she is definitely, yes." I realized that this was going to impact the lives of nearly everyone at the office—those who started five years prior, and even those who started five months ago, too.

"WOW, being so impactful for so many people will make me the happiest person on the planet," I thought. "I will be happy to say yes."

My situation was different than many of the employees, perhaps. I'd already realized that I was not going to stay on afterward, as I already had Pontera in the making. Moovit was already requiring my attention, and there were more start-ups that I wanted to build.

I was ready to move on. At the same time, there was another voice saying, "Wait a minute, we are in a dialogue with an investor that will be investing some $100–150 million in the company, which will give us the funding we need to become even more significant and more impactful."

Amir and Ehud were excited. It was definitely a life-changing event for all of us. We discussed it briefly. We all shared the gut feeling of saying yes.

So, we did. We said YES.

We quickly gathered the board of directors to get their blessing to enter into the negotiation and due-diligence phase.

With a $1 billion price tag, they gladly approved!

This is when the deal journey began.

We wanted to keep the negotiations a secret even from the employees, but if the buyer needed to do due diligence, what would happen if, all of a sudden, a bunch of corporate development types showed up? Our team would most definitely get it.

We spun the visit as a due-diligence trip for a new investor.

As we discussed with the potential acquiring partner the essence of the term sheet, they explained that, for them, secrecy was critical. If this deal leaked, there would be no deal.

As part of the term sheet dialogue, we told them that Microsoft was an investor in the company and they have ROFN (right of first notice) terms. We were legally bound to tell them we had an acquisition offer from a major-league player, but not the details. We were actually pretty sure that Microsoft, without proper maps, would make a bid for Waze, too, but they never did.

After approving the final version of the term sheet, due diligence began. Our potential acquirer came to our offices, and they were impressed with what we had built so far. After about a week, they went back to the US.

"This is not an investor doing due diligence," Samuel Keret, who was running sales, told me. "This is due diligence for an M&A transaction."

Up until that moment, very few people knew. We decided to share what was going on regarding the negotiations with the company's management; it simply didn't make sense to do otherwise.

A week later, the corporate development team came back to Israel for further discussions, at which point they presented some new conditions. In particular, that all key employees must relocate from our offices in Israel to the US.

We looked at each other and said, "This is not going to happen. There might be some people that will be OK with it, but most of them are not going to move."

We said no to the relocation. They then wanted to start new negotiations around how many of the staff members would relocate and which functions would move.

"We cannot even ask," we told them, "because we will need to tell people why we're asking and then the secrecy won't be kept anymore."

After about a month of negotiations and due diligence, it looked like we were stuck, mainly because of this future misalignment.

In our minds, they didn't know what to do with us. In their minds, we were being stubborn by insisting that the majority of the company would remain in Israel.

On May 9, 2013, the Israeli press reported that Facebook was in the final phase of due diligence to acquire Waze for a billion dollars; the rumors were more or less accurate; we *were* in the middle of a dialogue.

What the press didn't know is that we were *stuck* in the dialogue. The gap between the buyer's desire to relocate the team and our desire to stay as one company in Israel was too great, but it was the uncertainty about our shared future what got the deal stuck. Just a month before, I had imagined some $25 million on its way to my bank account. Now I didn't. What had started just about a few weeks ago and looked like the highest priority on their end (and definitely the highest priority on ours) became a low priority on the acquirer's side.

For us, it was back to fundraising and running the company.

That's when the term sheet from Google came up. This time, it was a much a better offer than before. It was a higher number: $1.15 billion in cash. The name, Waze, would stay, and there was mutual agreement about the vision to help drivers to avoid traffic jams. There was no plan to merge us into Google Maps.

It was also clear that Waze would remain in Israel. Our headquarters wouldn't even need to move to Google's offices in Israel, unless we choose to do so. As for our Palo Alto office, they would need to move to Mountain View where Google is based, although there were only about ten people in that office at the time, so we agreed.

We went back to the first buyer with whom we were negotiating, as we had a no-shop clause, and told them there was another offer that just came in, unsolicited. They simply said we were free to take it.

One of the items on Google's one-page term sheet was that they could close the deal in one week. We said yes and hoped that, this time, it would work out. Google was a better acquirer for us. They knew the space and, essentially, were our only serious competitor.

They were also the ones to realize that what we were building was great, both in terms of map, traffic, mapping capabilities, and the app itself, which was so much better than Google Maps for driving.

Imagine the roller-coaster journey of due diligence all conducted within a single week. (It turned out to be ten days.) Some of us, like Fej Shmuelevitz, who was running communities and at the same time reading every single word of the documents, didn't sleep for a week and, if we were able to catch a few hours of sleep, it was on the floor of our law office.

In some cases, we were looking at actual deal breakers during the due-diligence phase.

"Just give us a map to evaluate," Google told us at one point early on. So, of course, we sent them the map of Tel Aviv.

"This is great," they responded, "but it's in your backyard. Can you give us something else?"

We next sent them the file we had on the San Francisco Bay Area.

"This is great, too, but everyone in the world will polish their Bay Area map to a shiny level. Please give us something else."

I suggested we give them a list of countries to choose from, but what we really wanted was for them to pick Malaysia where Waze was very successful. Outside of Israel, we had the best map there, and it was 100 percent community made.

We sent them a list of countries including Chile, Brazil, Costa Rica, Malaysia, France, Italy, and Sweden—where we knew our maps were excellent.

What did they pick up? Malaysia.

That was essentially the end of the data-quality due diligence.

Then something else came up.

"You have partnership agreements in so many countries—Brazil, the rest of LATAM, Indonesia, South Africa," Google pointed out. "But we have our own geo partners in different places, so we don't need yours."

We basically agreed but suggested making the change only after the deal was done, as we felt we had plenty of time.

They accepted, but then, three days later, they changed their tune.

"We want all of your partnership agreements terminated," came the word from on high. That would have resulted in a couple million dollars to be paid in early termination fees. Google agreed to pay even if the deal fell apart.

Finally, Google required key employees and management to stay, and created an appropriate retention package for them. It worked: Nearly everyone stayed for that period of time. Some left shortly afterward. Noam remained with Google until 2021.

The deal closed on June 9, 2013.

THE ULTIMATE DNA

During the five and a quarter years of Waze's formal journey, we had two employees who passed away. The first was our office manager who died in a car crash. A senior developer died from cancer a few years later. Both were among our first hires.

We established a trust fund to keep the equity plan going for both of them, with their spouses as the beneficiaries. When Waze was acquired, both of the spouses became millionaires, along with about 75 percent of Waze employees.

All of Waze's employees had stock options, including the most junior on staff and even the janitor, whom we all loved. If there is something that I'm really proud of, it's the reward given to all those people that followed me over the years—at Waze, at Moovit, and in my other start-ups.

WHEN TO SAY YES

Saying "yes" to an exit offer will dramatically change your trajectory. Here are some very good reasons to say yes, and what you need to consider.

- Is this a life-changing event for you? If so, think positively about it.
- Is this a life-changing event for many of your employees? If so, think even more positively about the deal. If not, try to structure the deal so that it is.
- How do you envision the future? Are you willing to commit for a few more years to this journey?
- Are you tired of leading this journey? If so, then it might be time to exit.

Don't "average out" these considerations. Rather, use only the extreme answers. So, if you really are tired, and it is an OK deal, there is a way out for you.

If it is a dramatic event for you, and even if you could keep on running the business forever, I would still encourage you to think positively about the deal.

SECONDARY SHARES

I cannot reiterate this enough: Always sell secondary shares whenever you can and, in particular, when you go through the up-rounding journey.

Just imagine that you have good traction and, after some five years, you bring the company to a $250 million valuation. You raise some $50 million, and the round is oversubscribed. In this case, you should consider selling in the range of 10 to 20 percent of your holdings.

Say that you own 10 percent of the company. Ten percent of that—that is, 1 percent—means $2.5 million to take home.

Now, let's say that your start-up is making even better progress and, a year later, you can raise an additional $100 million at a $750 million valuation. Selling 1 percent means about $8 million to take home.

Then, another couple of years go by and you have reached a $5 billion valuation, in which case 1 percent means a $50 million to take home.

There are four reasons for selling secondary shares, and they are all super important:

- **Reward and recognition**—You are already some five to ten years into the making and have good traction, and you should be recognized and rewarded for this major achievement. You are very special to have brought the company to this place, and that deserves a celebration.
- **Patience to continue**—Once you're selling shares and taking money home, your appetite for a bigger deal increases. An entrepreneur that didn't sell secondary shares is more likely to sell the company earlier than someone who already made a significant amount of money.

- **Reduce risk in your portfolio**—If you're a young entrepreneur, more than 90 percent of your wealth may be hidden within the company. If I were your financial advisor, I would tell you that you must be out of your mind—this level of risk, having 90 percent of your assets in a single basket, is way too much.

- **Top-up**—Your board of directors wants you to be happy, patient, and motivated. If they think you don't have enough skin in the game, they will top-up your equity position with additional shares or options. If they don't do that, the next investor will (you may need to tell them to do it).

In some cases, when a secondary opportunity is on the table, the investors don't actually want the founders to sell secondary shares. They prefer to see hungry founders and they are afraid that a secondary deal or a mini-exit would reduce the founders' motivation.

In my experience, it is the other way around.

Tasting a mini-exit makes you more motivated and, in particular, willing to take higher risks.

When should you sell secondary shares?

- When you can and when it makes sense.
- When you can get a significant amount of money that matters to you and that is not at the expense of the company.
- When you're already several years into the making of the company, and you have the realization that this period is going to last several years more until you get to a liquidation event.

How much motivation and appetite will you have after such a secondary sale? I once read a research study in which people were asked, "How much more money do you need to feel it is enough?" The number was pretty consistent; it was always a factor of what they had, usually double.

So, someone with $50,000 in savings said $100,000 would make them feel it is enough, and someone with a $1 million said it was $2 million, and someone with $30 million said $60 million.

For people with very high aspirations, rather than double, it was 10x.

If this is the case, your motivation and appetite are not going to decrease; they will only increase if you sell secondary shares.

What about employees? It's exactly the same. If there is an opportunity for selling secondary shares, then you should include them, particularly those employees who have already spent a long time with the company.

Your job as a CEO is to take care of your employees. It will be the most rewarding part of the journey.

EXERCISING OPTIONS

The Israeli ESOP plan, as opposed to the American ISO plan, allows employees to exercise their options without any tax implications. The tax event is postponed until selling the shares. The plan we had at Waze allowed employees who left, or whose employment was terminated, to exercise the options within ninety days after the end of employment. At Waze, we had a guy who joined rather early and got some share options, as our model was that everyone gets options. After about a year, though, we fired him. He then had ninety days to exercise the vested options (in other words, buying his share options at the price they were set in the original agreement). It would have cost him about $10,000 out of pocket to exercise those options.

"I'm not going to exercise options for two reasons," he told me. "Ten thousand dollars is a bit too much right now for me. But, in particular, I don't believe in the company anymore."

"What changed?" I asked him.

"You let me go, so I don't believe in the company anymore," he replied.

"Did you believe in the company when you joined?" I followed up.

"Of course!" he said.

"Did you believe in the company ninety days ago?"

Again, he replied in the affirmative.

"So, what changed?"

"I told you," he said, now a bit more impatient. "It's the fact that Waze let me go!"

It turns out that most people are ego-driven. If they opt to leave on their own accord, they tend to still believe in the company and, therefore, will exercise their options.

If they were let go, however, what crosses the minds of most people goes something like this:

I think I'm really good. If they let me go, they don't know jack shit and therefore I don't believe in the leadership, which means the company is not going to be successful.

That guy missed an opportunity for about a quarter of a million dollars—what could have been a life-changing event for him at the time.

As a CEO, don't get involved in the question of whether ex-employees should be exercising their options. Depending on where you're based, it may even be illegal to provide such advice. What you *should* provide is a very simple and transparent explanation of the equity position of each employee when you hire them. Most likely you'll refresh that once a year.

Some companies are very vague about equity compensation, while others are very transparent. I suggest the following: Every once in a while (say every half year), pick ten random employees and ask them, "How many options (or RSU—restricted stock units) do you have? How much is that as a percentage of your holdings? How much is it worth today?"

In my opinion, they need to know.

A friend of mine used to work at Moovit in the early days. He helped them for a while and then left. He had some already-vested options and I urged him to exercise them.

"That's about five thousand dollars in cash and I'm kind of short," he told me.

"I will lend you the money," I assured him.

He exercised the options and was one of the people Nir called just before the transaction.

His $5,000 turned into about $150,000—a dramatic event for this person.

About thirty seconds after Nir's call, Nir rang me up to say that he was so excited; he could hear over the phone tears of joy.

Thirty seconds later, my friend called me up, saying that Nir called him.

ALWAYS BRING A DEAL

If you want to discuss a deal, start by bringing one . . . and then everything will become real.

When a real offer is on the table, you can start to think if you like it. Even if the timing is not right, even if you haven't made significant progress yet, or the valuation is still low—there is nothing like an offer to get things moving. It will be easier to raise capital, get the support of existing investors, and hire employees once you have a deal on the table, and afterward as well.

How might this look?

"What if we acquire you?" or "Would you be open to discussing an M&A?" or a meeting with the corporate development team whose job it is to acquire companies, or a banker saying, "I can get you a buyer at a nice price." But none of those are an offer.

An offer is a term sheet with the intent to acquire your company. "No-offer offers" are, in reality, due-diligence questions by a potential partner.

In the early days of Waze, Arkady Volozh, the CEO of Yandex (a Russian language search engine and web provider), visited Tel Aviv and we met.

"What if we offer you fifty million dollars to acquire Waze?" he said.

I told him that we would consider any offer and most likely decline.

Arkady used this method as a due-diligence question to understand how committed we were to the journey.

Some years later, he was visiting Israel again and was scheduled to meet Nir at Moovit.

I prepared Nir.

"He will ask you if you're for sale and will make a test-the-waters offer of fifty million dollars or maybe even more. No matter what the offer is, simply say no—it is just a due-diligence question."

The main reason to bring a deal to the table is to accelerate the process. Your company is very unique and there aren't many like it. If a buyer wants to buy you, they want to buy *you* and not someone else. As long as you're independent, there is no rush for that decision. The acquirer can acquire you today, tomorrow, next year, or whenever, regardless of the price.

But if there is a deal on the table, the opportunity to acquire you or even to invest in you may disappear and, therefore, a deal on the table accelerates the process. This deal may be for an M&A, a large funding round, or for filing for IPO.

IPO VERSUS M&A

There's a common saying in the business world: "Fake it until you make it." But that's not always the case.

While raising capital, your investors are hoping to hear that you plan to build a huge company that will become public eventually. This is exactly what you need to tell them. But the actual decision of going public is very different.

You should seriously consider going public if:

- You think you have something really big, you want to continue running it forever, and you are convinced this start-up of yours is a once-in-a-lifetime opportunity.
- You don't envision anyone acquiring your company.
- You have raised a lot of money at a very high valuation (which means the list of potential buyers is now much smaller).

Running a public company is very different. It entails a lot of headaches, and it is another major change in the direction of the company.

If you think you want that, then you need to speak with two to three CEOs who have taken their companies public in the last three years—not about the IPO road show but about the years *afterward*.

In many cases, it won't be up to you. M&A is an opportunity; IPO is the default. PE (private equity) is another opportunity that is somewhere in between.

The more progress you can make and the higher valuation you can command, some of the opportunities you had before will diminish and will no longer be an option. At $100 million, many companies may acquire you. At $1 billion, there are way fewer that may acquire you. At $10 billion, there are very few, if any.

At the end of the day, it all boils down to a few questions you need to ask yourself.

- Is this a life-changing event?
- Do you want to keep your company forever?
- Do you want to deal with the headaches of a public company?
- Do you have alternatives?

Once you can answer those questions, your path will be rather clear.

SAYING NO

To get the deal you want, you have to say NO to the deal you *don't* want.

One of my CEOs came to me one day and said there might be a dialogue for M&A. It was a private equity fund trying to combine a few companies to get a bigger market position.

"That's great," I said. "So, what's the deal?"

A few days later, he came back with a deal that looked like X in cash plus 2X in equity of the future combination. The amount for X was rather low, so even 3X was still rather low.

"If there is such a deal, would you like to take it?" I asked the CEO.

He said no.

I kept on digging.

"If it would be two, three, five or ten times more than they offered, would you consider it?"

"At five to ten times I will consider it," he said. "So, how should I negotiate to get to that point?"

"You say NO!" I said.

"That's it?" he asked

"Well, you can be more polite. You can say, 'Thank you for your consideration, but the answer is NO.'"

"Should I give the potential PE investor a guideline of what will make us interested?" the CEO continued.

"No!" I emphasized. "A simple no is the only relevant answer here. If they want to propose something else, they will. If you give them any room for negotiation, and they propose a ballpark figure of X, if you then say no, they may come back with something completely different."

The only way that you can significantly change the terms of the deal is through a competitive bid. If the buyer is afraid to lose the deal, the price can go up dramatically.

Losing a deal is not the same as "no deal." It means someone else will take it.

So, if there is an offer on the table and you say no, the buyer will walk away initially but may come back later (months or even a year later) with a new offer.

If, however, there is a competitive deal on the table, there is no option of coming back in the future and, therefore, the deal offer will improve dramatically.

SAYING NO IS NOT ALWAYS A GOOD IDEA

Somewhere in the "prehistoric ages" of the high-tech ecosystem (around the year 1999), a friend of mine was running a start-up in the email area. He got an offer to be acquired for $150 million.

At the time, it was a very high amount, and he was holding about 25 percent of the company, so it would have meant nearly $40 million for him.

The company's last round before that was $30 million at a $50 million pre-money valuation. Now, this was 1999—a period where unrealistic valuations were commonplace, somewhat similar to end of 2021 and beginning of 2022—and he was stunned by the idea of earning $40 million. He wanted to say yes.

My friend asked for my perspective.

"If you like the deal, it is a life-changing event for you, and you think you can fulfill your destiny under the new ownership, you should say yes."

But one of the investors from the last round nixed the idea.

"We've just invested in you in order to build a billion-dollar company, not just to earn 2X on our money. You are a world-class CEO. There's no way you cannot bring this company to a billion-dollar valuation within a couple of years."

The investor convinced my friend to say no. Then came the dot-com crash in the year 2000, followed by a long roller-coaster journey.

The next offer didn't come until 2005 and it was for just $30 million, this time with liquidation preferences. That meant zero dollars to my friend.

He said no again.

In the end, there was a very small deal some years later with no cash for him at all. Only a retention package.

I have other examples in which saying no turned out amazingly, but the most important part is that *you* are in the driver's seat and, even though there might be people screaming from the back seat, it is still you behind the wheel.

INVESTMENT BANKERS

When negotiating the deal at Waze, we held an internal discussion on whether we should hire an investment banker.

Investment banking is a segment of banking that helps companies with IPOs, M&As, etc., helping to find deals and opportunities, as well as acting as a consultant or a mediator in such deals. The major argument against hiring a banker was that there might only be a single-digit number of players in the market that were relevant for us. Those players had the deep pockets to pay the price, and one of them was already a shareholder (Microsoft). Moreover, if a potential acquirer wasn't thinking of us already, we were not going to get them to do so in a short time.

Today, I think very differently.

The ability for you to create a competitive offer in a very short time frame is limited; it is much easier for a banker to take on that task. In particular, the banker, through negotiation, will create more time for the competitive bids. You will not engage with an alternative offer before you have one; the banker will.

The other reason I think a banker is needed is simple. You have a limited ability to negotiate the deal. You haven't seen other deals negotiated with that buyer, and you are at the beginning of a relationship with them, so you are not sure you can negotiate like there is no tomorrow, since there *is* a tomorrow. A banker, however, can.

The key question is when to bring on the banker. The answer is when you tell yourself: "If there will be an offer at two times the price of the last round's valuation, I will consider it favorably." That's the time to start building a relationship with a banker.

When won't it work out? If you bring the banker to a situation where there is already an offer on the table and you expect them to negotiate on your behalf. Bankers don't like doing that.

While I was working at Comverse, we were looking to acquire a company out of Cambridge, Massachusetts, in the speech-recognition space. We put an offer on the table. They said yes, but quickly added, "Wait, we will let you know who our banker is in a few days."

The reality is that there wasn't enough time for them to generate competitive bids and the banker was unable to create an alternative. When it came time to negotiate, we finalized a deal that was actually *less* than our willingness to pay.

There is always room for negotiation, but in reality, negotiation is essentially a transfer of power via dialogue. Without alternatives, that power is limited.

If you want the deal, and you know it will be nearly impossible for you to say no, find someone who can easily say no, and send *them* to negotiate.

If you want the deal, you will often find yourself negotiating with multiple parties at the same time: the buyer, your family, your shareholders, and on behalf of other groups such as your employees.

Still, the deal may be sweet for you but sour for the last-round investors, or early investors. Remember the priorities: you, your family, your employees, and only then your investors.

THE ESSENCE OF AN M&A DEAL

What does a mergers and acquisitions deal look like? There are a few elements. Some are similar to an investment, like how much they are willing to pay. Others have to do with the "day after"—the vision and the business purpose of the acquisition, which is even more important.

Examine the deal in three dimensions:

1. **The mutual future.** Are you on board with the vision and the new mission resulting from the M&A? Can you see how the integration is going to work? Who is committed to it working on the buying organization's side? Do you like your new boss and your new position and title? How long are you committed to staying? Not only did you have the most challenging journey in your lifetime for the last decade, but now you're expected to stay three more years to work out the integration. How do you feel about that? What about the name of your company—will your brand continue to exist? Even if you don't care about the future, and you plan to leave as soon as

you can, and you are there only for the cash reward of the deal, you still have to sign up for the future, otherwise, there will be no deal. If the buyer doesn't believe you are up to the mutual future they envision, the buyer will walk away from the deal.

2. **The deal.** How much? Cash or equity? How much for the retention package for employees and you? Is there an "earn out," where part of the acquisition price is based on performance over time? If so, for whom, when, and based on what? How about a "holdback," where money is held in escrow to ensure that certain conditions are met by the seller before the funds are released? How much and for whom? Before you even speak about the dollar amount, figure out the future.

3. **You.** What is your vision and how does that compare with the new vision? Can you be successful? Can you even imagine yourself with a new boss and a different corporate DNA?

Regardless of the outcome, you must start the dialogue with agreement on the shared future and the role of your start-up in this new future. If there is no future, there is no merit to the deal.

You want very simple answers to several key questions:

- "Why do you want to acquire us?"
- "What's in it for you (the buyer)?"
- "How do you envision the future five years down the road and five days after the completion of the transaction?"

Even though the framework of the deal has already been discussed or presented, the first few days of dialogue should focus on the question of a mutual future. If you like the deal, but not the future, think of redefining the mutual future, and if you still don't like the mutual future, think of your employees before saying no—would you do this deal for them?

Let's turn back to the deal. Not all millions look the same.

- $100 million in cash is one kind of deal.
- $100 million in equity of a public company is something else.
- And $100 million worth of equity in another private company is completely different still.

In the first case, you, your shareholders, and your employees get cash.

The second case is fairly close to the first. Even assuming there might be some lock-up period where you, as an employee of a public company, cannot buy or sell shares for a while. This lock-up period may last a few months. In general, you will be able to cash out relatively quickly, and easily.

The third example, however, is very different. You've essentially replaced one potential outcome with a different one, and you have no idea when the new potential will materialize (if at all), nor do you know how big it will be.

RETENTION PACKAGES

The buyer knows that the team is super important. They are essentially buying the team plus the traction the team has created. A major concern for the buyer is that they will put tons of money into the deal; you, your management, and your employees will all have a life-changing event, and then leave.

So, the buyer will be looking for your commitment, hoping your word is trustworthy, but they will, at the same time, create a retention package for you, for your management, and for key employees to keep them rewarded throughout the integration period as well as afterward.

This retention package might be two to five years long. Let's say it is for a three-year period. An example of a deal with a retention package may look like this: $300 million, comprising $250 million for shareholders and a $50 million retention package to keep key employees for the next three years.

Now, let's say that you own 5 percent of the company on the day of the M&A. This is $12.5 million in cash plus more in retention.

How much more?

The buyer will make it significant for you—perhaps even $5 million a year for the next three years—which will probably be enough to make you stay. It's certainly significant enough to think about it!

But what if the cash you get is much more, say $100 million? There won't be enough in the retention package to make it significant compared to the $100 million in cash.

Let's say there is a $10 million-a-year retention package for the next three years. In this case, though, you have shares worth $100 million. The buyer may say you will be getting only $70 million in cash with the rest structured as an additional $30 million retention to be paid if you stay over the next three years. So, the retention package becomes significant enough compared to the cash on the first day.

In the Waze deal (the one that went through), Google offered $1.15 billion in cash. Of that, $75 million was for retention. We in the management thought that was not enough to keep key employees for the next three to four years.

So, we negotiated with the board of directors and the shareholders to change that to a $120 million retention package.

Google obviously agreed. Instead of cash going to shareholders, it would go to employees—much better for them.

But then Google pulled another trick: They asked the key management to give up on some of the cash and double it through the retention period.

So, for example, we would give up on $25 million and get $50 million during the next three years.

If you want to succeed in the years to come, retention is mandatory, not just for the buyer, but also for you, to be able to retain your team. Expect it to be part of the deal and assume there is no deal without it.

Who doesn't like retention packages? The shareholders! Because, essentially, retention means we are taking some of the shareholders' value and distributing it to the employees, and we are doing it once, on the day of liquidation. To an extent, it is the same as ISO or any other equity plan you're using.

If you have a generous equity plan, where the majority of employees are still unvested, the need for retention will be low. I've seen retention packages ranging from 5 percent to 50 percent of the deal, but the rule of thumb is simple: It must be enough to retain all key employees over the relevant period.

The word "enough," however, is challenging. How much is enough?

"EARN OUTS" AND "HOLDBACKS"

While a retention package is certainly needed, and there will be no deal without it, a completely different type of beast is the "earn out." It basically means the cash part of the deal is small, but it can double, triple, or quadruple itself if you step up to specific targets set by the acquiring partner.

While it sounds promising, it is in fact quite nasty.

It is nasty because someone is going to hold you accountable for your three-year plan and objectives but will not commit to providing a budget for those three years.

The ability of a start-up to provide accurate forecasts or targets for a year is nearly impossible; for three years, it is simply irrelevant.

Say that you have a B2B start-up, growing at 2.5x from last year, and you have seventy customers and a total ARR (annual recurring revenue) of $15 million. Your business plan suggests 3x growth next year, 2.5x the year after, and 2x in three years.

A cash plus retention deal might look like this: $300 million cash plus $75 million retention. Assuming you have 10 percent of the equity, that comes out to about $30 million in cash for you plus retention.

An earn-out deal could look like this: $100 million in cash; plus $50 million retention; plus $50 million if the first-year targets are met, $100 million for second-year objectives, and $150 million to meet the third-year milestones.

While this may look like a bigger, better deal, the amount of uncertainty is so high that the risk is simply too great.

Here are a few of the most common risks.

- It is not clear that you will be there to receive the earn out when the time comes.
- Your three-year plan was very ambitious and assumed the execution of a program and a budget, but you don't know whether you will have either or both of those.
- The buyer may change strategy and make your original plans irrelevant.

Keep in mind that earn out is for *all* shareholders, so you're going to work your ass off for the next three years to achieve those objectives, yet your reward is only 10 percent of the deal. Investors that are no longer even involved with the company will enjoy the benefits the most.

The biggest issue of an earn out is that, in most cases, it is not paid; something happens a few years into the journey.

"Holdback" is another necessary evil. This is where the buyer is basically saying, "I don't have enough time to do a thorough due diligence, and regardless, if it is going to be a big deal, we will face multiple lawsuits, so we are going to put X percent of the deal in what is essentially an escrow account to handle those potential events. That money will be released sometime in the far future, once it is clear there are no more claims."

There are multiple challenges here. Who's part of the holdback? Is it all shareholders? Just common shares? Or everyone except employees?

The second challenge is that this money was already paid by the buyer, so they don't care about it. Most of it essentially belongs to the investors of the acquired company, which the buyer doesn't care about either. And yet, the buyer holds the key for the holdback fund.

At the end of the day, don't count on getting the holdback, or at least not all of it.

Another weird deal I've seen is when a buyer acquires just 70 percent of the company. In this case, the question is: What happens to the remaining 30 percent of the shares and, in particular, what happens to the shareholders? There will be no further liquidity as the majority (the 70 percent) is not going to sell, nor do they need to buy the rest.

On one hand, this is a simple way to get a 30 percent discount. There are "put" and "call" options associated with the deal. So, for example, when buying 70 percent of a company, the buyer pays $X as the price per share. The buyer also has an option to buy the remaining 30 percent at a price that is slightly higher than $X, say 1.2X, within two to three years, and the seller has the option to sell that 30 percent at a price of slightly less than $X, say 0.8X.

The result is that, most likely, the buyer will acquire the entire company, but with 30 percent of it paid later.

FINANCIAL, TAX, AND LEGAL ADVISORS

I'm going to admit something shocking here: I like to pay taxes—it means there is profit, and profit is good. What I don't like is overpaying on my taxes because of a lack of planning.

About a year ago, an entrepreneur I've known for many years reached out and asked for my advice. He was in an M&A dialogue and had no clue what to say.

We met and I guided him on the deal's essence and what matters. I even made an introduction to a lawyer.

A couple of weeks later, he came back to me.

"The deal is nearly done," he said. "The buyer will acquire seventy-five percent of the shares today and agreed on profit-sharing moving forward, so there will be no call or put options on the rest of the twenty-five percent."

He told me that he was already a dozen years into his journey and the company went through several funding rounds. Nearly all of this entrepreneur's 9.9 percent holding was in options from the last round, which took place about a year prior.

We did a quick calculation together.

"In a $50 million deal, I have nearly ten percent, which is $5 million," he explained. "Seventy-five percent of that is $3.75 million. After a twenty-five percent tax rate, I'll be left with close to $3 million in cash, more than I ever made and certainly a life-changing event."

"Wait a minute," I interrupted him. "Your options are not in the capital gains tax bracket. You should get someone to help you before you close the deal, so you can make sure you're taxed at the lowest rate."

In Israel, tax regulations are such that employees who receive stock options, by and large, will be taxed at a 25 percent tax rate. (The regular tax bracket in Israel is a whopping 47 percent.) There is a special ruling from the Israel Tax Authority which stipulates that, if you're selling shares more than two years after the grant day, you can sell them as secondary shares or as part of an M&A with a lower capital gains tax bracket.

In an M&A deal, all proceeds from those options are taxed at a lower tax rate. So, essentially, you're exercising the options and selling the shares on the same day, and you can still enjoy being in the long-term capital gains tax bracket.

That wouldn't work in the US, however. If you are exercising your options and selling your shares on the same day (as in a secondary shares deal, for example), you will be taxed at the short-term capital gains rate—a much higher tax bracket.

The alternative is to exercise your options, then hold the shares for at least a year before selling them.

"But wait a minute," you may be asking about now. "How do I even know there will be a buyer one year down the road?"

The point to these stories: *You need a tax advisor to plan ahead, not just in the event of a deal.*

The reason that I recommend you meet with a financial advisor rather early, or at least as soon as your equity is worth something, is simple. The advisor will tell you that you're crazy. "Nearly one hundred percent of your financial assets are based on one company."

In fact, it is even more than that. Your salary and your 401(k) are also both based on a single company—yours.

What should you be doing instead?

Sell secondary shares. Again and again and again.

What about legal?

In general, you should have a legal point of view whenever you will be discussing deals and you want around-the-clock support once the negotiations start. If you have a dealmaker lawyer on your team, have them negotiate for you.

Nitzan Hirsch-Falk (H-F & Co. Law Offices) was our lead lawyer at Waze, Moovit, and he will be a part of my future deals, as well. He is a dealmaker, a risk-taker, and a good negotiator to boot, which is exactly what I want.

CONFLICTS OF INTEREST

The entire deal is, by definition, a major conflict of interest. The biggest challenge is that those conflicts shift, reshape, and change during the negotiation and transaction process.

Think of the basics.

Your investors care about the outcome of this deal *for them*. They will take the money and walk away, but you will need to stay. It's *you* who needs to deal with the day after tomorrow. They don't.

At the same time, you're negotiating with the acquirer, trying to get the best deal for your company and your shareholders.

But wait a minute—a second later, the buyer is the new shareholder and you actually have to work together for the next few years.

What about your employees?

You want them to get the best possible outcome of the deal, and to stick with you for the next years of the journey. This is your opportunity to make sure they are well rewarded.

It's very challenging trying to juggle all those interests and still make everyone happy. But you don't have to keep everyone happy. You just have to make sure you get the deal done (and then everyone *will* be happy), and remain committed to your company's DNA.

There are a few levers you can pull to shift the balance between today and tomorrow and between you, your employees, and the shareholders. Pull those levers carefully. Too much of anything may blow the deal and then everyone will clearly *not* be happy.

What levers can you pull?

- **Retention versus cash.** While high retention is good for the future and for employees, it is not good for investors. Best practice: Build enough into the budget to have a significant reward for employees over the next three years.

- **Who participates in a holdback?** You want to exclude employees. Investors want to exclude themselves. The best practice here is to apply this to *all* shareholders, including yourself and founders, so no one is easy on releasing money from the holdback.

- **Retention versus earn out.** In an earn out, everyone participates, including all the shareholders. In retention, it's just the employees who stay.

The biggest challenge, however, lies someplace else.

You are not in a good place to negotiate if you're trying to please everyone. So, LET SOMEONE ELSE *NEGOTIATE* the deal. That could be your lawyer or a trusted board member (assuming you have one).

The buyer, you should assume, is doing the same. The buying organization usually has a business unit that cares about this deal going through; it's the one that later on you will become part of. The negotiator, on the other hand, is on the buyer's corporate development team. They won't need to work with you the next day and therefore are in a much better position to negotiate.

MANAGING YOUR INVESTORS THROUGH THE PROCESS

If this is going to be a conflict-of-interest issue, then you and your investors are not on the same page. You will need to manage them through the process.

Let me put things into a little perspective here.

Your investors will get their own lawyers to negotiate their side of the deal in order to get the maximum for their shareholders.

Let's not forget, though, that these are *your* shareholders. They invested when you needed it, and they have their own rights to be protected and you, as CEO, should be responsive to their interests.

But there is no future for them in this company. They don't need to be there after the transaction. You do. To be successful later on, you will need your team, and you will need them to stay.

So, leave yourself room to negotiate with all parties—the buyer, your board, the investors, and your employees. Always account for uncertainty. For example, you may not have received the retention requirements yet, or it may be unclear if there will be an earn out or not.

At the end of the day, the existing shareholders are in the weakest position to negotiate. If they stand to make a significant amount of money, they are not going to object. At the same time, they cannot force you to take a deal.

THE DAY AFTER

The sun is still shining, but that's about the only thing that is the same after you close the deal. The "closing of the deal" extreme roller coaster is now over, and you are still in a state of euphoria, on one hand, and exhausted on the other.

You wake up the next morning and *everything* changes: your company's name; the journey, which has come to an end and restarted; your bank balance; your boss; the recognition from the many people who care.

But the most significant thing that's changed is that you have no idea who you report to, what your new objectives are, or who matters in the new organization. You were essentially dropped out of the blue into a working company with your entire division, and you now need to start a new journey.

What do you do first?

Gather the employees and tell them what's happening. You can say something along the following lines:

"This is what it means to you (you will become XYZ's employee next week), this is why we are doing it, this is the new vision, and I will be striving in the next few weeks to understand what it all means for us. Meanwhile, please be patient."

You go to your new boss with your management team and build a one-hundred-day plan.

Then you go back to your family and tell them, "Remember how I was missing for a long journey and was completely not here for the last three weeks while we were negotiating? Well, guess what? It will be a few more weeks like that."

Once you settle the plan, you go back to your team and explain the new objectives and targets. You reiterate the deal and then have a one-on-one dialogue with each staff member. Finally, you send them to HR and to the CFO to completely understand the new world and what the deal will mean for them.

I started my career at Comverse as a software developer and then moved to product and marketing. In 1994, I relocated to the US.

By 1997, Comverse, which was number two in the global voicemail market, had merged with the number three player, Boston Technology. Comverse was rather strong internationally and with mobile operators, whereas Boston was strong domestically with landline operators. Their market shares were fairly complementary.

On the day of the announcement, I was at Comverse's New York office. The president of the company gathered all the employees to tell us about the deal. He was in the midst of showing us a fifteen- to twenty-minute presentation when he paused and said: "While this is important, I'm pretty sure everyone cares about one thing—what's going to happen to me."

"You've got it all wrong," I immediately responded, in front of everyone. "We don't really care about what's going to happen to you, we care about what's going to happen to us!"

That's the most important thing—when there are changes, people care about themselves first. You have to address that right away, as rumors will begin circulating fast.

The Comverse–Boston Technology deal was rather simple—an equity exchange between two public companies—so there was no liquidity event for employees. Yet, the only thing people cared about was what was going to happen to them.

Up next was the famous NIH (not invented here) conundrum that is part and parcel of so many M&A events.

Comverse built a voicemail system, and so did Boston Technology. Which one would remain the platform of the future, and what would happen to all the people working on the other one?

In 1998, I moved back to Israel but I was still traveling back and forth extensively to the US. It took nearly a year to "break the ice" with some of the Boston Technology people. I learned that they had been highly suspicious of the deal. I wondered why.

The acquisition was constructed in such a way that none of the Boston Technology employees could be fired in the first year. But that resulted in them creating what turned out to be an unsubstantiated theory that, after a year plus one day, all of them were going to get fired. It was only when they saw that this was not the case that they started to share more and stop being so defensive.

Let me give you another perspective.

Google Maps had its navigation app, its own mapmaking technology, and sources of traffic data. We wondered: How long before they would swallow Waze completely, suck up all our IP (intellectual property), and get rid of all our people?

Indeed, there was not a single person at Waze whose mind these questions didn't cross.

In fact, many people I've met over the years asked me the same question: "Why *didn't* they merge everything into a single offering?"

Let me ask that same question differently.

For the Google Maps people, the question was the opposite: "Why in heaven are we acquiring another company that is doing exactly the same thing we do, and why did we promise them that we are not going to swallow them?"

When Google acquired Waze, it was with the understanding that Waze was a better, more functional app with seven times higher usage than Google Maps. If I had been at Google back then, I would probably have asked the same question I did when I was at Comverse: "What's going to happen to me?"

So, why does Google still have two map and traffic offerings and not one?

While I don't know the answer from the inside, as I didn't stay on at Waze after the sale, I can imagine the following.

If you have the number one and number two products in the market and you combine them into one single product, no one will be able to tell you that this one or that one is better, or which is going to remain the market leader. If you change your product dramatically, it is even possible that you will become less than "good enough," and people will churn and switch to something else.

When people get used to something, they don't want to change. And if you force them to, it is unclear that you will end up at the top.

TWO DAYS AFTER

So, you have made it through the first one hundred days of the integration. You've defined the objectives, the plans, the budget, and the compensation and retention packages. Congratulations! You are now running a division within a large corporation and not a start-up company.

While all the business objectives seem to be OK, and you know you can deliver them, it is the DNA that is different. You're now part of a much larger entity. This results in several changes:

- You cannot speak with the press; the public affairs department takes care of that.
- You cannot issue a newsletter to your users without the legal department "sanitizing" it.
- You cannot hire a candidate before the job opening has gone through the acquiring company's hiring policy.

- You find yourself fighting battles that you don't like, that in fact you hate. You start to rethink the whole deal.

You may wonder: *"How do I get out of this!"*

While I was not at Google, I did speak to my friends there. One day, one of them came over and said, "That's it; I've had enough!"

"What's wrong?" I asked him.

"It's like I need written approval to fart, and then it is only one type of fart that I'm allowed to make."

Another friend told me that the company was wasting so much money, but when he tried to say something, it seemed like no one cared.

Three months later, the first guy told me he was leaving. We spoke while we were riding our bicycles.

"What about retention?" I asked him. "If I recall correctly, you had a nice retention package in order for you to stay, right?"

"Damn right!" he replied.

It was close to $750,000 on an annual basis, something very significant for him.

"That's like two thousand dollars a day, right?"

"Yes," he said. "Or about one hundred dollars an hour—even when you sleep!"

"So during this bike ride, you were making one hundred dollars, and now that we are drinking coffee on the beach you are also making one hundred dollars, right?"

He nodded in acknowledgment.

"Great, so let's keep riding on the weekends and rediscuss this again in three months," I said. "If you still want to leave, then leave, but it will be with two hundred thousand dollars more."

He stayed.

You should stay, too. After all, if you're not there, no one will be able to take care of your team nor deliver the expected results. You said you will, and your word still counts. After about one to two years, start to look for someone to replace you, so you can leave if you want.

There are no right or wrong decisions, just a decision to be made.

THE COMMITMENT TO STAY

This is one that's easily made but not easily kept.

Once you've decided that you would like to accept the offer—maybe it was a life-changing event or maybe you were getting tired and worn out from the journey—regardless of the reason, the commitment to stay is part of the deal.

But it is also a double-edged sword.

If you tell the buyer you don't want to stay, they won't buy, because they need you.

If you tell them you'll stay but just for two years and not for four years, you send a signal that you do not believe in the vision or in your ability to deliver on it.

So, you end up saying OK to whatever they are asking.

Here are a few final tips when it comes to negotiating and staying.

1. Let someone else negotiate on your behalf. You should signal nothing but the commitment to deliver. The main message should be, however, that there is nothing in the world that you will be able to deliver in four years and you won't be able to deliver in three.
2. Don't worry about the journey to come in the new organization. If you don't want to stay, you will find a way out.
3. Create a different spread of retention; otherwise major attrition is what will happen after the end of the retention package!

Nothing prepares you for this major switchback on your journey. Part of it is that your life has changed forever and part of it is that these are like three completely different periods within a very short time—before the offer, during the transaction, and the day after. Each is different, as if there is no connection between them.

STARTIPS

- **When to sell**—If the deal is a life-changing event for you, start to think about it positively. If you also like what the day after is going to look like, think about the deal even more positively.

- **Four things to consider**—The most important things to think about are you, your team, today, and tomorrow.

- **A better deal**—There might be a better deal, but to get one, you will need to "bake" it for a while. An investment banker may be able to get you what you need if you approach one ahead of time.

- **The transition from the day before to the day after**—This will be the most extreme transition of your life: Everything changes, not once but multiple times.

- **Read this chapter again** when you are about to discuss an offer.

Happylogue

Writing this book was a project I started with the vision of help- ing entrepreneurs increase their likelihood of being successful, and for a good reason: The world needs you! The world needs more and more successful entrepreneurs with a mission of solving problems and making our world a better place.

I hope you found some insights that will serve you on your entrepre- neurial journey.

Let me take this opportunity to summarize the most critical takeaways from the previous chapters.

- **Building a start-up is a journey of failures**—You try something and it doesn't work and then you try another thing that doesn't work until you try something that finally *does* work. Therefore, the most important rule to increase the likelihood of success is to try *more*, and the way to try more is by **failing fast**.
- **There is no such thing as a bad idea**—Entrepreneurs must embrace and encourage failure as a way to move forward within their organizations.
- **Users**—There are a few critical rules about users that you and your product team must accept. First, users belong to different groups. Innovators, early adopters, and the early majority are the main categories that will matter to you. A user from one group cannot understand the emotions and mindset of a user from another group; therefore, you have to meet different users and understand their issues and perceptions.

The second important rule is that, de facto, most of your users in the first few years are going to be first-time users. No one can have a first-time experience for the second time. Thus, the only way for you to get a sense of it is to *watch* first-time users.

- **Product-market fit**—This is the most important part of your journey. If you figure out PMF, you are on the path to being successful. If you don't, you will die. It's as simple as that. PMF is measured in *only* one way—retention. For B2C products, that's easy: It's when users are coming back. For B2B (or when the customer is paying), retention is measured by renewals. Even before retention, you will need to figure out conversion. How are users getting to the value? *Conversion is a derivative of simplicity, and retention is a derivative of value.* Without conversion and retention, you will die.

- **DNA = People**—At the end of the day, if you have the right DNA for your company, this will be the journey of your life. If not, it will be a nightmare of your life. Don't tell yourself, "In my next company I will do things differently." Do it now. "Today is the first day of the rest of your life" may be a cliché but it's also true!

- **Firing is more important than hiring**—If there is someone who doesn't fit, the sooner you disengage from that person, the better off you will be. Keep in mind that, if there is someone who doesn't fit, everyone knows that, and usually you will be the last one to know. Once you fix it, everyone will be relieved. But how do you know? For every person you hire, after one month, ask yourself a very simple question: "Knowing what I know today, would I hire this person?" If the answer is no, fire that person straight away. If the answer is yes, tell them that. If the employee doesn't report to you, go to his or her direct manager and ask the same question. Awesome organizations are those that fire quickly.

- **Exit**—Go back and read chapter 13 when a possible exit is becoming relevant. It may feel remote right now, but it will be critical once you're getting close.

MORE WAZE STORIES

Often, when I tell stories about Waze, I will hear more stories from users that can be added to my list. I'm pretty sure you have a few of those, as well.

For example, I was once called "Moses of the roads" in Canada. On several occasions, I heard people say: "You set me free," or "You empowered me to drive."

There was a guy who offered me thousands of dollars that he said he owes me due to saving him from speeding tickets.

I have even been considered a marriage counselor for stopping the fights in the car over which route to take.

But I owe one of the best stories to one of my sons.

Some years back, he had just started to drive. He really liked being behind the wheel.

One day, I asked him to drive me to the airport.

"I can't, Dad," he said somberly. "My phone is broken."

"What do you mean you can't?" I countered. "Here are the keys, here's the car, drive me to the airport!"

"No, no, no, you don't understand. My phone is broken," he replied. "I don't know how to get there."

I scratched my head for a second, then said, "You know what, I'll be in the car with you. I'll tell you how to get there!"

Then he added, "And how will I get *back home?*"

So, we lose our orientation but not our logic!

INVEST WITH ME

While I have heard many stories from Waze users over the years, I've heard one question even more frequently.

"Can I invest in your start-ups?" or "Can I invest with you?"

I've invested in a dozen start-ups and I keep on investing in them further as they evolve. I follow a very specific philosophy of doing good and doing well—essentially, solving problems and making the world a better place.

I have developed a very specific practice, joining way before the start-up is established and focusing on three key parts: the problem, the CEO, and my guidance and mentorship, from prelaunch through the launch of the company and then through the entire journey.

At the end of the day, my goal is to increase the likelihood of the start-up to succeed and to add value exactly where I am needed on one hand and where I enjoy the most on the other.

Throughout the last decade or so, I've tried multiple investing models. I was a pre-seed investor to companies like Pontera (previously FeeX), FairFly, Engie, and others. I then became a lead seed investor through co-investing with friends and other investors in companies such as SeeTree and Refundit.

Together with a partner, Ariel Sacerdoti, we created an investment vehicle called "The Founders Kitchen" through which we have invested in all my start-ups, including Pontera, Refundit, Kahun, Engie, SeeTree, Zeek, Dynamo, WeSki, Fibo, Livecare, and more.

Nowadays, I am back into co-investment models, which lead into my start-ups. This model is very different. I don't have a deal flow like other investors. I only invest in my own start-ups—those that were already built and those that I will be building in the future.

If you find this book valuable—if it actually helped you to become more successful—then I would ask you to do two more things, please:

1. Share your insights with your fellow entrepreneurs and, in particular, with your management team.
2. Pay it forward: When the time is right, find a young entrepreneur to guide and mentor.

Acknowledgments

I would like to thank my fellow Waze founders Ehud Shabtai and Amir Shinar. I am so glad we started this journey back in 2007. Thank you for being who you are, for sharing the vision, the focus, and DNA of an amazing workplace that changed the lives of so many, me included.

Noam Bardin, Waze wouldn't have become so successful without you. I am happy that you accepted our offer to join Waze as CEO, and grateful for many years of an amazing journey, through both the hard times and the wins.

The Waze team—starting from the management team we established in the very early days with Fej Shmuelevitz, Samuel Keret, Yael Elish, Di-Ann Eisner, and Anat Eitan, to all the amazing people we brought on board over the years. The journey, together with you, was pretty amazing. I don't think we could have done this without you, nor that I would have wanted to do it any other way.

Adi Barill, this book would not have been published without you, my book partner and coeditor. From concept through publication, you have been a true partner and rainmaker, bringing your expertise to outlining, writing, editing, marketing, and everything in between.

My CEOs—Nir Erez, Yoav Zurel, Aviel Siman-Tov, Daniel Zelkind, Israel Telpaz, Ziv Tirosh, Nimrod Bar-Levin, Orr Kowarsky, Yotam Idan, Roi Kimchi, Eitan Ron, Alon Schwartzman, Roy Yotvat, Greg Moran, and Peri Avitan. You all have been, and still are, taking part in the journey to change the world for the better, and disrupt inefficient markets. I am honored that you let me become valuable to you and, in particular, allowed me to learn so much through you. I wouldn't have gained so many insights without you.

I would also like to thank all the teams in all my start-ups. The ones that succeeded, and the ones that didn't. Thank you for taking the risk, and dedicating so much effort to being a part of working to change people's lives.

Noga—my wife and the love of my life, who was there when I first had the idea to write a book, accompanied me in my travels around the world, and joined one hundred book meetings and a similar number of speaking events, empowering and supporting me through this journey.

Kids—Charlie, Ido, Tal, Eran, Amit—thank you for being such a significant part of my life, willing to pay the price of me being busy all the time and accepting who I am, always following one of my dreams. You have been an inspiration to me, and I proudly see you following my path in your entrepreneurial thinking and doing. Out of all my creations, you are by far my most successful.

Dad—I still miss him, my greatest inspiration and mentor, with the wisdom and empowerment to follow my dreams, and to constantly try. My dad was very sharp, and occasionally would be able to abstract an essence into a few simple words. For example, "Even a dog is not going to leap if you hang the meat from the ceiling" to describe setting unreachable targets. Unfortunately, he passed away in January 2007, without seeing the Waze journey, or this book. My mom passed away in May 2022, while I was working on the book's final edits, and didn't get to see it published. Both my parents influenced me greatly, and people who know both me and them often say, "You tell stories as your mom did" or "You think exactly like your dad."

Sometime in November 2018, I presented my story at my mother's assisted living facility to people with an average age over 85. Prior to that, my mom was under a lot of pressure. She worried, "What if it won't make the right impression, what if he speaks way above the understanding level of the audience? *What if this and what if that?*" I tried to calm her, saying she is an awesome storyteller and I've learned from her how to tell a good story. It didn't help.

When I present to a large audience, it is rather hard to see everyone, so I pick several people to watch and talk to as if I'm telling my story to them. At this event, one of these people was my mom, who was sitting fairly close to me. She was on edge before we started, but I saw her laugh and relax shortly after I started talking.

The presentation was a blast and afterward she was walking around the hall, proud like a peacock, and presented me to everyone. Then she told me, "You should write a book." It wasn't the first time it had crossed my mind, but it was the conviction that I needed. This was when I decided to write *Fall in Love with the Problem, Not the Solution*. In that sense, this book became to be part of her last will.

I would also like to thank Jim (James Levine) from Levine Greenberg Rostan Literary, who has accompanied me on this book journey, showing me around this "new territory." To BenBella Books and Matt Holt, who believed in the book and partnered with us to bring my story to the public, and the team at BenBella: Katie Dickman, Mallory Hyde, Brigid Pearson, Jessika Rieck, and Kerri Stebbins.

Brian Blum—thank you for helping shape and interpret the initial book vision and ideas into a coherent plan and then supporting the writing process.

My appreciation to the broader team: Nurit Blok, the graphic designer, and Ofer Ziv, the website builder who help me get my messages across to my audiences.

I would like to also thank the more than one billion users of Waze, Moovit, and the rest of my start-ups. Without you, this story would never have existed.

To all the tens of thousands of people around the world, who heard me tell my story and made me improve my lectures and workshops through their questions and comments, thank you. I hope this book will enrich you and make you more successful.

Special thanks to my readers and to all the people I have not mentioned but who influenced my journey.

Index

About the Author

Uri Levine (http://urilevine.com) is a passionate entrepreneur and disruptor, and a two-time "unicorn" builder (duocorn). He cofounded Waze, the world's largest community-based driving traffic and navigation app, which Google acquired for $1.1 billion in 2013, and is a former investor and board member in Moovit, the Waze of public transportation, which Intel acquired for $1 billion in 2020. Levine also heads The Founders Kitchen, a company-builder fund.

Levine's vision in building start-ups is to disrupt inefficient markets and improve underfunctioning services, focusing on solving "BIG problems" and saving consumers time and money while empowering them and changing the world for the better. Among Uri's start-ups are Pontera, FairFly, Refundit, and SeeTree, and he is always working on the next one.

Uri has been in the high-tech business for the last thirty years, half of them in the start-up scene, and he has seen everything ranging from failure to moderate success to big success. He is a world-class speaker on entrepreneurship, disruption, evolution vs. revolutions of markets, mobility, and start-ups. In his presentations and workshops, he shares the lessons learned from his experience of both triumphs and defeats.

Levine is a BA graduate from Tel Aviv University. He served in the Israeli army at special intelligence unit 8200. In his public activity, he serves on the board of trustees of Tel Aviv University and also mentors young entrepreneurs. In 2015, Levine, together with Ehud Shabtai and Amir Shinar, was named as one of 100 visionaries by Genius 100 Foundation.